PARTY, POLITICS, AND THE POST-9/11 ARMY

PARTY, POLITICS, AND THE POST-9/11 ARMY

Heidi A. Urben

Rapid Communications in Conflict and Security Series
General Editor: Geoffrey R.H. Burn

CAMBRIA PRESS

Amherst, New York

Library of Congress Cataloging-in-Publication Data

Names: Urben, Heidi A., author.
Title: Party, politics, and the post-9/11 Army / Heidi A. Urben.
Description: Amherst, New York : Cambria Press, [2021] |
Series: Cambria rapid communications in conflict and security series |
Includes bibliographical references and index. |
Summary: "Using a range of survey tools to glean insights into changing norms within the
US military, this book provides a particularly valuable window into the political beliefs and
behavior of active-duty (primarily US Army) officers. With its presentation of contemporary
data, discussion of new dynamics created by social media, large number of questions for
future research, and pragmatic policy recommendations, this book offers significant findings
to be pulled that will improve the dialogue within professional military education and in
senior military leader's writings to their colleagues and guidance to the forces and is an
important resource for policy makers, practitioners, and scholars"-- Provided by publisher.

Identifiers: LCCN 2021022547 (print) | LCCN 2021022548 (ebook) |
ISBN 9781621966180 (library binding) | ISBN 9781621966197 (paperback) |
ISBN 9781621966067 (pdf) | ISBN 9781621966074 (epub)

Subjects: LCSH: United States. Army--Officers--Political activity. | United States.
Army--Officers--Attitudes. | Civil-military relations--United States. | Military
ethics--United States. | Political culture--United States. | United States. Army--
History--21st century. | Social surveys--United States. | Public opinion--United States.

Classification: LCC UB413 .U73 2021 (print) | LCC UB413 (ebook) |
DDC 324.273088/355--dc23

LC record available at https://lccn.loc.gov/2021022547

LC ebook record available at https://lccn.loc.gov/2021022548

TABLE OF CONTENTS

LIST OF TABLES

List of Figures

Foreword

Peter D. Feaver

"I am wearied to death all day with a variety of perplexing circumstances—disturbed at the conduct of the militia, whose behavior and want of discipline has done great injury to the other troops, who never had officers, except in a few instances, worth the bread they eat."

—George Washington,
letter to Lund Washington, September 30, 1776

"It concerns me to think that anyone wearing the uniform of a soldier or a sailor, an airman, marine, or guardian or coast guardsmen, would espouse these sorts of beliefs [political extremism], let alone act on them. But they do. Some of them still do. We've got to be better than that."

—Lloyd Austin,
video message to all hands, February 19, 2021

American leaders from George Washington to Lloyd Austin have, from time to time, expressed concern about the caliber and conduct of the people serving in uniform. These concerns are usually balanced, even overmatched, by strong dollops of pride, confidence, and genuine affection for the same collective body of servicemen (and now servicewomen). And these concerns are tempered with caveats. Washington was talking about the irregular militia and keen to develop a cadre of professional soldiers who, he believed, would not suffer from these defects. Austin was talking about a military more professionalized and better-trained than anything Washington could have imagined—but Austin also emphasized that the problematic element was an infinitesimal fraction of the overall force.

Yet a common thread runs through these and countless other examples that could be assembled: a conviction that the strength of the US military turns to a great extent on the human factor, particularly the quality of the rank and file. A military that is otherwise well-equipped but is disordered—whether through chronic ill-discipline or through the poison of factionalism—will not adequately provide for the common defense.

Accordingly, theorists of American civil-military relations have long focused on the orientation of the men and women who serve in uniform as one of the key pillars undergirding the health of the armed forces, and thus the security of the Republic. This orientation—sometimes called the "military mind" or "professionalism" or "the military viewpoint"—encompasses a wide range of values, attitudes, opinions, and even behaviors that collectively describe what the military is thinking. Theorists do not agree entirely on what the military should be thinking, but they all agree that—whatever it is—it is an important component in healthy civil-military relations.

Theory begets empirics. If it is important, then it should be measured and tracked.

And here is the rub. If it is measured and tracked, then it can be debated and contested—and theorists, including some of the very same theorists who have identified this as a crucial factor in civil-military relations, have also worried that too much attention and debate is likely to stir up the very same factionalism and politicization that is the hallmark of a troubled force.

Military leaders have paid attention, alternating between wanting to know as much as possible about the thought orientation of the force and worrying that investigating the same will stir up trouble. Some high-profile academic studies, including a large one I helped lead, may have done just that.

This has resulted in a situation where the scholar must trade off access and scope. One can work with military officials to get close access to the force, but in exchange one must accept limits on the scope of what one can investigate. Or one can explore as wide-ranging a set of questions as one wishes, but at a distance, catching military personnel where one can. It is impossible to maximize both access and scope at the same time.

This brings us to Heidi Urben's important contribution in this monograph. Dr. Urben has balanced this trade-off as well as any scholar in recent times and with it has made a valuable contribution to our understanding of the orientation of the US military. To be sure, even this superior study had to make practical concessions. The most important is that she focuses just on US Army officers, current and prospective. Given the post-Capitol insurrection concerns about extremism in the ranks, the latter is a more serious limitation than the former. But her choices in this study's scope are sensible, and the result is admirable.

The book is both timeless and timely. Dr. Urben is engaging several decades of scholarship and bringing fresh data to bear on these well-established questions. Yet the book is arriving in the wake of a particularly turbulent period of civil-military relations where the questions she is asking—does the US military have a political orientation and if so, will that lead to behaviors that are problematic for the health of American democracy—are so fresh as to be almost raw.

Along the way, Dr. Urben has developed a special niche focus on social media, charting a path that the rank and file have long since galloped down and yet one that barely shows up on the mental maps of civil-military theorists or, until lately, senior military leaders themselves. She is right to hone in on this aspect of the topic. It is the place where there is the most room for policy refinements, and Urben is well-positioned to help leaders sort their way through this thorny issue.

Urben's careful parsing of the data leads her to an equally careful cautionary conclusion: The data do not point to an imminent crisis in the orientation of the military, but they do reinforce the concerns. She sees erosion in the foundation of American civil-military relations, not the sharp rupture of a sudden earthquake. Yet she offers much more than a lamentation. Contra the quip attributed to Mark Twain, Urben does not merely talk about politicization in the military without doing anything about it. Rather, she sets out a sensible five-step program of realistic steps that policy makers can take to shore up the foundations. None are quick fixes, but collectively they are likely to be efficacious in addressing the problems Urben highlights for our attention.

Urben tops these off with a teaching guide suitable for junior commanders to use in training and education at the unit level. Such a guide is precisely the sort of tool Secretary Austin was reaching for in his all-hands message. If one suspends disbelief for the sake of a rhetorical flourish, one can even imagine General Washington seeing some value in such a device as he sought to build an American military from scratch.

We have come a very long way from the problems that wearied Washington, but if we are not careful—if we do not pay heed to what Urben is saying here—we may find ourselves facing troubles no less wearying.

ACKNOWLEDGEMENTS

This book has been more than a decade in the making. It never would have come about had retired Colonel Isaiah "Ike" Wilson III, retired Brigadier General Mike Meese, and retired Brigadier General Cindy Jebb not paved the way for me to pursue my PhD while on active duty in the US Army and eventually teach in the Department of Social Sciences at West Point. Their persistence and good cheer in waging seemingly insurmountable bureaucratic battles on behalf of the many rotating faculty in the "Sosh Department" not only made my own research possible, but they motivated me to pay it forward with the same enthusiasm to assist junior officers with similar broadening opportunities in the latter half of my US Army career.

I am particularly thankful to Tom Kelly, former Deputy Undersecretary of the Army, who green-lighted my dissertation survey of US Army officers back in 2009 and provided the necessary top cover to field the survey to such a large segment of the officer corps. I literally would not have been able to conduct that survey without the help of Colonel David Lyle and the Office of Economic and Manpower Analysis (OEMA) at West Point who hosted my survey. David, in particular, provided expert counsel on my survey instrument, and I owe him and OEMA a debt of gratitude. My dissertation committee of Mark Rom, Clyde Wilcox, and Peter Feaver made every part of my dissertation better and the entire process of writing it an enjoyable journey. I remain indebted to Peter, more than anyone, who from day one, has encouraged me and countless other civil-military relations scholars with unmatched generosity. He is the type of mentor everyone deserves but not everyone is lucky enough to find. The truth is, we're all just trying to live up to his superb example and produce something that has a fraction of the value his work has had over the past three decades.

When I was a research fellow at the National War College from 2015 to 2016, Stephen Mariano and Stephanie Zedlar were instrumental in facilitating my social media survey to be fielded at the National Defense University (NDU). I am thankful to Joe Collins for his helpful feedback on that project and for his friendship over two decades that first began at Bagram Airfield, Afghanistan and continued at Georgetown and NDU. More recently, I am grateful to the leadership at NDU, especially Laura Junor at the Institute for National Strategic Studies, for the invitation to serve as a Visiting Research Fellow and for enabling surveys of NDU students since 2017. I owe a special thank you to Brett Swaney who has done so much of the leg work to field these surveys at NDU, and I also appreciate Marybeth Ulrich for facilitating the fielding of two waves of the survey at the Army War College.

I am grateful to supportive colleagues in the Sosh Department at West Point—Lieutenant Colonel Heidi Demarest, Colonel Suzanne Nielsen, and Rachel Sondheimer—who graciously allowed me to survey West Point cadets on multiple occasions and are dear friends. Their scholarship has greatly influenced mine, and cadets at West Point are lucky to have them as mentors and educators.

Jason Dempsey continues to set the benchmark for generosity. Years ago, when I was working on my dissertation, he sent me feedback while he was deployed to Afghanistan, which still amazes me to this day. His work has inspired my own, and I am thankful for his outstanding feedback on this project as well. Risa Brooks, Sue Bryant, and Major Michael Robinson have been cherished collaborators over the past few years, and their work has made mine better. I am particularly grateful to Risa for her thoughtful feedback on portions of this book. Jay Parker deserves a special round of thanks. It was Jay who encouraged me to write this book and connected me with Cambria Press. Without Jay's optimism and nudging, I'm not sure I would have ever written this book.

Portions of chapter 3 build upon survey data I first published in an article in *Armed Forces and Society*, entitled, "Wearing Politics on Their Sleeves: Levels of Political Activism of Active Duty Army Officers," *Armed Forces and Society* 40, no. 3 (Spring 2014): 568-591. Additionally, portions of chapter 5 build on survey data I first published in an article in *Orbis*, entitled, "Party, Politics, and Deciding What Is Proper: Army Officers' Attitudes after Two Long Wars," *Orbis* 57, no. 3 (Summer 2013): 351-368. I am also appreciative of Bill Eliason and Jeff Smotherman's help in publishing an earlier version of my social media study, entitled, *Like, Comment, Retweet: The State of the Military's Nonpartisan Ethic in the World of Social Media* through NDU Press. Portions of that study are included in chapter 4.

I am grateful to Geoffrey Burn, Toni Tan, David Armstrong, and the entire team at Cambria Press for all their support, encouragement, and unbelievable efficiency throughout this process. I am also indebted to the anonymous reviewers selected by Cambria Press for their excellent input and suggestions. All errors in this book, of course, are mine alone.

Finally, I want to thank my family for their support over this past year, which included my retirement from the army and the COVID-19 pandemic that has affected us all. They have been a constant source of encouragement and much needed humor during a challenging year. I am especially grateful to my mom, Tharba Urben who diligently read every word of this book multiple times. I doubt that she found civil-military relations as interesting as her fiction book club, but she never let on.

PARTY, POLITICS, AND THE POST-9/11 ARMY

CHAPTER 1

INTRODUCTION

We have a chance that we will lose the American people if we let the military become politicized.[1]

—Admiral Michael Mullen, US Navy, ret.

Throughout the All-Volunteer Force era, but chiefly since the 1990s, the military has faced charges of growing politicization.[2] While both the armed forces and civilian political leaders bear responsibility for any politicization, this study examines the extent to which behavior by the uniformed military over the past decade may have contributed to the institution's gradual politicization and the erosion of its nonpartisan ethic. Politicization of the armed forces is both a broad and vague claim, but Alice Hunt Friend's definition is a good starting point: "a politicized military exercises loyalty to a single political party and/or consistently advocates for and defends partisan political positions and fortunes."[3] The charge of politicization within the military can be further broken down into three main claims: that the military, particularly its officer corps, has become—or has appeared to become—too partisan, too politically vocal, and too resistant to civilian control.

Central to the "too-partisan" claim has been the concern that the officer corps tends to consistently embrace or align itself with one party—a factor that could, in turn, cause the public to view the military as an interest group and ultimately affect the public's overall trust in the armed forces. This particular charge started gaining traction in the late 1990s with the publication of Tom Ricks' book, *Making the Corps*, which suggested the officer corps was disproportionately conservative and Republican and out of step with the American public.[4] Around the same time, Ole Holsti published twenty years' worth of survey data on military officer attitudes, finding that the officer corps moved from being majority Independent to majority Republican over time.[5] Peter Feaver and Richard Kohn's Triangle Institute for Security Studies (TISS) study published in 2001 confirmed similar levels of ideological conservatism and strong Republican Party affiliation within the officer corps.[6] Implicit in the claim that the military has become too partisan is that some combination of the military, civilian leaders, and the American public has *perceived* the military to be partisan. A preference for voting for one party over the other, even in decisive numbers, is not by itself an indicator of politicization. The widespread perception that the military favors one party—beyond the act of voting —contributes to the charge of politicization.

The "too politically vocal" charge centers on the assertion that those in uniform (and especially retired members of the military) are increasingly abandoning the norms of nonpartisanship and neutrality in the public sphere, especially on social media, by participating in partisan political discourse without restraint. The early years of the Clinton administration were often viewed as the nadir in civil-military relations, marked by several, high-profile instances of vocal criticism by senior military officers directed against the commander in chief.[7] The advent of social media, however, enabled service members' political opinions to be broadcast further and wider than ever before.[8] It may be that members of the military are no more politically vocal today than they were in the 1990s, but social media provides further reach for their commentaries, along with written, lasting, public records.

Retired officers—especially retired flag officers—have contributed to the perception of a politically vocal officer corps through a rise in partisan endorsements during election campaigns and an increased willingness to publicly criticize the president. This was evident in the 2006 "revolt of the generals," when six retired generals spoke out against the Bush administration's handling of the Iraq War, and in multiple instances during the Trump administration, when large numbers of retired flag officers criticized Donald Trump's leadership on a variety of issues.[9] Although a small portion of the entire living, retired flag-officer population makes partisan endorsements or engages in partisan political commentary in public, these retired officers are rarely met with public criticism for their political outspokenness from their peers or active-duty flag officers. The ambivalence about retired officers wading into partisan politics among the public and active-duty service members contributes to uneven support for the norm of nonpartisanship being extended into retirement.

The "too-resistant" assertion suggests uneven adherence by members of the military to their civilian superiors. Being resistant to civilian control does not just mean defying lawful orders outright or even the various ways the military can "shirk" as outlined in Feaver's principal-agent model.[10] It can manifest itself in more nuanced ways, such as members of the military exhibiting a lack of respect for civilian officials, believing that national security officials should have served in uniform in order to be respected, or advocating that senior military leaders should insist on having their way during deliberations with civilian officials about the use of force. When members of the military operate in this fashion, they fail to adhere to Feaver's admonition that "civilians have the right to be wrong."[11] And while partisanship need not be the main driver behind such resistance, when it is, it constitutes an alarming threat to civilian control.

These three claims do not exist separately in a vacuum, and for politicization of the military to truly occur, all three factors would have to be present and intertwined with one another. To fully assess these claims, however, a comprehensive understanding of how politics and partisanship manifest themselves in the officer corps is needed. Scholars and journalists alike rely, perhaps too much, on a handful of now-outdated surveys of military personnel, such as Holsti and James Rosenau's Foreign Policy Leadership Program surveys that ran from 1976 to 1996, Peter Feaver and Richard Kohn's TISS Survey from 1998–1999, or Jason Dempsey's 2004 surveys of US Army–enlisted personnel and West Point cadets.[12] The media and the public also tend to put too much stock in surveys that outlets such as the *Military Times* conducts of its readership, glossing over the fact that their samples are by no means representative of the entire active-duty military.[13] Such surveys arguably gain the widest public spread, however. This was evident when the *Military Times* published a poll in August 2020 suggesting more active-duty troops planned to vote for Joe Biden over Donald Trump, which was then carried widely by other prominent news outlets and featured in one of Biden's campaign advertisements.[14] Lastly, there can be a tendency to conflate veteran attitudes with current service members' attitudes, especially because it is easier to survey veterans than active-duty service members. This is problematic, given the diversity and age span of veterans in the United States. Vietnam War–era veterans constitute the largest block of living veterans today, and the median veteran age is 65, but there is little to suggest these veterans, for example, would be a suitable proxy for those currently serving today.[15]

All these shortcuts—relying on older survey data or skewed samples or using veteran attitudes as a proxy for active-duty attitudes—are understandable and symptomatic of a broader challenge: it is difficult to survey active-duty service members, especially about their partisan political attitudes. In fact, over the past decade, it has gotten even harder. The Department of Defense and each of the services have tried to mitigate the amount of survey fatigue across the force by instituting tighter controls on surveys—in addition to the normal Institutional Review Board protocols which all human subjects research must undergo.[16] Strict oversight of human subjects research is to be expected, especially within the federal government, but centralizing approval for surveys at the very top of an organization with more than one million people in it results in fewer large-scale, and thus more reliable, surveys. My own survey research benefited from the fact that I was an insider at the time —an active-duty army officer largely surveying other officers. It is even more difficult for outside researchers to obtain the necessary approvals and navigate the bureaucratic hurdles necessary to conduct large-scale survey research of service members' attitudes.

This book aims to build upon past survey research, focusing exclusively on the attitudes of active-duty army officers. Drawing upon original survey research conducted over the past decade, this book explores the roots of the three politicization claims—that the officer corps is too partisan, too politically vocal, and too resistant to civilian control— through an in-depth analysis of the attitudes of serving army officers. This project centers on a large-scale, random-sample survey (n=4,248) of active-duty army officers' political and partisan attitudes (2009), as well as two targeted surveys of West Point cadets and officers attending senior service college conducted in 2015–2016 (n=537) and again from 2017–2020 (n=1,218). While these samples are not true panel data, they allow us to compare the views of US Army officers in order to gauge the extent to which their political views have changed over time—in this case, at three critical junctures in the post-9/11 era: shortly after the inauguration of President Barack Obama, amidst the wars in Iraq and Afghanistan; near the end of the Obama administration, just prior to the 2016 election; and during President Donald Trump's administration.

This book focuses primarily on the political attitudes and behavior of active-duty US Army officers, although the results can be extrapolated to the other services' officer corps as well. As the largest branch of service and one that bore a large share of the burden fighting the post 9/11 wars of Iraq, Afghanistan, and elsewhere, it offers the richest opportunity for an in-depth study of military officers' political views and views regarding the norms of civil-military relations during wartime. Although this book focuses on the findings from multiple surveys of active-duty officers and cadets—including one large-scale, random-sample study— the samples are not intended to reflect the entire US Army. This study focuses on officer attitudes—and within the officer corps, often an even narrower sampling of senior officers or "up-and-comers"—those likely to be tapped for advancement through promotion and selection for exclusive military schooling. As Jason Dempsey found, US Army–enlisted and noncommissioned officers tend to have more diverse partisan and political views and are typically more representative of society compared to the officer corps, which accounts for only about 20 percent of the US Army.[17] However, the attitudes and behavior of the officer corps carry more weight in determining the broader tenor of civil-military relations in the United States and the degree to which norms are either upheld or deteriorate across the force. Because of that, their attitudes are the focus of this book.

CIVIL-MILITARY RELATIONS IN A TIME OF WAR SURVEY (2009)

The Civil-Military Relations in a Time of War Survey, henceforth referred to as the CMR Time of War Survey, focused on the party affiliation and political views of US Army officers. By design, it replicated many of the same questions of military officers in past surveys so that the views of army officers could be compared over time. From April 24, 2009 through May 11, 2009, the opt-in CMR Time of War Survey was administered via the internet to a random sample of over 21,000 army officers via their official army email addresses.[18] The random sample consisted of officers in the ranks of lieutenant through colonel, amounting to 30 percent of the total active-duty army officer population at the time, and was representative of the larger army population in terms of the breakdown by gender, race, education level, specialty, rank, source of commission, years of service, and age.

Table 1. CMR Time of War Survey (2009) Demographic Comparison to Active-Duty Army Officer Population.

	Survey Sample		Active Duty Army Officer Corps	
	n	%	N	%
Lieutenants	704	16.9	14,175	19.5
Captains	1133	27.1	27,886	38.4
Majors	1060	25.4	15,886	21.9
Lieutenant Colonels	870	20.8	9,728	13.4
Colonels	408	9.8	5,027	6.9
TOTAL	4175	100.0	72,702	100.0
Men	3342	86.2	60,244	82.9
Women	537	13.8	12,458	17.1
TOTAL	3879	100.0	72,702	100.0
White	3030	78.6	53,050	73.0
Black	296	7.7	9,199	12.7
Hispanic	219	5.7	4,057	5.6
Other	309	8.0	6,396	8.8
TOTAL	3854	100.0	72,702	100.00
20-24 age group	250	6.4	5,771	7.9
25-29 age group	636	16.3	17,275	23.8
30-34 age group	675	17.3	14,129	19.4
35-39 age group	799	20.5	14,407	19.8
40-44 age group	806	20.7	11,536	15.9
45-49 age group	464	11.9	6,210	8.5
Over 50 age group	273	7.0	3,372	4.6
TOTAL	3903	100.0	72,702	100.0
Service Academy	715	17.0	10,442	14.4
ROTC	2258	53.5	37,996	52.3
OCS	681	16.2	11,837	16.3
Other	564	13.4	12,427	17.1
TOTAL	4218	100.0	72,702	100.0
Some College	13	0.3	2,166	3.0
College Graduate	1241	31.8	41,435	57.0
Graduate Degree	2139	54.8	28,562	39.3
Other/UNK	510	13.1	539	7.4
TOTAL	3903	100.0	72,702	100.0

Source. CMR Time of War Survey (2009).
Note. Army population data provided by the Office of Economic and Manpower Analysis at the US Military Academy.

General officers were excluded from the random sample to preserve their anonymity, given that there are only roughly 300 general officers on active duty in the army at any given time.

The response rate for the survey was 20 percent, with a total of 4,248 respondents. For the most part, respondents in the CMR Time of War Survey were representative of the larger army officer corps population in terms of key demographic variables, and because of this, the variables are not weighted. With regard to gender, race, and source of commissioning, survey respondents closely mirrored the overall army officer population, with less than a five-percentage point difference between the sample and population by each category.

POLITICS AND SOCIAL MEDIA SURVEY (2015–2016)

The Politics, the Military, and Social Media Research Survey, henceforth referred to as the Politics & Social Media Survey, examined the social media habits of military officers, including the degree to which members of the military express their political views on social media sites. Unlike the CMR Time of War Survey, the Politics & Social Media Survey was not a true random-sample survey but relied upon the observations of a sample of military officers attending the National Defense University (NDU) and cadets attending the United States Military Academy at West Point. While West Point cadets are future officers still in a pre-commissioning status, this book refers to the entire sample of both NDU students and West Point cadets as military elites, following a classification used in similar past research.[19]

To avoid potential social-desirability bias, the Politics & Social Media Survey primarily asked respondents questions about their observations of the behavior and attitudes of their military and nonmilitary friends on social media, as opposed to asking respondents to report details about their own political expressions on social media. While this approach may have reduced the likelihood of respondents underreporting or overreporting in possible attempts to provide what they believe are "the correct" answers to somewhat-sensitive questions, it is not without its own limitations. Chiefly, it relied upon survey respondents to serve as accurate observers of their friends' political expressions on social media, and this, of course, entails some bias. Nonetheless, given the dearth of survey research on political attitudes and participation by members of the military and the untapped arena of how such attitudes play out on social media, this sample of convenience is sufficient to draw some initial conclusions about the behavior and attitudes of members of the military at the intersection of politics and social media.

From December 1–18, 2015, and again from January 14–21, 2016, this opt-in, internet-based survey was administered to military officers enrolled in the five main colleges within NDU: the National War College, the Dwight D. Eisenhower School for National Security and Resource Strategy, the College of International Security Affairs (CISA), the Information Resources Management College (now called the College of Information and Cyberspace), and the Joint Forces Staff College (JFSC). The majority of officers surveyed across NDU were students attending senior service college, although officers enrolled in CISA and JFSC were not exclusively senior-service-college students. Students attending CISA also included a cohort at Fort Bragg enrolled in the Joint Special Operations Master of Arts Program, and officers surveyed in JFSC included those enrolled in both the Joint Advanced Warfighting School and Joint and Combined Warfighting School. From December 8–18, 2015, the same survey was administered to sophomore cadets at the US Military Academy enrolled in the core course, "Introduction to American Politics." All cadets are required to take Introduction to American Politics while at West Point, usually during their sophomore year, therefore this population represents roughly half of the class of 2018.

The response rate for the survey was 44 percent, with a total of 537 respondents. With West Point cadets accounting for 58 percent of the sample, the majority of respondents (70 percent) were affiliated with the

US Army. While this sample is by no means intended to be representative of the entire US military or the officer corps for that matter, it does provide unique insights into the tenor and volume of political activity on social media by the military, both active duty and retired. Most significantly, it provides a suitable sample of military elite opinion, bookended by those on the path to commissioning and senior officers approaching the pinnacle of their careers.

Table 2. Politics & Social Media Survey (2015–2016) Demographics.

	Survey Sample	
	n	%
West Point Cadets	307	58.5
O3s	3	0.6
O4s	31	5.9
O5s	156	29.7
O6s	28	5.3
TOTAL	525	100.0
U.S. Air Force	80	15.3
U.S. Army	369	70.4
U.S. Coast Guard	5	1.0
U.S. Marine Corps	20	3.8
U.S. Navy	50	9.5
TOTAL	524	100.0
18-24 age group	307	58.5
25-29 age group	0	0
30-34 age group	6	1.1
35-39 age group	36	6.9
40-44 age group	119	22.7
45-49 age group	44	8.4
50-54 age group	13	2.5
Over 55 age group	0	0
TOTAL	525	100.0

Source. Politics & Social Media Survey (2015–2016).

NATIONAL DEFENSE UNIVERSITY CIVIL-MILITARY RELATIONS SURVEYS (2017–2020)

The third and final survey central to this book involves another military elite sample hosted at NDU, the NDU Civil-Military Relations Survey, henceforth referred to as the NDU CMR Survey. From December 2017 to March 2020, military officers from each of the services enrolled in the various colleges within NDU and the Army War College (AWC), along with cadets at the US Military Academy were surveyed in seven waves. West Point cadets were surveyed in December 2017 and January 2018; NDU students were surveyed from January to April 2018, from February to April 2019, and from October to December 2019; and AWC students were surveyed from April to June 2018 and in March 2020. These waves are part of an ongoing NDU project aimed at assessing military elite attitudes—not unlike the Foreign Policy Leadership Project, which surveyed NDU students every four years from 1976 to 1996. By holding the survey instrument constant and surveying the same professional military education venues, this project aims to measure to what extent elite attitudes vary or remain constant over time. The response rate for all seven waves of the survey was 38 percent, and the sample is evenly split between NDU and AWC students (n=621) and West Point cadets (n=597). Like the Politics & Social Media Survey sample, the NDU CMR Survey sample is predominantly army (72 percent).

Of note, the final wave of the survey referenced in this book was completed in March 2020—just as the coronavirus pandemic was beginning in the United States, but far before its devastating, wide-reaching effects were fully realized. This final wave also predated the turbulence of the summer of 2020 associated with nationwide Black Lives Matter protests in response to the killing of George Floyd, the 2020 presidential campaign and election and its aftermath, and finally the insurrection on the US Capitol in January 2021.

Table 3. NDU CMR Survey (2017–2020) Demographics.

	Survey Sample	
	n	%
West Point Cadets	597	49.0
O4s	92	7.6
O5s	388	31.9
O6s	141	11.6
TOTAL	1218	100.0
U.S. Air Force	177	14.5
U.S. Army	884	72.6
U.S. Coast Guard	7	0.6
U.S. Marine Corps	51	4.2
U.S. Navy	98	8.1
TOTAL	1217	100.0
Men	999	82.2
Women	217	17.9
TOTAL	1216	100.0
White	882	72.9
Black	95	7.9
Hispanic	63	5.2
Other	170	14.1
TOTAL	1210	100.0
18-24 age group	590	48.5
25-29 age group	6	0.5
30-34 age group	20	1.6
35-39 age group	78	6.4
40-44 age group	291	23.9
45-49 age group	180	14.8
50-54 age group	44	3.6
Over 55 age group	8	0.7
TOTAL	1217	100.0

Source. NDU CMR Survey (2017–2020).

While the findings of this survey represent a recent snapshot of senior army officer attitudes on their partisan leanings, it is unclear to what extent the extraordinary events of 2020 and January 2021 may have further shaped the political attitudes and party loyalties of those in uniform. Additional survey research is certainly required.

OUTLINE OF THIS PROJECT

This book, heavy on empirical observations from these three original surveys, aims to answer five central questions about the officer corps' politics in the post-9/11 era. First, how stable are the partisan and political attitudes of the officer corps, and how has the political makeup of the officer corps evolved? Second, what forms of political activity do officers engage in, and is such activity in keeping with Department of Defense directives that govern and restrict political behavior? Third, what are the nature and extent of active-duty service members' political expressions on social media, and are they consistent with the norm of nonpartisanship? Fourth, how do those on active duty view politically outspoken retired flag officers and the suggestion that the norm of nonpartisanship should extend into retirement? Lastly, do the partisanship and ideology of those in uniform matter? Do officers' partisan political attitudes impact their views of civil-military relations, the role senior military leaders and civilian policy-makers should play during wartime, and the institution of the armed forces itself? Or is concern about the politics of those who serve today much ado about nothing?

Chapter 2 addresses the partisan affiliation and political ideology of army officers serving in the All-Volunteer Force era, particularly during the post-9/11 wars.[20] It identifies the determinants of officers' partisan affiliation, assesses the durability of officers' partisan and political attitudes, and compares the partisanship and ideology of military officers over time throughout key junctures in the All-Volunteer Force era, by looking at past survey research. This chapter also examines the charge that the officer corps has become consistently conservative and Republican.

Chapter 3 explores the levels of political participation, activism, and outspokenness of active-duty army officers and examines to what extent they participate in traditional forms of political expression, including those allowable activities outlined in Department of Defense Directive (DoDD) 1344.10, *Political Activities by Members of the Armed Forces*. From the simple act of voting to more overt acts of partisanship, it compares the types of political activities army officers engage in and reports on officers' attitudes on the appropriateness of such public political behavior for the active-duty force. Lastly, it examines the correlation between party affiliation and levels of political activism among army officers.

Chapter 4 examines the nature and extent of political expressions by army officers in the realm of social media. DoDD 1344.10, which governs political conduct by members of the military, was last updated in 2008, before the evolution of social media. This chapter examines whether the political activities by members of the military are in keeping with the norm of nonpartisanship and the DoD directive. It also analyzes what effect party affiliation and ideology might play in army officers' political activities online.

Chapter 5 takes on the unsettled issue of the role retired officers play in partisan politics. Richard Kohn famously argued that, like "princes of the church," retired four-stars never truly retire but continue to speak for the institution after they have left uniform.[21] Since 1988, an increasing number of retired general and flag officers have endorsed presidential candidates on both sides of the aisles, and in several high-profile instances, retired general and flag officers have publicly criticized the sitting president, secretary of defense, and chairman of the Joint Chiefs of Staff. This chapter examines active-duty officers' views of the role that retired officers, especially retired general and flag officers, play in the public sphere. It also examines to what extent such views may vary based on partisan affiliation and ideology.

Chapter 6 examines the opinions of military elites on interactions between senior military leaders and civilian policy-makers. From decisions on the use of force to the roles of senior military leaders during wartime, this chapter reports on the attitudes of military elites towards their civilian overseers. It also examines to what degree military elite opinions on these issues have changed over the past twenty years, and to what extent such changes could be attributed to partisan rationalization or motivated reasoning. Finally, it considers the role partisanship and political ideology play in shaping officer attitudes on such civil-military interactions. Chapter 7, the conclusion, takes stock of the state of nonpartisanship in the officer corps. It returns to the construct on politicization offered at the outset of this chapter to evaluate, based on the empirical findings of this book's survey data, if indeed the officer corps has become too partisan, too vocal, and too resistant to civilian oversight. The chapter closes with recommendations for senior military leaders and their civilian superiors as how to best promote the norm of nonpartisanship in the armed forces.

Readers, especially those serving on active duty, who are looking for a more practical application of the nonpartisan ethic beyond the legalistic, if not incomplete, DoDD 1344.10 will find that in Appendix A —A Guide to Instilling the Nonpartisan Ethic at the Unit Level. DoDD 1344.10 provides a list of political dos and don'ts for members of the military but avoids a deeper discussion on the more important issue of whether or not members of the military should engage in certain political activities, even if they are permitted. Moreover, most officers are simply not exposed to DoDD 1344.10 in their pre-commissioning programs or throughout their careers; and coupled with the scant attention paid to civil-military relations writ large in professional military education, most officers probably have not spent much time thinking about the norm of nonpartisanship. This appendix can serve as a useful tool for O-5 and O-6-level commanders specifically, providing them suggestions on how to best facilitate professional development discussions with their officers about the nonpartisan ethic.

When retired General Joseph Votel, former commander of US Central Command, recently reflected on the importance of the military remaining apolitical or nonpartisan, he observed:

> This is not a 'nice to do' thing; it is an absolute necessity in our constitutional system. When the military is viewed as having been politicized, it throws our American institutions out of balance and diminishes trust and confidence in our democratic form of government.[22]

If there is any silver lining to the charges the military has become politicized, it may be the renewed introspection ongoing within the ranks, along with leaders rightly viewing the nonpartisan ethic as integral to the profession.

Notes

1. McLaughlin, "'Sickening': Here's Why One Retired Military Officer Spoke Out Against Trump."
2. This is by no means a comprehensive list but shows that concerns of military politicization have been prevalent since the late 1990s. See Ricks, *Making the Corps*; Ricks, "The Widening Gap Between the Military and Society"; Holsti, "A Widening Gap Between the U.S. Military and Civilian Society"; Holsti, "Politicization of the United States Military"; Bacevich and Kohn, "Grand Army of the Republicans"; Exum, "The Dangerous Politicization of the U.S. Military"; Barno and Bensahel, "The Increasingly Dangerous Politicization of the U.S. Military"; Risa Brooks, "What Can Military and Civilian Leaders Do to Prevent the Military's Politicization."
3. Friend, "Military Politicization."
4. Ricks, *Making the Corps*.
5. Holsti, "A Widening Gap Between the U.S. Military and Civilian Society."
6. Feaver and Kohn, *Soldiers and Civilians*.
7. See chapter 4 for greater detail, and for one of the more notorious examples, see Schmitt, "General to Be Disciplined for Disparaging President."
8. Urben, *Like, Comment, Retweet*.
9. Cloud, Schmitt, and Shanker, "Rumsfeld Faces Growing Revolt by Retired Generals"; and Kablack et al., "The Military Speaks Out."
10. Feaver, *Armed Servants*
11. Ibid.
12. Holsti, "A Widening Gap Between the U.S. Military and Civilian Society"; Feaver and Kohn, *Soldiers and Civilians*; and Jason K. Dempsey, *Our Army*.
13. This is by no means to denigrate the *Military Times* surveys. They are useful for their consistency—in that they poll their readership every year. Their results, however, should be heavily caveated, given the skewed nature of their samples.
14. Shane, "Trump's Popularity Slips in Latest Military Times Poll." The poll was featured in subsequent articles in the *Washington Post*, *Time*, *USA Today*, *US News & World Report*, and *NBC News*, among others and featured in a Biden campaign ad, entitled, "No Wonder," that ran on

October 30, 2020, https://www.youtube.com/watch?v=d1Kwr1eJQMw& feature=emb_title.

15. Vespa, *Those Who Served*.

16. In 2015, the Department of Defense issued Department of Defense (DoD) Instruction 1100.13, *DoD Surveys*, which requires any survey of more than one component (e.g., more than one service or entity) to obtain approval from the Undersecretary of Defense for Personnel and Readiness. See Department of Defense, *DoD Surveys*, DoD Directive 1100.13 (Washington, DC: Department of Defense, 2017), https://www.esd.whs.mil/Portals/ 54/Documents/DD/issuances/dodi/110013p.pdf?ver=2019-04-08-125316 -290. Similarly, in 2019, the U.S. Army issued Army Regulation 25-98, *Information Management Control Requirements Program*, which requires all internal Army surveys of 100 individuals or more to be approved by the Headquarters, Department of the Army. The Army regulation is clear that its intent is, at least in part, to reduce the overall number of surveys administered to Army personnel: "To avoid overburdening Soldiers and DA Civilians, it is required that Army organizations obtain approval before administering an Army internal survey." See Department of the Army, *Information Management Control Requirements Program*, Army Regulation 25-98 (Washington, DC: Department of the Army, 2019): 13, https://armypubs.army.mil/epubs/DR_pubs/DR_a/pdf/web/ARN20910_ R25_98_ADMIN_FINAL.pdf.

17. More recent survey research of 9/11 veterans suggests enlisted and non-commissioned officers may be more apt to identify as Republicans today, however. See Liebert and Golby, "Midlife Crisis?," 119.

18. Until approximately 2013 when Army Knowledge Online (AKO) email transitioned to the Department of Defense enterprise email, all soldiers in the army were required to maintain an AKO email account, their primary work email addresses. The survey was created using SelectSurvey.net and hosted by the Office of Economic and Manpower Analysis at the U.S. Military Academy, which generated a random sample of 21,811 army officers from the US Army personnel databases.

19. Holsti, "Of Chasms and Convergences," 20.

20. Party identification and party affiliation of active-duty members and/or veterans are based exclusively on their self-professed preferences.

21. Kohn, "General Elections."

22. Votel, "An Apolitical Military Is Essential."

CHAPTER 2

PARTY AND IDEOLOGY

CONTINUITY AND CHANGE IN THE OFFICER CORPS

> I can estimate that at least 80% of military ballots I saw were
> straight ticket Democrat or simply had Joe Biden's name filled in
> on them. I had always been told that military people tended to be
> conservative, so this stuck out to me.[1]
> —Unnamed Republican poll watcher in Michigan

Is the officer corps in the All-Volunteer Force era consistently conservative
and reliably Republican, as this poll watcher seemed to think? In other
words, despite protracted wars, changes of presidential administration,
and changing demographics in both society and the military, are the
partisan and ideological attitudes of officers stable? This chapter examines
the political ideology and partisan identification of army officers in the
post-9/11 era and what determines these attitudes, including whether
factors pertaining to service in the army shape officers' partisanship.
It explores what variance, if any, has occurred over time in partisan
affiliation and ideology in the officer corps, as well as in an individual
officer's career in the US Army. Lastly, it examines how officers perceive
their fellow officers' partisanship and ideology, so as to investigate the
degree to which the officer corps' politics are well-known among those
in uniform.

CONSERVATIVES, THE REPUBLICAN PARTY, AND THE ALL-VOLUNTEER FORCE

In 1997, journalist Tom Ricks' book, *Making the Corps*, an in-depth profile of a Marine platoon in basic training, was one of the first popular accounts to suggest that a sociopolitical chasm had developed between American society and the Marine Corps—and all branches of the military for that matter. One of the defining characteristics of this gap, in Ricks' estimation, was the growing Republican leanings of the officer corps. Among Ricks' assertions was that for *junior* officers "open identification with the Republican Party [had become] the norm" and cited informal surveys of West Point cadets to bolster his claims.[2] While Samuel Huntington had long referred to the "military mind" as conservative, Ricks portrayed an officer corps that had become unabashedly polarized to the far right of the political spectrum.[3]

Social scientists wishing to study the political attitudes of military officers since the advent of the All-Volunteer Force have traditionally focused on a handful of studies. First, on four-year intervals from 1976 to 1996, Ole R. Holsti and James Rosenau conducted a series of surveys of military and civilian elites entitled the Foreign Policy Leadership Project (FPLP). The military respondents in the FPLP surveys primarily consisted of senior officers (O-5s and O-6s) in attendance at the National War College or assigned to the Pentagon.[4]

The FPLP surveys found among senior military officers surveyed from 1976 to 1996 an increasing preference for the Republican Party and a decline in the percentage of officers who indicated they were Independents.[5] For example, in 1976, only 33 percent of respondents identified as Republicans, but by 1996, this figure had increased to 67 percent. Similarly, the percentage of respondents claiming to be Independents declined from 46 percent in 1976 to 22 percent in 1996. Holsti observed a similar trend regarding political ideology. The percentage of officers who identified as somewhat or very conservative increased from 61 percent in 1976 to 73 percent in 1996, while the percentage of those describing themselves as somewhat or very liberal decreased from 16 percent to just 3 percent.[6] While the FPLP surveys were immensely valuable in comparing attitudes over time, the military sample was quite small, limiting the extent to which conclusions could be drawn about the military's political attitudes.

Peter Feaver and Richard Kohn's Triangle Institute for Security Studies (TISS) *Survey on the Military in the Post-Cold War Era* conducted during 1998–1999 was closely patterned after Holsti and Rosenau's prior work, comparing the attitudes of military and civilian elites, but the TISS Survey included a much larger military sample and was more comprehensive in scope.[7] The 81-question TISS Survey conducted over the fall of 1998 through the spring of 1999 was a landmark study for its breadth and depth.[8] While it focused on far more than the political attitudes of military elites, the TISS Survey, along with the FPLP study, is the most widely cited in terms of partisan attitudes of military elites in the post–Vietnam War era. Like the FPLP study, the TISS Survey found similar rates of party affiliation and political ideology for military elites, with 64 percent of respondents identifying with the Republican Party, 8 percent with the Democratic Party, and 17 percent as Independents.[9] Likewise, 67 percent of military elite respondents described themselves as conservative, while less than 5 percent claimed to be liberal, and 28 percent moderate.[10]

In 2004, Jason Dempsey's Citizenship & Service Survey (C&S Survey) was administered to both enlisted and active-duty officers serving in the army and represents the greatest contribution to understanding how enlisted and active-duty officers' political attitudes vary.[11] He found that while 63 percent of commissioned officers described themselves as conservative, only 32 percent of enlisted soldiers did.[12] Moreover, while he did not explicitly query his respondents on party affiliation, he created a novel party affiliation algorithm to predict respondents' party affiliation based on their responses to other questions in the survey. Under this algorithm, he predicted that while more than 64 percent of lieutenant colonels and colonels (the main focus of the FPLP and TISS samples) would affiliate themselves with the Republican Party, only 18 percent of junior enlisted soldiers, 21 percent of noncommissioned officers, and 36 percent of senior noncommissioned officers would do the same.[13] Dempsey's C&S Survey is the most comprehensive survey to suggest that the army is not as politically homogenous as perhaps previously thought—in contrast to the poll watcher's quote at the beginning of this chapter.[14] Dempsey also surveyed 885 cadets at the US Military Academy on the eve of the 2004 election. As with his findings on the political views of army officers, Dempsey found most West Point cadets identified with the Republican Party (61 percent)—a figure that exceeded his predicted Republican Party affiliation for lieutenants (44 percent) in his C&S Survey.[15] Of most concern, Dempsey found that most West Point cadets tended to conflate officership in the army with affiliation with the Republican Party.

The Stability of Partisan Attitudes

A substantial amount of political science literature suggests that people's partisan attitudes and political ideology are highly stable. In their pioneering work on partisan identification, *The American Voter*, Campbell, Converse, Miller, and Stokes argued that partisanship is an enduring psychological attachment, learned at an early age, primarily through familial socialization, and solidifies as one grows older. They attributed much of the stability in partisan attitudes to the existence of a "perceptual screen through which the individual tends to see what is favorable to his partisan orientation. The stronger the party bond, the more exaggerated the process of selection and perceptual distortion will be."[16] This perceptual screen makes it difficult for people with strong partisan loyalties and well-developed political attitudes to process information that does not adhere to their preexisting partisan loyalties and thus unlikely that strong partisans will change their attitudes and partisan identification.

Green, Palmquist, and Schickler argued that party affiliation is akin to membership in a social group. It has an enduring quality and reflects part of one's *identity*—far more than just a political opinion and thus is resistant to fluctuations in political events. Green et al. took Campbell et al.'s perceptual screen one step further, concluding that political events have little impact on partisan identity, and they made an important distinction between short-term changes in political opinions and long-term changes in partisan identification:

> Partisans neither shed their attachments when their party performs poorly nor maintain their attachments by shutting out bad news. On the contrary, the public does take notice of political events, and news tends to affect Democrats and Republicans in similar ways. Seldom, however, does the political or economic environment change in ways that would impel Democrats and Republicans to relabel themselves.[17]

Alternative assessments of party affiliation and political ideology offer a more dynamic view, however. Most notable is Morris Fiorina's *Retrospective Voting*, which argued that voters are constantly forming a "running tally" of party performance in their minds.[18] Fiorina challenged Campbell et al.'s assertion that partisanship is enduring and highly stable and instead offered a far more dynamic vision of party affiliation, one in which voters are continuously assessing and updating their evaluations of party performance. Using data from the Survey Research Center's 1956–1960 panel study, Fiorina tested his model of party identification as a running tally of retrospective evaluations and found that "retrospective evaluations can play a major role in moving individuals up and down the party identification scale."[19] Fiorina acknowledged some degree of durability in partisan identity and that when partisan change does occur, it may manifest itself in incremental changes along a spectrum as opposed to wholesale relabeling. He also conceded that strong partisans are less likely to be swayed by retrospective evaluations than weak partisans.

The steady shift among military officers towards the political right and the ensuing gap that emerged between military and civilian elites from the late 1970s to the late 1990s raised several questions, many of which have not been sufficiently answered with past survey research. Does something about military service cause its officers to become more conservative and affiliated with the Republican Party? Or does the All-Volunteer Force continuously attract individuals who happen to be politically conservative and Republican? While surveys of military officers over the past 40 years have included questions on political ideology and partisan identification, little attention has focused on ideological and partisanship changes and the role the military as an institution may play in this. Should there be a connection, or worse, causation between service in the military and identification with the Republican Party, it would most certainly raise valid questions about a politicized military.

As influential as the aforementioned FPLP and TISS surveys were in their scope, they are now dated. Even Dempsey's surveys are now over 16 years old and were conducted just three years after the war in Afghanistan began; at the time of this writing, America's 20-year war in Afghanistan has just ended. Suffice it to say, history has happened: two protracted wars that resulted in the deaths of more than 5,000 American service members, a global financial crisis, the election of the nation's first black president, and the model-breaking election of Donald Trump to the presidency, rise of populism, and ensuing schism within the Republican Party. The COVID-19 pandemic should be added to this list, but data from the three surveys cited in this book precede the pandemic. Any one of these political events could theoretically have been cause for army officers to reevaluate their partisanship and political leanings, and a reexamination with updated data is thus merited.[20]

This chapter revisits the partisan identification and political ideology of army officers, drawing comparisons to past surveys but focusing particularly on the post-9/11 era. It also examines the determinants of partisan identification for army officers, paying particular attention to whether factors associated with service in the US Army itself might shape partisan attitudes. In addition to examining the trends in ideological and party identification in the officer corps over time, this chapter explores to what extent officers change their attachment to a political party or ideology during their careers. Lastly, it examines perceptions of the officer corps' politics among officers themselves and how much those perceptions match reality.

PARTY IDENTIFICATION OF ARMY OFFICERS, POST-9/11

As stated earlier, few comprehensive surveys exist to chart the party identification and political ideology over time of members of the military, let alone active-duty army officers specifically. In order to draw a longer but more consistent comparison over time—and include the FPLP and TISS surveys from the late 1980s and late 1990s, respectively—lieutenants, captains, and majors are excluded from this comparison, zeroing in solely on army lieutenant colonels and colonels. Admittedly, this reduces the sample size and restricts the explanatory ability somewhat because lieutenant colonels and colonels make up only 20 percent of the active-duty army-officer corps. Nonetheless, it does provide a gauge of *senior* officers' viewpoints over time, which carries weightier implications for civil-military relations, especially as it pertains to the dialogue and interaction between the military and its civilian overseers.

Table 4 displays the party identification of army lieutenant colonels and colonels over time, drawing upon the FPLP (1988 and 1992) and TISS (1998–1999) surveys, as well as the CMR Time of War Survey, Politics & Social Media Survey and the NDU CMR Survey. The first thing that stands out is the remarkable consistency in the percentage of senior army officers affiliating themselves with the Republican Party over the past 30 years. In each of the six referenced surveys, the majority of senior army officers reported identifying with the Republican Party, and in three of the last four surveys, over 60 percent of senior officers self-identified as Republicans. In addition, in every survey, the number of Republican senior army officers outnumbered Democrats and pure Independents combined, and in the most recent survey, Republicans outnumbered Democrats by more than six to one.

Table 4. Party Identification of Senior US Army Officers Over Time.

	Democrats	Independents	Republicans	Other/No Preference
		percent checking each option		
FPLP Survey, 1988 (n=49)	14.3	30.6	49.0	6.1
FPLP Survey, 1992 (n=49)	8.2	24.5	59.2	8.2
TISS Survey, 1998-1999 (n=114)	5.3	17.5	66.7	10.5
CMR Time of War Survey, 2009 (n=1,216)	13.2	16.2	65.6	5.0
Politics & Social Media Survey, 2016 (n=51)	15.7	15.7	51.0	17.7
NDU CMR Survey, 2018-2020 (n=256)	10.2	22.3	61.3	6.3

Source. FPLP Survey (1988 and 1992), TISS Survey (1998–1999), CMR Time of War Survey (2009), Politics & Social Media Survey (2016), NDU CMR Survey (2018–2020).
Note. Data reflects responses from active-duty army lieutenant colonels and colonels only.

The one anomaly looks to be the relative dip in Republican Party affiliation among respondents in the Politics & Social Media Survey; at 51 percent, it was the lowest reported Republican affiliation among senior army officers since the 1988 FPLP survey. However, another data point stands out: roughly 18 percent of respondents in the 2016 survey reported "other" or "no preference" for their party affiliations—a percentage that was nearly three times the amount for that category in preceding and subsequent surveys. It could be that some officers surveyed in January 2016 were turned off by both eventual nominees for president and suppressed their true affiliations when surveyed, opting instead for "other" or "no preference." In an October 2016 *Military Times* poll that asked who respondents would vote for if the election were held that day, 34 percent responded with "third party" instead of Donald Trump or Hillary Clinton, yet exit polls after the election found only 5 percent of military and veteran voters cast their ballots for third-party candidates.[21] Whatever the reason, it is possible that a portion of those who claimed "other" or "no preference" in the Politics & Social Media Survey were really Republicans, considering 61 percent of a virtually identical cohort of officers surveyed two to four years later identified as Republican and only 6 percent selected "other" or "no preference."

Although the percentage of respondents identifying as Democrats remained less than 15 percent for most of the six surveys referenced in table 4, the percentage of those identifying as Independents has fluctuated somewhat. The high-water mark was in the 1988 FPLP survey, where nearly 31 percent of respondents identified as Independents, but the percentage dropped to just over 15 percent in 2016 before rebounding to 22 percent in the NDU CMR Survey from 2018 to 2020. It remains to be seen if this upward trend will continue and whether officers who previously identified as Republicans may be more apt to identify as Independents in the coming months and years.

A methodological note worth noting is that the CMR Time of War Survey, the Politics & Social Media Survey, and the NDU CMR Survey employed a seven-point partisan identification scale (strong Democrat to strong Republican). The seven-point scale, used in the American National Election Studies (ANES) surveys since 1952, provides greater fidelity on partisan attitudes and a better gauge of the strength of partisanship. To ensure a consistent comparison to the FPLP and TISS surveys, which employed a three-point partisan identification scale (Democrat, Independent, and Republican), table 4 follows the same methodology used by the ANES and counts "leaners" as partisans. This is also consistent with past scholarship that suggests Independents who lean Democrat or Republican are "largely closet Democrats and Republicans."[22]

Table 5 displays the results for the seven-point partisan identification scale for senior army officers. This chart highlights two important observations that are hidden in the three-point partisan identification scale in table 4: a declining percentage of strong Republicans and increasing percentage of weak Republicans and Independents who lean Republican. In the CMR Time of War Survey, 27 percent of army lieutenant colonels and colonels self-identified as strong Republicans—the largest category on the seven-point scale in that survey. However, the percentage of strong Republicans in the Politics & Social Media Survey and NDU CMR Survey was almost half of that (15 and 14 percent respectively) in the CMR Time of War Survey. Despite ongoing debates regarding increased polarization in the American electorate, partisanship among Republicans in the officer corps has actually weakened since 2009.[23] Taken more broadly, 15-20 percent of respondents in the Politics & Social Media Survey and NDU CMR Survey were classified as strong partisans in either party. And although the largest single category on the seven-point scale in 2009 was strong Republican, the largest single category in both 2016 and during 2018–2020 was Independent who leans Republican.

Table 5. Party Identification (7-point scale) of Senior US Army Officers (2009–2020).

	Strong Democrat	Weak Democrat	Lean Democrat	Independent	Lean Republican	Weak Republican	Strong Republican	Other/No Preference
				percent checking each option				
CMR Time of War Survey, 2009 (n=1,216)	4.1	2.9	6.2	16.2	24.8	13.8	27.0	5.0
Politics & Social Media Survey, 2016 (n=68)	5.9	0.0	11.8	17.7	29.4	13.2	14.7	7.4
NDU CMR Survey, 2018-2020 (n=256)	0.4	2.3	7.4	22.3	31.6	15.6	14.1	6.3

Source. CMR Time of War Survey (2009), Politics & Social Media Survey (2016), and NDU CMR Survey (2018–2020).
Note. Data reflects responses from active-duty US Army lieutenant colonels and colonels only.

The percentage of respondents identifying as pure Independents or Independents who lean one way or the other increased over the past decade—from 47 percent in 2009 to 59 percent in 2016 to 61 percent during 2018–2020. These are important findings for the broader discussion of whether the officer corps has become politicized. Although the number of officers affiliating with the Republican Party vastly outnumber Democrats, and strong partisans are far more likely to be Republican than Democrats, the majority of senior officers surveyed over the past decade are weak or leaning partisans.

One additional comparison is worth examining—the partisan identification of those just beginning their careers as officers in the army. Table 6 displays the findings of party affiliation for West Point cadets and army lieutenants on a three-point scale, and table 7 reports the findings for a seven-point scale. Three things stand out. First, again, is the remarkable consistency in party identification over time with little variance from the TISS Survey to the three more recent surveys conducted. Had a seven-point party identification scale been employed in the TISS Survey, its results may have more closely mirrored the findings from the other three surveys. Some of the respondents who identified as Independents (21 percent) in the TISS Survey may have actually been Independent leaners, and the relatively large percentage who answered "other" or "no preference" creates some ambiguity compared to the more recent surveys. For the most part, however, the results look similar. Second, while a majority of cadets and lieutenants affiliated themselves with the Republican Party, they were smaller majorities compared to their more senior officer counterparts, and the largest single category in all three surveys was Independents who lean Republican.

Table 6. Party Identification of West Point Cadets and US Army Lieutenants Over Time.

	percent checking each option			
	Democrats	Independents	Republicans	Other/No Preference
TISS Survey, 1998-1999 (n=256)	8.6	21.1	48.8	21.5
CMR Time of War Survey, 2009 (n=646)	23.7	14.9	52.9	8.5
Politics & Social Media Survey, 2016 (n=303)	27.7	10.9	55.5	5.9
NDU CMR Survey, 2017-2018 (n=596)	24.8	18.3	54.4	2.5

Source. TISS Survey (1998–1999), CMR Time of War Survey (2009), Politics & Social Media Survey (2015–2016), and NDU CMR Survey (2018–2020).

Note. Data reflects responses from West Point cadets for the TISS Survey, Politics & Social Media Survey, and NDU CMR Survey and from army lieutenants for the CMR Time of War Survey.

Table 7. Party Identification (7-point scale) of West Point Cadets and US Army Lieutenants (2009–2020).

	percent checking each option							
	Strong Democrat	Weak Democrat	Lean Democrat	Independent	Lean Republican	Weak Republican	Strong Republican	Other/No Preference
CMR Time of War Survey, 2009 (n=646)	5.9	5.9	11.9	14.9	20.3	15.5	17.2	8.5
Politics & Social Media Survey, 2016 (n=301)	3.7	7.0	17.3	10.6	25.9	14.3	15.3	6.0
NDU CMR Survey, 2018-2020 (n=596)	4.5	4.9	15.4	18.3	21.6	16.4	16.3	2.5

Source. CMR Time of War Survey (2009), Politics & Social Media Survey (2015–2016), and NDU CMR Survey (2018–2020). *Note.* Data reflects responses from West Point cadets for the Politics & Social Media Survey and NDU CMR Survey and from army lieutenants for the CMR Time of War Survey.

Lastly, a larger proportion of cadets identified as Democrats than senior officers did—about one-quarter of cadets compared to roughly 5 to 10 percent of lieutenant colonels and colonels. This is noteworthy and suggests one of at least three things might happening over time: first, this could be a generational phenomenon, whereby the individuals commissioning into the officer corps today may be less apt to identify with the Republican Party than past cohorts. If true, this will be borne out if the cadets and lieutenants surveyed here advance to become lieutenant colonels and colonels and maintain their political leanings. Second, it could be that these cadets and lieutenants who initially identify as Democrats end up switching their affiliation to Independent or Republican the longer they stay in the army. If this was, in turn, due to socialization effects within the army, it would raise real concerns about politicization within the officer corps. Or third, perhaps this could be evidence of self-selection. Officers who make the army a career could be more likely to be Republican, and officers more apt to self-identify as Democrats may leave the service before reaching the ranks of senior army officers. This last option is also concerning because it carries the possibility that these junior officers leave the military because they hold minority viewpoints within the officer corps and find military culture to be unwelcoming or incompatible with their beliefs. While any of these three explanations cannot be definitively proven without additional data and research, it is a theme that will be revisited several times in this chapter.

POLITICAL IDEOLOGY OF ARMY OFFICERS, POST-9/11

In *The Soldier and the State*, Samuel Huntington argued that there is such a thing as a "military mind," and it is conservative and realistic, and his theory has been backed up with strong empirical findings throughout the All-Volunteer Force era—at least for the officer corps.[24] Table 8 shows the results of the ideological self-classification of senior army officers, oriented along a seven-point scale going back to the 1988 FPLP survey and also includes data from Dempsey's C&S Survey.

Table 8. Ideology of Senior US Army Officers Over Time.

	percent checking each option						
	Very Liberal	Liberal	Slightly Liberal	Moderate	Slightly Conservative	Conservative	Very Conservative
FPLP Survey, 1988 (n=49)	0.0	0.0	4.1	26.5	57.1	12.2	0.0
FPLP Survey, 1992 (n=130)	0.0	0.0	4.1	30.6	51.0	12.2	2.0
TISS Survey, 1998-1999 (n=130)	0.0	0.8	6.2	29.2	50.8	12.3	0.0
C&S Survey, 2004 (n=125)	0.0	2.9	9.2	18.2	23.7	41.7	4.3
CMR Time of War Survey, 2009 (n=1,215)	0.7	3.5	5.8	23.1	22.6	35.2	9.0
Politics & Social Media Survey, 2016 (n=67)	1.5	3.0	11.9	31.3	20.9	23.9	7.5
NDU CMR Survey, 2018-2020 (n=249)	0.0	2.8	3.6	36.1	28.5	22.9	6.0

Source. FPLP Survey (1988 and 1992), TISS Survey (1998–1999), C&S Survey (2004), CMR Time of War Survey (2009), Politics & Social Media Survey (2016), NDU CMR Survey (2018–2020).

Note. Data reflects responses from active-duty US Army lieutenant colonels and colonels only.

The consistent use of the seven-point ideological scale (very liberal to very conservative) across each of these surveys provides a greater level of fidelity in understanding the political views of senior army officers. As with their party identification, the political ideologies of lieutenant colonels and colonels has remained relatively constant over the past 30 years, insofar as most officers self-identify as conservative in each of the reported seven surveys, a sizeable minority self-identify as moderate, and hardly anyone self-identifies as liberal.

A closer exploration of the seven-point scale over time reveals a trend, however. Since Dempsey's C&S Survey in 2004, the percentage of respondents who self-identified as moderate has steadily increased —from 18 to 36 percent in the 2018–2020 NDU CMR Survey. Similarly, the percentage of those who identified as conservative declined from a high of 42 percent in 2004 to 23 percent in 2018–2020. There are many possible examples for this, but each requires additional investigation to confirm. The least likely scenario is that senior officers serving today are simply less conservative as a generational cohort. This seems doubtful since the senior officers surveyed in 2016 and from 2018 to 2020 were the junior officers of the mid-to-late 1990s who were the focus of analyses by Tom Ricks and others because they were deemed to be so conservative. A second possibility may be found in the close correlation between ideology and party during a time of intense polarization. A weakening in ideological intensity corresponds with the observed weakening in partisan intensity among Republicans in the ranks of senior officers. It is possible that a decline in intensity of both conservative ideology and affiliation with the Republican Party reflects a dissatisfaction among senior army officers with Donald Trump or the direction of the Republican Party, but it is unclear based on this survey data alone.

Table 9 lists the political ideology of West Point cadets and army lieutenants across six surveys dating back to the TISS Survey and includes Dempsey's two surveys from 2004. As with the senior officers, a majority of cadets and lieutenants self-identify as conservative, though not as strongly as the senior officers. In fact, in the two most recent surveys conducted, the proportion of cadets self-identifying as conservative was just under 50 percent. Moderates accounted for about a third of cadet responses in the most recent surveys, and about 20 to 25 percent of cadets have identified as liberal over time. As with party identification, while the majority of cadets or lieutenants surveyed landed on the right side of the political spectrum, they were more balanced and more politically diverse than the senior officers surveyed.

At the very least, it should be acknowledged that cadets enrolling in the US Military Academy today exhibit greater gender and racial diversity than ever before. When Dempsey conducted his survey of cadets in 2004, just six percent of the Corps of Cadets was African American and 15 percent were women.[25] Meanwhile, in the class of 2023, which enrolled at West Point in June 2019, 15 percent were African American and 24 percent were women.[26] Based on these demographics alone, it should not be surprising that the political and partisan attitudes of cadets surveyed in 2016 and 2017 are less conservative or more moderate than cadets surveyed in 2004 or 1999. Given the consistently high rates of affiliation of senior army officers with the Republican Party and their propensity to identify as conservative, the real question, as this chapter broaches in the next sections, is whether these more liberal-leaning or moderate cadets will end up making the army their career.

Table 9. Ideology of West Point Cadets and US Army Lieutenants Over Time.

	percent checking each option						
	Very Liberal	Liberal	Slightly Liberal	Moderate	Slightly Conservative	Conservative	Very Conservative
TISS Survey, 1998-1999 (n=272)	1.5	2.9	10.7	21.3	39.7	13.6	1.1
Cadet Pre-Election Survey, 2004 (n=886)	1.0	8.5	10.1	19.4	20.7	34.1	6.3
C&S Survey, 2004 (n=82)	0.0	14.3	10.2	23.0	24.8	24.6	3.1
CMR Time of War Survey, 2009 (n=641)	1.4	7.5	9.4	29.6	19.5	26.2	6.4
Politics & Social Media Survey, 2016 (n=305)	2.3	7.9	14.8	30.2	17.7	22.0	5.3
NDU CMR Survey, 2017-2018 (n=580)	0.9	9.1	12.1	28.3	22.6	22.6	4.5

Source. TISS Survey (1998–1999), Cadet Preelection Survey (2004), CMR Time of War Survey (2009), Politics & Social Media Survey (2015–2016), and NDU CMR Survey (2018–2020).
Note. Data reflects responses from West Point cadets for the TISS Survey, Cadet Preelection Survey, Politics & Social Media Survey, and NDU CMR Survey and from US Army lieutenants for the C&S Survey and CMR Time of War Survey.

DETERMINANTS OF PARTISAN IDENTIFICATION IN THE POST-9/11 OFFICER CORPS

What are the factors that shape and determine the partisan affiliations of army officers? Table 10 reports the results of logistic regressions of affiliation with the Republican Party and Democratic Party against a host of explanatory variables from the CMR Time of War Survey. With more than 4,000 survey responses, it offers the best opportunity to model partisan affiliation within the army officer corps, especially because of the large number of demographic variables collected. As expected, a conservative political ideology and having parents who are Republicans are the strongest predictors of Republican Party affiliation for army officers, while being liberal and having parents who are Democrats are the strongest determinants of affiliation with the Democratic Party.

Race and gender are also important, and mostly expected predictors of party affiliation. In the Republican model, dummy variables for being white, Hispanic, and male positively affect affiliation with the Republican Party while being black has a negative effect. While those are the expected impacts for whites, blacks, and men, the finding for Hispanics is somewhat counterintuitive, especially because Hispanics voted for Barack Obama in 2008 by a margin of more than two to one.[27] In the Democratic model, being a woman and being black both positively predict affiliation with the Democratic Party—again, expected results. Little of this is earth-shattering: the politics that officers inherit from their parents and demographics such as race and gender matter most in determining their party affiliation. In this regard, army officers differ very little from their civilian counterparts.

Table 10. Logistic Regression Analysis of US Army Officers' Party Identification.

Dependent Variable = Republican Party ID (dummy)		Dependent Variable = Democratic Party ID (dummy)	
Conservative	2.51***	Liberal	3.10***
	(0.09)		(0.20)
Rep Parents	1.07***	Dem Parents	1.85***
	(0.09)		(0.19)
Age	-0.13	Age	0.00
	(0.07)		(0.14)
Men	0.33*	Women	0.90***
	(0.13)		(0.22)
White	0.83***	White	-0.29
	(0.14)		(0.28)
Black	-1.04***	Black	1.62***
	(0.24)		(0.41)
Hispanic	0.83***	Hispanic	-0.22
	(0.22)		(0.41)
Grad Degree	0.04	Grad Degree	0.21
	(0.11)		(0.23)
Evangelical	0.40***	Evangelical	-0.63**
	(0.11)		(0.24)
South	-0.04	South	0.05
	(0.11)		(0.22)
Combat Arms	0.15	Combat Arms	0.22
	(0.11)		(0.23)
Combat Svc Spt	-0.03	Combat Svc Spt	0.16
	(0.11)		(0.23)
Yrs of Service	0.01	Yrs of Service	-0.01
	(0.01)		(0.04)
Rank	0.17*	Rank	-0.06
	(0.08)		(0.19)
USMA	-0.02	USMA	-0.00
	(0.16)		(.31)
ROTC	0.05	ROTC	-0.07
	(0.11)		(0.25)
Family Service	-0.08	Family Service	-0.28
	(0.09)		(0.18)
		Junior Officers Separating	0.64*
			(0.31)
Pseudo R^2	0.34	Pseudo R^2	0.39
Log Likelihood	-1715.59	Log Likelihood	-456.23
N	3859	N	1456

Source. CMR Time of War Survey (2009).
Note. Entries are logit coefficients with standard errors in parentheses. * $p<.05$, **$p<.01$, ***$p<.001$.

Since interpreting coefficients from logit regressions often fails to convey the real substance at hand, simulations of predicted party affiliation allow for a more meaningful interpretation of the effect some of these key variables have on party identification.[28] For example, a conservative officer whose parents are Republicans has a 72 percent chance of affiliating with the Republican Party. If that hypothetical conservative officer with Republican parents is a white male, the probability of him being a Republican jumps to 89 percent. Likewise, a liberal officer whose parents are Democrats has a 91 percent likelihood of self-identifying as a Democrat. While not a perfect correlation, a conservative political ideology and having parents who are Republicans are the strongest predictors of affiliation with the Republican Party. The same holds true for liberals and having parents who are Democrats with identifying with the Democratic Party.

Michael Desch once noted that "the typical American military officer today is southern, white, conservative, likely to identify with the Republican Party, to be quite religious, and increasingly he's likely to be an evangelical Protestant."[29] While the portrait may be somewhat accurate, it suggests a conflation between affiliation with the Republican Party and white, male, evangelical officers from the south that is worth testing. Roughly three-quarters of evangelical or born-again Christians voted Republican in presidential elections going back to at least 2004 when the Pew Research Center started closely tracking this, so it seems natural that being an evangelical Christian would serve as a predictor for an army officer's affiliation with the Republican Party.[30] While being evangelical does predict Republican Party identification for army officers— and negatively predicts affiliation with the Democratic Party—growing up in the south had no impact on Republican or Democratic party affiliation, despite the fact that southerners constituted 22 percent of the survey sample.

Explanatory variables related to service in the army such as commissioning source, specialty, years of service, and having immediate family members who served in the military had no effect on affiliation with the Republican or Democratic parties. The only true service-related variable that impacted party identification is rank, which had a positive effect on affiliation with the Republican Party, even when controlling for age and years of service. The higher the rank an officer attains in the army, the more likely they will identify as Republican. While this research has shown that junior officers tend to have higher rates of affiliation with the Democratic Party than senior officers, this trend has been apparent over time, going back to the FPLP and TISS surveys—contrary to what Tom Ricks observed in the late 1990s, when junior officers stood out for being staunch conservative Republicans.[31] As suggested earlier, one of at least three things may be happening: a generational impact might be at play, but its effects will not be seen until the junior officers surveyed most recently reach the rank of lieutenant colonel or colonel; officers might become more conservative and Republican the longer they stay in the army; or the officers who are less likely to affiliate with the Republican Party might end up leaving the army relatively earlier in their careers, while those who choose to make the army a career generally tend to be conservative Republicans.

Respondents in the CMR Time of War Survey were asked whether they were in the process of leaving the army or would be within the next six months. Overall, 306 officers reported that they were planning on leaving the army, 100 of whom had completed less than ten years of service. Among the 100 junior officers preparing to leave the army, 37 percent described themselves as Democrats, 11 percent as Independents, and 44 percent as Republicans. Similarly, junior officers preparing to leave the army were also more likely to be centrist or left of center, with 54 percent professing to be liberal or moderate, compared to 45 percent of lieutenants and captains overall. Finally, as table 10 indicates, being a junior officer separating from the army has a significant, positive effect on army officers' affiliation with the Democratic Party.

This is an area that merits further research. While rank was the only service-specific variable to have an effect on the party identification of army officers, the fact that the attrition rate for junior officers is characterized by a higher affiliation with the Democratic Party than for those who make the army a career begs the obvious question: is the officer corps' political leanings a contributing factor to junior officers leaving the army? This question cannot be answered with the results of these surveys alone, but it is worth examining more closely, perhaps in qualitative exit surveys of junior officers who decide to leave the army. From a normative standpoint, the officer corps' preference for the Republican Party is not by itself a significant concern for the profession, as many others have pointed out over the years.[32] It is a concern, however, for an institution that claims partisan neutrality, especially if the officer corps' political leanings are somehow pushing officers with minority viewpoints out of the army.

Survey data from the NDU CMR Survey that was conducted from 2017 to 2020 offer another opportunity to examine the determinants of partisan identification within the officer corps and see if any noteworthy changes are evident since the CMR Time of War Survey was conducted in 2009. A few caveats are worth noting: first, in order to run logistic regressions with the 2017–2020 survey data, the full sample, including officers from each of the services (not just army officers, although army officers constitute the overwhelming majority of the sample), is used. Second, the CMR Time of War Survey was a random-sample survey of army officers in the ranks of lieutenant through colonel, whereas the NDU CMR Survey consists of responses of West Point cadets and senior-service-college students and lacks responses from midgrade officers (captains and majors). Lastly, the NDU CMR Survey did not include the range of independent variables that the CMR Time of War Survey had, namely religion, region in the country where respondents grew up, and service-specific variables such as source of commissioning and specialty (e.g., combat arms, combat support, etc.).

Table 11. Logistic Regression Analysis of the US Army Officer Corps' Party Identification Over Time.

	Dependent Variable = Republican Party ID (dummy)			Dependent Variable = Democrat Party ID (dummy)	
	2009	2017-2020		2009	2017-2020
Conservative	2.56***	2.69***	Liberal	3.32***	4.03***
	(0.09)	(0.16)		(0.13)	(0.25)
Republican Parents	1.08***	1.20***	Democratic Parents	1.55***	2.16***
	(0.09)	(0.16)		(0.12)	(0.26)
Age	0.00	0.10	Age	-0.14***	-0.14
	(0.03)	(0.06)		(0.04)	(0.08)
Men	0.37**	0.34	Women	0.85***	0.34
	(0.12)	(0.21)		(0.14)	(0.26)
White	0.82***	0.84***	White	-0.40*	0.24
	(0.14)	(0.23)		(0.19)	(0.31)
Black	-0.94***	-0.73	Black	1.65***	1.35***
	(0.23)	(0.41)		(0.23)	(0.41)
Hispanic	0.76***	0.26	Hispanic	0.03	1.35**
	(0.21)	(0.39)		(0.27)	(0.47)
Grad School	0.07	-0.19	Grad School	0.10	0.27
	(0.10)	(0.25)		(0.14)	(0.35)
Family Service	-0.08	-0.07	Family Service	-0.23*	-0.21
	(0.09)	(0.16)		(0.11)	(0.21)
Pseudo R^2	0.33	0.38	Pseudo R^2	0.40	0.49
Log Likelihood	-1754.1	-520.3	Log Likelihood	-1100.3	-315.3
N	3903	1215	N	3903	1215

Source. CMR Time of War Survey (2009) and NDU CMR Survey (2017–2020).
Note. Entries are logit coefficients with standard errors in parentheses. * $p < .05$, ** $p < .01$, *** $p < .001$.

Table 11 reports the results of logistic regressions on the affiliations of army officers with the Republican and Democratic parties against the same set of independent variables. As with the regressions highlighted in table 10, the explanatory variables with the biggest impact on party affiliation remain respondents' ideology and the party affiliation of their parents. While gender was a predictor of partisan identification (men for Republicans, and women for Democrats) for the 2009 data, it is not statistically significant with the data from 2017 to 2020. Nor is rank or grade, which is not pictured in table 10. Race remains an important determinant in all the models—white continuing to be a predictor of Republican Party affiliation, and black a predictor of Democratic Party affiliation. Notably, party affiliation for Hispanics flip-flopped in the NDU CMR Survey, moving from having a positive effect on an affiliation with the Republican Party in 2009 to predicting identification with the Democratic Party in the 2017–2020 surveys. This corresponds with recent voting trends, in which 69 percent of Hispanics voted for Democratic congressional candidates in the 2018 midterm elections.[33]

On the surface, the lack of an effect of graduate-school education on party affiliation seems surprising and counter to most political science research that finds postgraduate education tends to predict affiliation with the Democratic Party.[34] However, army officers do not truly mirror the rest of society in this regard, and their graduate-school experiences are also quite different. Of the 256 US Army lieutenant colonels and colonels surveyed in the NDU CMR Survey, 88 percent reported they already had a graduate degree from a civilian institution. In the post-9/11 era, many army officers obtain master's degrees online or in conjunction with their enrollments in professional military education—often in classrooms populated almost entirely with other military officers.[35] Thus, what holds true for advanced education with most Americans may not apply in the same fashion with army officers.

Change in Partisan Identification and Political Attitudes

Partisan and ideological changes within the officer corps have been hinted at in this chapter but not definitively settled. Certainly, examining the partisan identification and ideology of the officer corps over time gives a sense of continuity or shifting allegiances and beliefs, but it cannot conclusively answer the question if individual army officers change their partisan affiliation or political beliefs after they joined the army. Table 12 examines responses from senior army officers surveyed in the CMR Time of War Survey and the NDU CMR Survey on whether their partisan affiliation has changed since joining the army.

In 2009, 67 percent of respondents indicated their party affiliation had not changed much since joining the army, and another 16 percent reported they felt less attached to either party. But any evidence of partisan relabeling or weakening looks miniscule at best—just 4 percent of Democrats and 5 percent of Republicans reported being less attached to their own party. Instead, 72 percent of Republicans reported no change in their party identification, while 11 percent of Republicans reported feeling more attached to their party since joining the army. Meanwhile, 58 percent of Democrats reported no change, but 26 percent felt an even stronger attachment to the Democratic Party—hardly evidence that something about serving in the army makes officers suddenly become Republicans. Surely, there can be ideological reasons behind Democrats' intensified feelings for the Democratic Party, but it could also be a byproduct of being a political minority in the army—being exposed to views by their Republican peers who far outnumber them could cause Democrats to solidify their affinity for the Democratic Party. Of note, 90 percent of Independents reported either not changing their affiliation or growing less attached to either party.

Table 12. Change in Senior US Army Officers' Partisan Identification.

Party Affiliation Change Among Senior Army Officers
percent indicating their partisan affiliation has changed since being in the Army

CMR Time of War Survey, 2009

	No Change in Party ID	More Attached to a Party	Less Attached to Either Party
Total (n=1,216)	67.0	11.5	16.2

	No Change in Party ID	Less Attached to Either Party	More Attached to Own Party	Less Attached to Own Party
Democrats	57.5	11.9	26.3	4.4
Independents	50.3	40.1	N/A	N/A
Republicans	72.0	11.3	11.2	5.4

NDU CMR Survey, 2018-2020

	No Change in Party ID	More Attached to a Party	Less Attached to Either Party
Total (n=256)	39.1	10.6	35.9

	No Change in Party ID	Less Attached to Either Party	More Attached to Own Party	Less Attached to Own Party
Democrats	34.6	30.8	23.1	11.5
Independents	26.3	59.7	N/A	N/A
Republicans	45.2	26.1	12.7	15.9

Source. CMR Time of War Survey (2009) and NDU CMR Survey (2018–2020).
Note. Data reflects responses from active-duty US Army lieutenant colonels and colonels only.

Together, these findings dispute any notion that service in the army somehow pushes its officers to the political right. Rather, officers who identified with the Democratic Party showed no signs of relabeling, or even moderation for that matter, and Independents generally remained Independent. Overall, the majority of officers reported that their party affiliation had not changed much since joining the army, and for those who did indicate their affiliation had changed, their party attachments solidified; there is no evidence to support wholesale partisan relabeling, especially relabeling that has occurred as a result of service in the army.

Data from the 2018–2020 surveys paint a different picture, however. Although 67 percent of respondents reported having experienced no changes in their party identification in 2009, only 39 percent reported no change during 2018–2020. Meanwhile, 36 percent reported being less attached to either party—doubling the figure from 2009. The same held true for partisans: the percentage of Democrats and Republicans who reported being less attached to their own party tripled from 2009. Equally, the percentage of Democrats and Republicans who reported being less attached to either party more than doubled from 2009. Certainly, these findings are in line with continued reporting on Americans' low confidence levels in institutions in general today.[36] But, in a time when there are increased concerns about intense negative partisanship and elite partisan polarization—not to mention concerns of politicization of the military—military elites are weakening their partisan ties, not deepening them.

Changes in political ideology for senior army officers proved to be more dynamic than partisan identification, with approximately 54 percent of respondents indicating their political beliefs had changed since joining the army when surveyed in 2009 and 59 percent in the 2018–2020 NDU CMR Survey (see table 13). Among those who reported changes in their beliefs in 2009, the majority (26 percent) indicated they became more conservative or less liberal.

Table 13. Change in Senior US Army Officers' Political Ideology.

Senior Army Officers' Political Ideology Change
percent indicating their political views have changed since being in the Army

CMR Time of War Survey, 2009	I am more liberal or less conservative	I am more moderate	I am more conservative or less liberal	No, my political views have not changed much
TOTAL (n=1,220)	11.8	16.2	26.2	45.8
Democrats	28.3	17.0	16.4	38.4
Independents	16.3	27.1	16.3	40.3
Republicans	8.1	13.8	31.1	47.0
Liberals	45.1	10.7	10.7	33.6
Moderates	10.4	33.2	12.8	43.2
Conservatives	7.3	11.4	33.2	48.1

NDU CMR Survey, 2018–2020	I am more liberal or less conservative	I am more moderate	I am more conservative or less liberal	No, my political views have not changed much
TOTAL (n=256)	18.8	19.9	19.9	41.4
Democrats	34.6	15.4	23.1	26.9
Independents	22.8	24.6	14.0	61.4
Republicans	15.9	19.8	24.8	42.0
Liberals	31.3	12.5	18.8	37.5
Moderates	30.0	32.2	11.1	26.7
Conservatives	10.7	13.3	25.3	50.7

Source. CMR Time of War Survey (2009) and NDU CMR Survey (2018–2020).
Note. Data reflects responses from active-duty army lieutenant colonels and colonels only.

Yet, when the same question was posed again in 2018–2020, the directional change was equally split among respondents who said they had become more conservative or less liberal (20 percent), more moderate (20 percent), or more liberal or less conservative (19 percent).

The trend observed where an increasing percentage of senior army officers reported being less attached to either party is observable for partisans and their ideologies, too. In 2009, 33 percent of Democrats indicated their political views had become more moderate, become less liberal, or had become more conservative since joining the army—a percentage that edged upwards to 38 percent in 2018–2020. The shift in ideological moderation was even more pronounced for Republicans. In 2009, 22 percent reported they had become more moderate, less conservative, or more liberal, and by 2018–2020, that figure climbed to 36 percent. To be fair, 67 percent of Republicans who participated in the NDU CMR Survey from 2018–2020 reported their political views had not changed much or that they had become more conservative or less liberal, so this should not be construed as a significant leftward shift among Republican military elites. Over a third of Republicans admitting to becoming more moderate in their ideologies is not trivial, though.

These findings suggest that both party affiliation and political ideology for army officers are fairly durable over time and that service in the army may have little impact on political attitudes over one's career. In the most recent survey of senior army officers, an increasing number indicated they were less attached to either party. In addition, partisans on both sides of the aisle admitted their political views moved more towards the center than in past years. While more than a quarter of respondents reported becoming more conservative or less liberal in 2009, this dissipated by 2018–2020, and there is no evidence to support a large-scale, rightward shift within the ranks of active-duty army officers—at least not today. If anything, while their party and ideological labels may have remained the same, officers appear to be softening their partisanship and moderating their ideologies somewhat.

PERCEPTION OF THE OFFICER CORPS' PARTISANSHIP AND IDEOLOGY

What about how senior army officers view the officer corps' politics? Where do they believe their fellow officers stand in terms of party affiliation and political ideology? Comparing officers' perceptions against their own reported self-identification not only allows us to gauge how accurate their perceptions are but also to see how their assessments vary based on their own partisanship and ideologies. In both the CMR Time of War Survey and NDU CMR Survey, respondents were asked to describe generally the officer corps' party affiliation and could choose one of four options: that most were Republicans, that some were Republicans and some were Democrats, that most were Democrats, or that they were not sure.

Table 14, which lists the findings, shows that while 61 percent of senior army officers in 2009 felt most officers were Republican, only 41 percent believed that was the case a decade later. Conversely, the proportion of senior officers who thought some were Democrats and some were Republicans more than doubled from the CMR Time of War Survey to the NDU CMR Survey—jumping from 22 percent to 48 percent. The only real constant is virtually no one in both surveys thought the officer corps comprised mostly Democrats.

In 2009, senior officers' perception of the officer corps' partisanship was fairly accurate: 60 percent of officers in the ranks of lieutenant through colonel who were surveyed in the CMR Time of War Survey self-identified as Republicans (as did 66 percent of senior officers), and 61 percent of senior army officers thought the officer corps was mostly Republican. Meanwhile, 74 percent of senior officers who were Democrats thought most of the officer corps was Republican—a higher proportion than Republicans who thought so (62 percent). This is not unexpected; senior officers who were Democrats may have been more conscious of holding a minority viewpoint in the officer corps and more apt to describe the institution as almost universally preferring the Republican Party.

Table 14. Senior US Army Officers' Perceived Party Identification of the Officer Corps Over Time.

	Generally speaking, how would you describe the officer corps? percent checking each option			
	Most are Democrats	Some are Democrats and Some are Republicans	Most are Republicans	Not Sure
CMR Time of War Survey, 2009 (n=1,215)	0.4	21.7	60.8	17.2
Democrat	1.3	15.6	74.4	8.8
Independent	0.5	23.4	54.8	21.3
Republican	0.0	23.2	62.1	14.7
NDU CMR Survey, 2018-2020 (n=256)	0.0	48.1	40.6	11.3
Democrat	0.0	57.7	30.8	11.5
Independent	0.0	47.4	38.6	14.0
Republican	0.0	47.8	43.3	8.9

Source. CMR Time of War Survey (2009) and NDU CMR Survey (2018–2020).
Note. Data reflects responses from active-duty army lieutenant colonels and colonels only.

For all these reasons, the findings from the NDU CMR Survey a decade later are so surprising. Surveyed between 2018 and 2020, 61 percent of senior army officers self-identified as Republican, but only 41 percent thought the majority of the officer corps was Republican (table 14). Moreover, Democratic officers—who, as a minority in the military, have historically been fairly cognizant of the officer corps' political leanings to the right—were less likely than their Republican peers to suggest the majority of the officer corps was Republican in the NDU CMR Survey. In a total flip, only 31 percent of Democrats thought the officer corps was mostly Republican—down from 74 percent in 2009—compared to 43 percent of Republicans who thought so.

What might explain this dramatic shift in perceptions, especially since the actual partisan makeup of the officer corps really has not changed much over time? There are at least two possible explanations, both of which are hard to prove without more data. First, after decades of concerns about the military consistently leaning toward the right, officers surveyed here could have been prone to some social-desirability bias. It might "look better" if the officer corps was perceived to be equally split between Democrats and Republicans, and thus more representative of society, even if it is not. Respondents may have felt compelled to falsify their true attitudes here—confusing bipartisanship with nonpartisanship. Second, this could have reflected a Trump effect within the officer corps, where Democrats and disaffected Republicans had been vocal in their opposition to Trump in the workplace during his administration. This could have created the perception among senior officers that the officer corps was more heterogeneous, even though it really was not. In other words, some respondents might have mistakenly concluded that anti-Trump sentiments within the officer corps meant there were fewer Republicans in the officer corps than in previous years, but this is little more than speculation, and more survey research is required. The related phenomenon of political outspokenness within the officer corps on social media will be explored in greater depth in chapter 4.

Respondents were also asked how they would generally classify the officer corps' political views, using the same seven-point scale they used in describing their ideologies. Figure 1 graphically depicts senior army officers' self-professed political ideologies against their perceptions of the officer corps' ideologies in a boxplot. In both the CMR Time of War Survey and the NDU CMR Survey, a stronger majority of senior officers assessed the officer corps to be conservative than the proportion of officers who self-identified as conservative. For example, from 2018 to 2020, 57 percent of army lieutenant colonels and colonels self-identified as conservative, but 81 percent perceived most of the officer corps to be conservative.

Figure 1. Senior US Army Officer Ideology Versus Perceived Ideology of the Officer Corps.

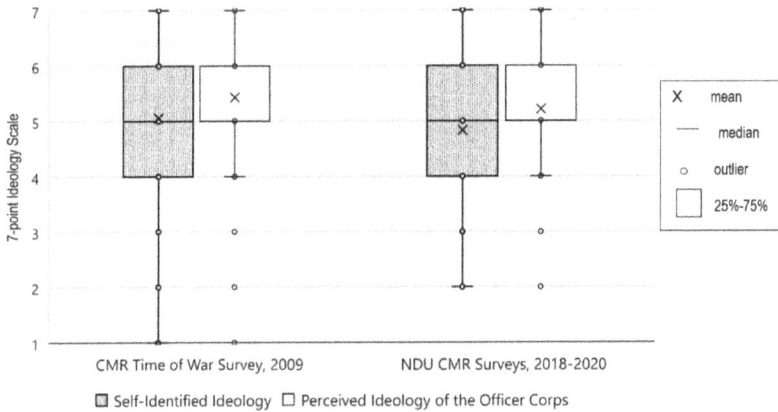

Source. CMR Time of War Survey (2009) and NDU CMR Survey (2018–2020).
Note. Data reflects responses from active-duty army lieutenant colonels and colonels only.

The senior officers' accurate perceptions of the officer corps' ideologies makes their recent inability to correctly assess officers' partisanship so intriguing, especially given senior officers' accuracy in describing the officer corps' party identification a decade earlier. This, too, gives credence to the idea that respondents' inability to accurately assess the officer corps' partisan identification may be rooted in some sort of Trump effect. In other words, respondents could have misconstrued disapproval for Trump within the officer corps as evidence of partisan relabeling, when it really might have only amounted to disapproval of the president.

CONCLUSION

At first blush, the quote that led off this chapter from the unnamed poll watcher, who assumed all military voters were Republican, seems understandable, even if prone to wild generalizations. Data from the CMR Time of War Survey, Politics & Social Media Survey, and NDU CMR Survey paints an army officer corps—especially its senior ranks—that is consistently conservative and reliably Republican, continuing a long-standing trend in the All-Volunteer Force era first observed in the FPLP and TISS projects. Despite that consistency, most officers serving today are weak partisans, and within the ranks of senior army officers specifically. A smaller percentage self-identify as strong Republicans compared to a decade ago, while more profess to be Independents who lean Republican than any other category on the seven-point party identification scale. The majority of junior officers and West Point cadets are also conservative Republicans, but not in the numbers of their senior officer counterparts, and a non-trivial number of younger officers do identify with the Democratic Party in sharp contrast to senior officers. The findings presented here do not suggest that officers simply become more conservative or Republican the longer they stay in the army. Rather, junior officers who are in the process of leaving the army are more likely to affiliate themselves with the Democratic Party, while officers who make the army a career tend to be Republicans. From the survey data in this book, the motivations of junior officers who leave the army are unclear but are surely varied; any suggestion they might be leaving because of the political or cultural makeup of the officer corps is concerning and should be investigated by senior army leaders.

The major determinants of army officers' partisan affiliation are unsurprising and relatively constant: their ideology, race, and gender as well as their parents' party identification are the factors that most strongly predict affiliation with the Republican or Democratic parties. While there is no evidence that service-specific variables, such as career specialty, source of commissioning, or having family members who served in the military, shape partisan attitudes, in the CMR Time of War Survey, officers' rank did positively affect an army officer's affiliation with the Republican Party. The higher the rank an army officer achieves, the more likely they are Republican.[37]

There is no evidence from any of the aforementioned surveys to suggest that service in the army pushes officers to the right of the political spectrum or to affiliate themselves with the Republican Party. In fact, data from the most recent NDU CMR Survey found significant dissatisfaction with both parties among senior officers, with a large portion of respondents professing to be less attached to the party with to which they claimed affiliation. While this dissatisfaction did not result in partisan relabeling and could have been little more than a negative reaction to President Trump, the strength of partisanship in the officer corps at the beginning of the third decade in the 2000s appears to be waning. While respondents were not queried specifically on why they were inclined to distance themselves from their party, it is hard to think it was not in response to the fractured state of politics and increased polarization since the 2016 election, and perhaps a direct response to the election and presidency of Donald Trump or the shifts ongoing within the Republican Party.[38] Future survey research of the officer corps during the Biden administration may offer additional insights on the strength of partisanship within the officer corps and to what degree this recent trend towards weak partisanship may have been a reaction to Trump specifically.

Recent surveys highlighted here not only found that the officer corps was consistently conservative, but that its conservatism was well-known among serving, senior army officers. This is an important observation that will be further analyzed in the next chapters and should not be overlooked: the only way an officer can size up the politics of the officer corps is if officers routinely and freely express their political views in the workplace. It is the only explanation that can account for senior officers' stunning accuracy and consistency in pinpointing the officer corps' political ideologies over time.

NOTES

1. Fahrenthold, Helderman, and Hamburger, "In Poll Watcher Affidavits, Trump Campaign Offers No Evidence of Fraud."
2. Ricks, *Making the Corps*, 280–281; and Ricks, "The Widening Gap Between the Military and Society." See also Bacevich and Kohn, "Grand Army of the Republicans."
3. Huntington, *The Soldier and the State*, 79.
4. Of note, Holsti and Rosenau only asked military respondents to identify their branch of service in 1988 and 1992, therefore, we can only isolate active-duty army officer responses in these two particular datasets (n=49 for both years). This will come into play later in the chapter when officers' political views are compared over time.
5. Holsti, "A Widening Gap Between the U.S. Military and Civilian Society," 11.
6. Ibid., 13.
7. The TISS survey included a military elite sample of 723 officers, most of whom were enrolled in senior service college; 115 of those military elites were Army lieutenant colonels and colonels.
8. Many of the TISS questions had subset or multi-part questions, and the entire survey included more than 200 questions in total. As a result, the TISS dataset has proven to be rich empirical resource for students of civil-military relations.
9. Holsti, "Of Chasms and Convergences," 28.
10. Ibid.
11. Dempsey's total sample of 1,188 soldiers included 535 active-duty army officers. See Jason K. Dempsey, *Our Army*, 7.
12. Jason K. Dempsey, *Our Army*, 75.
13. Ibid., 102.
14. Jason K. Dempsey's survey truly was a landmark one, and there has not been a comparable survey of active duty enlisted and noncommissioned officers' political attitudes since his was published.
15. Jason K. Dempsey, *Our Army*, 166.
16. Campbell et al., *The American Voter*, 133.
17. Green, Palmquist, and Schickler, *Partisan Hearts and Minds*, 111.
18. Fiorina, *Retrospective Voting in American National Elections*.
19. Ibid., 96.

20. MacKuen, Erikson, and Stimson, "Macropartisanship."
21. Those surveyed in *Military Times* polls tend to be subscribers and are more often are career Soldiers, but not necessarily all are officers. Shane, "Trump's Popularity Slips in Latest Military Times poll."
22. Keith et al., *The Myth of the Independent Voter*, 4.
23. Dimock et al., "Political Polarization in the American Public."
24. Huntington, *The Soldier and the State*, 59–79.
25. Jason K. Dempsey, *Our Army*, 162.
26. Fink, "West Point's Newest Class Has More Minority New Cadets."
27. Lopez, "The Hispanic Vote in 2008."
28. Simulations were run using Clarify software. See King, Tomz, and Wittenberg, "Making the Most of Statistical Analyses."
29. Moran, "In New England, a Sense of Abandonment."
30. Martinez and Smith, "How the Faithful Voted."
31. It should be noted that the lieutenants that Tom Ricks wrote about in the mid-to-late 1990s are today's colonels, who are generally found to be more conservative than junior officers serving today.
32. Betros, "Political Partisanship and the Military Ethic in America"; Collins, "Combining the Roles of Actor and Observer"; and Hooker, "Soldiers of the State."
33. Krogstad, Flores, and Lopez, "Key Takeaways About Latino Voters in the 2018 Midterm Elections."
34. Pew Research Center, "A Deep Dive into Party Affiliation."
35. This factor prompted retired Lieutenant General David Barno to reflect, "We have people getting two and three master's degrees during their time on active duty without ever having to encounter a civilian." Bryant and Urben, "Reconnecting Athens and Sparta."
36. According to Gallup's 2020 poll on trust and confidence in institutions, only 36 percent of Americans report having "a great deal" or "quite a lot of confidence" in the fourteen surveyed institutions. Brenan, "Amid Pandemic, Confidence in Key U.S. Institutions Surges."
37. As mentioned earlier, rank or grade did not have a statistically significant effect on Republican or Democratic party affiliation in the NDU CMR Survey regression. However, the NDU CMR Survey did not include lieutenants and captains, as the CMR Time of War Survey, and its sample of majors was also very small. A larger sample size with respondents from all ranks and grades would likely find rank to be a statistically significant explanatory variable.

38. Corasaniti, Karni, and Paz, "'There's Nothing Left': Why Thousands of Republicans Are Leaving the Party"; and Kollman and Jackson, "Trump Radicalized the Republican Party."

CHAPTER 3

ACTS OF CITIZENSHIP
OR PARTISANSHIP?

POLITICAL ACTIVITY IN THE OFFICER CORPS

Politics is beyond the scope of military competence, and the participation of military officers in politics undermines their professionalism, curtailing their professional competence, dividing the profession against itself, and substituting extraneous values for professional values. The military officer must remain neutral politically.[1]

—Samuel P. Huntington,
The Soldier and the State

This chapter explores the levels of political participation, activism, and outspokenness of active-duty army officers and examines to what extent they participate in traditional forms of political expression, including those allowable activities outlined in Department of Defense Directive (DoDD) 1344.10, *Political Activities by Members of the Armed Forces*. From the simple act of voting to more overt acts of partisanship, it analyzes the types of political activities army officers engage in and reports on officers' attitudes on the appropriateness of such public political behavior for the active-duty force. Lastly, it examines the correlation between party affiliation and levels of political activism among army officers to assess whether the officer corps has become politicized.

Measuring Political Activity in the Officer Corps

In *The Soldier and the State*, Huntington's objective control model centers on a military that is "politically sterile and neutral" and avoids participating in politics at all costs.[2] While Huntington fails to delineate what exactly might constitute participation in politics or what political neutrality means, it is safe to assume the only form of political behavior Huntington might have been comfortable with members of the military engaging in is the private act of voting. Voting is the most basic form of political participation, and for many officers it is the only partisan act in which they regularly engage. Historically, the ability for service members stationed far away from home to vote was difficult, and it took years, several wars, and legislation to ensure service members' full enfranchisement, as Donald Inbody has chronicled.[3] Voter turnout by those in uniform, especially absentee voting, has been aided during the All-Volunteer Force era by the Uniformed and Overseas Citizens Absentee Voting Act (UOCAVA) of 1986 and the emphasis the military has placed—and Congress has mandated—on affording all service members the opportunity to vote.[4] The UOCAVA was amended in 2009 by the Military and Overseas Voter Empowerment (MOVE) Act, providing additional protections and removing additional barriers to voting for service members stationed overseas.[5]

Political behavior by members of the military is regulated by DoD Directive 1344.10, which provides guidelines on permissible—albeit traditional and arguably dated—forms of political activity. In short, the directive allows members of the armed forces to participate in the political process as private citizens, but they must avoid the appearance or suggestion that their actions are officially sanctioned by the Department of Defense. For example, members of the military are allowed to vote and can express their personal opinions on political candidates as private citizens, but they cannot speak in front of a partisan political gathering. Service members may put a bumper sticker on their cars, but they cannot put a political poster in their yards if they live on a military installation. One may write a letter to the editor expressing their personal political views, with the caveat that their views do not reflect those of the Department of the Defense, but they cannot publish partisan articles soliciting votes for a particular candidate. A glaring omission in the directive pertains to political commentary on social media—which will be addressed in greater detail in chapter 4—but is largely a function of the directive not being updated since 2008.

On one hand, the Department of Defense actively encourages service members to vote, especially while stationed overseas, while on the other, it painstakingly enumerates restrictions on political activity by those on active duty. Alice Hunt Friend and Jim Golby have described this phenomenon in the All-Volunteer Force—and the inevitable tension that results—as a "hybrid approach," whereby partisan expression in uniform is forbidden but as private citizens is encouraged.[6] This duality can be problematic for service members to navigate and is reflected not only in the quotations that lead off this chapter, but in the messages penned by the chairman of the Joint Chiefs of Staff in *Joint Force Quarterly* on the eve of recent presidential elections. In advance of the 2008 election, Admiral Michael Mullen, then chairman of the Joint Chiefs of Staff, wrote:

> We are first and foremost citizens of this great country, and as such have a right to participate in the democratic process...What I am suggesting—indeed, what the Nation expects—is that military personnel will, in the execution of the mission assigned to them, put aside their partisan leanings. Political opinions have no place in cockpit or camp or conference room. We do not wear our politics on our sleeves. Part of the deal we made when we joined up was to willingly subordinate our individual interests to the greater good of protecting vital national interests...The only thing we should be wearing on our sleeves are our military insignia.[7]

Retired General Martin Dempsey, Mullen's successor, echoed a similar sentiment four years later, on the eve of the 2012 election, writing, "As citizens we should stay informed, and we are, of course, entitled to exercise our right to vote. But understanding the issues, even understanding the candidates, is different than advocating for them."[8] And in 2016, then Chairman General Joseph Dunford continued the consistent messaging, writing:

> Every member of the Joint Force has the right to exercise his or her civic duty, including learning and discussing—even debating —the policy issues driving the election cycle and voting for his or her candidate of choice. Provided that we follow the guidance and regulations governing individual political participation, we should be proud of our civic engagement. What we must collectively guard against is allowing our institution to become politicized, by how we conduct ourselves during engagements with the media, the public, or in open or social forums.[9]

The messages, striking in their consistency, reflect the "hybrid approach" and are positive, optimistic messages that speak to service members' civic virtue and selfless service. They also good examples of what the teaching of norms looks like in practice—carefully crafted and well-timed by the most senior member of the military. At the same time, these messages also reflect the inherent tension associated with the hybrid approach— a recognition that in practice, service members do, in fact, have a hard time compartmentalizing their personal political views while in uniform —and need to be reminded, probably more frequently than once every four years, to keep their politics private.

To truly answer the question on the degree of politicization within the armed forces, and its officer corps specifically, a full accounting of its political behavior is required—beyond just its historical party-affiliation rates. And as with data on party affiliation, accurate data on the officer corps' political behavior is difficult to obtain because the military is loath to have its members' political behavior and attitudes explored in depth. Survey data, however, can shed further light on the nature and extent of political expressions by active-duty officers and whether their behaviors are in keeping with the norms Huntington envisioned and recent chairmen of the Joint Chiefs have articulated.

VOTER TURNOUT AND VIEWS OF VOTING IN THE OFFICER CORPS

The Department of Defense's Federal Voting Assistance Program (FVAP) tracks voter turnout for all active-duty members of the armed forces—enlisted and officers combined. According to FVAP data, just 46 percent of active-duty military-service members voted in the 2016 presidential election, down from 59 percent in 2012; and 53 percent in 2008.[10] By this measure, with the exception of the 2004 election, military-voter turnout has been generally on par with overall voter turnout levels among the voting-age public during the post-9/11 era.[11] However, as the FVAP notes, active-duty military members are not representative of the broader American voting public in terms of age, gender, mobility, and education level, so direct, unweighted comparisons between the voting public and active-duty military voters can be misleading.

Understanding and reporting accurate voter-turnout levels within the officer corps over time, however, is even more difficult because FVAP data does not distinguish between enlisted and active-duty officers. Moreover, just as the active-duty military is not representative of society, the officer corps is even less so. Simply based on age and socioeconomic variables, we should expect officers to have higher voter-turnout levels than enlisted members and the voting-age public. Table 15 reports self-professed voter-turnout results for military officers during the 2008 and 2016 elections along with their intentions to vote in the 2020 election, as queried in the CMR Time of War Survey and NDU CMR Survey. In 2009, 81 percent of army officers in the ranks of lieutenant through colonel indicated they voted in the 2008 election—nearly 30 percentage points higher than the FVAP's measure of active-duty service member turnout that year.

Table 15. Military Officers' Views of Voting and Their Voter Turnout (2008–2020).

	Members of the active duty military should vote	Voter Turnout in 2008	Voter Turnout in 2016	Anticipated Voter Turnout in 2020
	Percent checking "agree" or "strongly agree"	percent who reported they voted	percent who reported they voted	percent who reported they plan to vote
TOTAL	92.5	81.3	72.7	89.3
O1-O3s	92.0	77.3***	N/A	N/A
O4-O6s	93.0	84.4***	75.4	89.3
Democrats	93.4	89.8*	85.7*	98.4
Independents	87.0	77.7	73.5	80.7
Republicans	95.0	85.7*	68.6*	91.5
(n)	3,986	4,090	264	354

Source. CMR Time of War Survey (2009) and NDU CMR Survey (2018–2020).
Note. Party identification is displayed for O4-O6s only. Differences between Democrats and Republicans are significant at * p < .05. Differences between O1-O3s and O4-O6s are statistically significant at *** p < .001.

A smaller percentage of lieutenants and captains (77 percent) than majors, lieutenant colonels, and colonels (84 percent) reported voting in 2008, and this is consistent with long-standing political science scholarship on voting behavior, which finds that education, age, and income are the strongest predictors of voting.[12] Additionally, Independents were less likely than both Democrats and Republicans to indicate they voted in 2008, suggesting either partisan affiliation helps drive military voters to the polls or that military Independents are more apt to subscribe to the philosophy that officers, in the tradition of George Marshall and others, should refrain from voting. Regardless, army officers who self-identified as Independents still reported a voter-turnout rate higher than the voting public in 2008, so not too much should be inferred from this one finding.

Jason Dempsey's 2004 Citizenship & Service (C&S) survey queried army officers on whether they voted in the 2000 election. According to his survey of 535 army officers in the ranks of lieutenant through colonel, 68 percent indicated they had voted in the 2000 election—a lower turnout rate than the 2009 CMR Time of War Survey reported but a figure more on par with reported army-officer turnout in 2016.[13] Among a sample of midgrade to senior military officers in each of the services surveyed in the NDU CMR Survey, 73 percent reported they voted in 2016, and 89 percent indicated they planned to vote in 2020.[14] Voter turnout among midgrade and senior officers in 2016 dropped nine percentage points from 2008 and is in line with the decreased active-duty military-voter turnout levels in 2016 reported by the FVAP. This decline in the officer corps' voter turnout may be rooted, at least partially, in the high unfavorability ratings for both Donald Trump and Hillary Clinton in the 2016 campaign.[15] Of note, however, Republican officers experienced a greater decline in self-reported turnout between 2008 and 2016. In 2009, among midgrade to senior officers who self-identified as Republicans, 86 percent reported they voted in the 2008 election, but just 69 percent of a similar sample indicated they voted in 2016—a remarkable 17-percentage-point drop-off. Midgrade to senior officers who identified as Democrats or Independents experienced only a four-percentage-point decline in turnout. So, despite high unfavorability ratings for both presidential candidates in 2016, Republican officers were more likely to sit this election out than Democrats or Independents. Despite this relative apathy in the officer corps in 2016—and it should be noted that such apathy still resulted in a 73 percent self-identified voter turnout—projected voter turnout for midgrade to senior officers in 2020 rebounded in dramatic fashion, with 89 percent of respondents indicating they planned to vote.

The self-reported voter-turnout figures for army officers should be regarded with a caveat because they undoubtedly reflect some degree of overreporting. Vote overreporting is common in election-related surveys, even in the long-standing American National Election Studies (ANES) because respondents often feel compelled to misrepresent their voting histories, exhibiting a social-desirability response bias.[16] Some scholars have also argued the ANES voter-turnout levels have become even more inflated in recent years due to both declining response rates and measurement issues.[17] Additionally, with both the CMR Time of War Survey and the NDU CMR Survey, the high levels of self-reported voter turnout may also reflect some sampling bias in that the respondents most likely to complete surveys voluntarily on civil-military relations may also be the ones who are most interested in politics and vote in elections in the first place.[18] Having said that, army officers probably do not overreport at the same rate of the civilian public, as Dempsey observed in his two surveys of army personnel in 2004.[19]

Even accepting that the self-reported voter-turnout rates for officers may be slightly inflated, and despite the difficulty with measurement comparisons between active-duty military voters and the overall voting-age public, the current corpus of literature suggests something about military service might make members more predisposed to voting than the general public. Jeremy Teigen found that veterans vote at higher rates than non-veterans, and this is especially the case among the World War II, Korean War, and post-Vietnam/All-Volunteer Force cohorts, suggesting some military socialization effects were at play.[20] Additionally, a 2018 survey by Syracuse University's Institute for Veterans and Military Families (IVMF) found that 77 percent of active-duty military officers view voting as a civic duty.[21] And as table 15 also shows, most army officers embrace the norm of affording all soldiers the opportunity to vote. In 2009, approximately 93 percent of army officers agreed with the statement that members of the military should vote, and there is little variance among demographic groups. Independents were the group least likely to agree with the statement, but only relatively speaking; 87 percent of them still felt members of the military should vote. Therefore, given the near unanimity among army officers that members of the active-duty military should vote, their high self-reported rates of actual and anticipated voter turnout may not be that off the mark.

Moreover, despite occasional calls from some within the military profession to abstain from voting as a sign of one's commitment to nonpartisanship, as Generals Grant, Marshall, and Eisenhower did, army officers serving today categorically reject such a notion.[22] According to the 2018 IVMF survey, less than two percent of active-duty military officers believed it was not appropriate for members of the military to vote.[23] And it is not just junior-ranking officers who ardently support members of the military voting. Lieutenant Colonel Matthew L. Cavanaugh's *New York Times* op-ed in 2016 that advocated for active-duty officers to refrain from voting was swiftly met with countering op-eds by two prominent retired general officers.[24] In more recent times, General David Petraeus was one of the few general officers who publicly acknowledged he refrained from voting while on active duty—a practice he took with him into retirement—but findings from the CMR Time of War Survey, among others, suggest that is a minority viewpoint in today's officer corps.[25]

LEVELS OF POLITICAL ACTIVISM AND INTEREST

The CMR Time of War Survey queried army officers on six different forms of political participation, each of which are activities allowable under DoDD 1344.10. Respondents were asked whether they had ever, as private individuals and not representing the army, donated money to a candidate or political party; worn a campaign button or put a bumper sticker on their cars; ever encouraged other members of the military to vote; joined a partisan or nonpartisan club and attended meetings; expressed their personal opinions on political candidates or issues to others; or attended a partisan or nonpartisan political fundraiser, meeting, rally, debate, convention, or any other political activity as non-uniformed spectators. Table 16 displays the results for respondents who answered "yes" to these six questions. The two activities recording the highest number of responses were also the two most benign types of political activity of the six: encouraging other members of the military to vote and expressing their personal political opinions to others. Nearly 80 percent of army officers surveyed indicated they had encouraged others in the military to vote during an election, a figure which increased as one grew more senior in rank (74 percent of lieutenants indicating so, compared to 90 percent of colonels). Taken together with the earlier findings on officers' high self-reported voter-turnout levels and their attitudes that members of the military should vote, this draws a portrait of an officer corps fully committed to voting in the All-Volunteer Force era.

Approximately 74 percent of officers surveyed also indicated they had at one point expressed their personal opinions on political candidates or issues to others during an election or campaign, but there is a slight variance depending upon officers' party affiliation. Nearly 80 percent of Republicans indicated they had expressed their political opinions to others, compared to 72 percent of Democrats and 67 percent of Independents. With Republicans forming the majority of the officer corps in the All-Volunteer Force era, their increased likelihood to express their political views to others may indicate they believe others in the officer corps share their same political leanings, or they simply feel less constrained in their political speech—a theme that will be addressed again in this book with additional survey findings.

Table 16. Political Activism of US Army Officers (2009).

	Gave money to an individual candidate running for office or to a political party	Wore a campaign button or put a campaign sticker on your car	Encouraged other members of the military to vote	Joined a partisan or non-partisan political club and attended its meetings	Expressed your personal opinion on political candidates or issues to others	Attended a partisan or nonpartisan political fundraiser, meeting, rally, debate, convention, or any other political activity as a non-uniformed spectator
			percent checking each option			
TOTAL	20.1	13.2	79.7	5.5	74.1	11.8
Lieutenants	14.1	14.8	74.0	7.4	71.4	13.7
Captains	16.9	13.4	77.6	6.0	73.2	12.7
Majors	20.1	12.4	80.2	5.4	77.3	12.5
Lt Colonels	25.8	13.6	81.6	4.4	74.6	9.3
Colonels	28.2	10.2	89.5	2.8	73.7	9.4
Democrats	28.3***	17.5*	79.7	5.5	71.9***	14.5
Independents	14.3	6.7	76.5	4.2	67.0	9.4
Republicans	19.7***	13.7*	81.7	6.7	79.6***	11.8
(n)	4,089	4,089	4,081	4,079	4,082	4,067

Source. CMR Time of War Survey (2009).
Note. Differences between Democrats and Republicans are statistically significant at *** $p < .001$ and * $p < .05$.

The four remaining indicators of political participation—which are far more overt measures— show much lower levels of activism by army officers. Less than six percent of respondents indicated they had ever joined a political club, and approximately 12 percent responded that they had attended a political fundraiser, rally, convention, debate, or meeting. Approximately 20 percent of army officers surveyed reported they had donated money to a candidate running for office or a political party at some point in their lives, and roughly 13 percent of officers reported they had worn a campaign button or put a bumper sticker on their cars. Additionally, only seven percent of army officers reported both making a campaign donation and putting a bumper sticker on their cars, and just two percent indicated they had participated in all six forms of political activity—scant evidence of a uniformly politically active officer corps.

According to time-series data from the 2008 ANES, approximately 11 percent of Americans donated money to a candidate or political party (compared to 20 percent of army officers) and 19 percent wore a campaign button or put a bumper sticker on their cars during the 2008 election (compared to 13 percent of army officers). With these two comparisons at least, army officers are somewhat on par with the American public in terms of levels of political activity, although army officers made monetary contributions to campaigns at a higher rate than the general public. The CMR Time of War Survey data from 2009 also reflects consistency with Dempsey's 2004 C&S Survey, where 18 percent of army officers reported having donated money to campaign and 16 percent indicated they displayed a campaign button, sticker, or sign.[26]

As expected, in all six measures of political activity, Independents were less politically active than Democrats and Republicans. Democrats, however, were more likely to donate to political candidates, than Republicans and Independents. Although the question asked if respondents had *ever* done any of these activities and was not simply restricted to the 2008 election (unlike similar ANES questions which are election-year specific), the higher levels of campaign donations by Democrats could reflect their recent support for the candidacy of Barack Obama in 2008. More noteworthy than the partisan finding on campaign donations, however, is the fact that over a quarter of lieutenant colonels and colonels —the most senior officers in the sample—admitted to donating money to a campaign. It is an unambiguously partisan act, but one that senior officers perhaps thought was private, in contrast to displaying a bumper sticker on their cars or a sign in their yards. They may have been unaware that donors who contribute $200 or more to federal election campaigns can be easily tracked online through sites such as OpenSecrets.org, putting their partisanship out there in the public domain.[27] As Jason Dempsey has noted, "while the act of donating money to a candidate or campaign is a semiprivate affair, it probably signals a stronger and more explicit commitment to a political cause than either displaying a bumper sticker or voting."[28] That over a quarter of senior officers made financial contributions to a candidate running for office or a political party is at least in tension with the kind of politically neutral professionalism which Huntington envisioned for the officer corps.

Another way to measure US Army officers' level of political engagement is to gauge their levels of political interest, free from the constraints of military service and DoDD 1344.10. Respondents in the CMR Time of War Survey were asked if they would consider participating more fully in politics after their careers in the military. As shown in table 17, 42 percent of army officers indicated they would consider becoming more involved in politics and campaigns; 29 percent expressed interest in running for political office someday; and 28 percent indicated they might join or work for an interest group. Although these are purely hypothetical scenarios, they demonstrate a significant level of political interest among army officers. There is nothing normatively wrong with military officers wanting to enter politics or simply becoming more involved in politics after they are out of uniform, but that roughly one-third of all officers indicated such interest is nonetheless noteworthy for a profession that ostensibly eschews politics.

Table 17. Political Interest of US Army Officers (2009).

	Following my career in the military, I would consider the following:		
	Becoming more involved in politics and campaigns	Running for political office	Joining or working for an interest group
	percent checking "agree" or "strongly agree"		
TOTAL	41.5	28.5	28.4
Lieutenants	41.1	33.2	24.2
Captains	41.4	29.4	26.8
Majors	41.6	28.8	26.9
Lieutenant Colonels	42.0	25.1	32.7
Colonels	42.3	25.9	35.4
Men	43.8	31.0	29.5
Women	30.3	14.3	24.8
Democrats	47.8*	28.2	35.7***
Independents	34.7	24.8	24.8
Republicans	43.1*	30.8	28.9***
(n)	4,079	4,075	4,057

Source. CMR Time of War Survey (2009).
Note. Differences between Democrats and Republicans are statistically significant at *** p < .001 and * p < .05.

As with the political-activism measures, Independents were less interested in getting involved in politics than Democrats and Republicans. Democrats were slightly more likely than Republicans to indicate interest in becoming more involved in politics and campaigns and in joining or working for an interest group. Additionally, a gender gap exists regarding political interest among army officers, with men displaying a greater interest in politics than women. For example, while 44 percent of men stated they would consider getting more involved in politics and campaigns after military service, only 30 percent of women did. Similarly, 30 percent of men would consider running for office someday, compared to just 14 percent of women. This finding, now more than 10 years old, may no longer be accurate—or, even if it is accurate, it is not necessarily indicative of the interest among female veterans in running for elected office today. In 2018, an unprecedented fourteen female veterans ran for Congress, and in 2020, that record was shattered with twenty-eight female veterans on the ballot.[29] To be sure, male veterans running for Congress in 2020 outnumbered female candidates by more than five to one, just as men greatly outnumber women in the military, and thus among veterans too. Greater electoral success among female veterans—as was seen in the 2018 midterm elections—could prompt greater interest among women serving in the military to consider running for political office someday.[30]

These findings of significant political interest within the officer corps are at odds with what many civil-military relations scholars note has been a side effect of the military's apolitical stance: a dislike of politics altogether. Retired Lieutenant Colonel Brian Babcock-Lumish noted, "being called 'political' by one's military peers is almost universally considered a slur on one's character..."[31] Similarly, retired Commander Dayne Nix observed, "military members generally view politics with distaste, if not downright hostility. Many view themselves as separate from and morally superior to politicians, whom they see engaged in political turf wars and nasty electoral campaigns."[32] While seemingly contradictory, it is possible that some army officers simultaneously hold two positions: a distrust of politics and politicians as well as the feeling they could probably "do it better" if they were involved in politics. These themes, especially army officers' views of politicians, elected leaders, and the society they are sworn to defend, will be examined in greater detail in chapter 5.

POLITICAL EXPRESSIONS BY THOSE ON ACTIVE DUTY

While the previous measures may help describe the levels of political activity and interest within the officer corps, they do not tell the whole story and cannot definitively answer the broader question about the extent to which the officer corps may be politicized in the post-9/11 era. First, the measures of political activity highlighted in table 16 are *allowable* activities under DoDD 1344.10. Second, while they may give a sense of how politically engaged army officers are, they do not by themselves suggest an inappropriate amount of politics in the workplace. Lastly, officers' interest in becoming more involved in politics after their careers in the military is by no means suggestive of politicization or normatively inappropriate behavior on active duty.

DoDD 1344.10 is best known for its list of dos and don'ts regarding political behavior, but the directive actually provides a fair amount of latitude to service members in exercising their First Amendment rights. However, the norms associated with a nonpartisan military go beyond regulations and directives. These norms suggest that even if certain behaviors and activities are allowable under DoDD 1344.10, they may not be appropriate, and service members should exercise great caution in undertaking any type of political activity. Table 18 displays the results from two survey questions aimed at gauging mid-to-senior grade army officers' adherence to the norms of a nonpartisan military, measured by whether they feel active-duty members should publicly criticize civilians in government and whether those on active duty should be allowed to express their political views like any other citizen. These two questions have been posed in three different surveys over the past 20 years, allowing for a comparison of views over time.

Approximately 86 percent of US Army majors, lieutenant colonels, and colonels surveyed in the 1998–1999 Triangle Institute for Security Studies (TISS) agreed with the notion that those on active duty should not criticize senior civilians in government, and responses were generally consistent across party lines. During the 2009 CMR in a Time of War Survey, however, only 75 percent of army majors, lieutenant colonels, and colonels agreed—even though, again, responses were generally consistent among Democrats, Independents, and Republicans. While the majority of officers still gave the normatively correct response, a decline of ten percentage points a decade after the TISS study is significant and may reflect the toll from the wars in Iraq and Afghanistan as well as an ensuing decline in army officers' trust in government, regardless of which political party is in power at the time.

During the NDU CMR Survey conducted from 2018 to 2020, the percentage of mid-to-senior grade army officers who felt that active-duty service members should not publicly criticize senior civilians in government rebounded back up to 85 percent, but potential evidence of partisan rationalization or motivated reasoning was unearthed that was not evident in the previous two surveys. While 91 percent of Republicans felt active-duty military members should refrain from publicly criticizing civilians in government, only 68 percent of Democrats did. The over-whelming majority of Republican respondents, surveyed when a Republican president occupied the White House, suggested those on active duty should not criticize senior civilian government officials—compared to a smaller proportion of Democrats who were likely opposed to the occupant of the Oval Office at the time. This suggests that officers today may temper their adherence to certain professional norms depending on their partisanship and who is president at the time.

Table 18. US Army Officers' Views of the Military's Role in Society Over Time.

	percent checking "agree" or "strongly agree"	
	Members of the active duty military should not publicly criticize senior members of the civilian branch of government	Members of the active duty military should be allowed to publicly express their political views just like any other citizen
TISS Survey, 1998-1999 (n=211)	85.7	35.7
Democrats	90.9	36.4
Independents	88.9	36.1
Republicans	85.8	35.5
CMR Time of War Survey, 2009 (n=2,200)	74.7	33.4
Democrats	73.7	36.3
Independents	73.4	27.6
Republicans	75.5	34.9
NDU CMR Survey, 2018-2020 (n=288)	85.1	16.0
Democrats	67.6***	24.3
Independents	82.5	12.7
Republicans	90.6***	14.1

Source. TISS Survey (1998–1999), CMR Time of War Survey (2009) and NDU CMR Survey (2018–2020).
Note. Data reflects responses from active-duty US Army majors, lieutenant colonels, and colonels only. Difference between Democrats and Republicans is statistically significant at *** p < .001.

A similar trend can be seen with regard to officers' views of the appropriateness of constraints on active-duty service members' political speech. During the TISS Survey, 36 percent of army majors, lieutenant colonels, and colonels felt those on active duty should be able to publicly express their political views just like any other citizen, compared to 33 percent in the CMR Time of War Survey a decade later. Both findings are alarming, with a third of midgrade to senior officers essentially rejecting the norm of members of the military keeping their politics private. On the surface, the findings in the NDU CMR Survey are encouraging, as only 16 percent of respondents surveyed between 2018 and 2020 agreed with the notion that active-duty military should be free to express their political views publicly—possibly another reaction to the political polarization that grew during the Trump administration. Upon closer examination, there may again be evidence of partisan rationalization, with 24 percent of Democrats believing active-duty service members should face no constraints in their political expression, compared to just 14 percent of Republicans, although the difference is not statistically significant. These findings that suggest partisan rationalization may be occurring within the officer corps, while discouraging, are consistent with recent research of the American public's views on critical norms of civil-military relations, which will be discussed in chapter 6. If the interpretation of this data is correct, adherence to important norms of civil-military relations within the officer corps may be on shaky ground and colored by one's partisanship.

There is at least one encouraging finding buried in the data here. While not displayed in table 18, with both questions, as officers advanced in rank, they were more likely to give the normatively correct answer. For example, while only 61 percent of lieutenants surveyed in 2009 agreed that active-duty military should not criticize senior civilians in the government, 82 percent of colonels did. Similarly, 38 percent of lieutenants felt it was appropriate for active-duty military to publicly express their political views like anyone else, compared to just 26 percent of colonels. These findings also held true for the NDU CMR Survey, with senior army officers more apt than junior officers to favor restrictions on active-duty military members' political speech. The longer officers stay in the army, the more likely they are to embrace the professional norms of the institution—in this case, the norm of a nonpartisan military.

POLITICS IN THE WORKPLACE

To gauge whether officers truly are bringing their politics into the cockpit, camp, or conference room, as Admiral Mullen warned against, the CMR Time of War Survey and the NDU CMR Survey (2017–2020) also queried senior officers specifically about political discourse and behavior at work, as shown in table 19.

Nearly half of the army lieutenant colonels and colonels surveyed in 2009 indicated that politics was something often talked about at work— a figure that dipped slightly to 43 percent during the NDU CMR Survey. Democrats and Independents witnessed the largest decline—10 and 16 percentage points, respectively—while attitudes among Republican senior officers generally stayed about the same in both surveys. If, in fact, fewer army officers were discussing politics between 2018 and 2020 compared to 2009, it is unclear exactly what was behind this, including whether or not it was a case of senior officers becoming more attuned to the norm of nonpartisanship and avoiding potential conflicts at work. In any regard, 40 to 50 percent of senior army officers reporting that politics is often talked about at work indicates political discourse among officers at work is a common occurrence.

Senior officers were also asked how often they felt uncomfortable expressing their political views at work. Theoretically, those who indicate a greater degree of discomfort might do so because they feel it is inappropriate for members of the military to be discussing politics at work, or because they are uncomfortable sharing their political views, believing theirs to be a minority position at work.

Table 19. Senior US Army Officers' Views of Politics in the Workplace.

	Talking Politics at Work *percent checking "agree" or "strongly agree"*	Degree of Discomfort *percent checking "often" or "almost always"*
	Politics is something often talked about at work	How often do you feel uncomfortable about expressing your political views with your co-workers?
CMR Time of War Survey, 2009	48.9	32.8
Democrats	52.0	45.1***
Independents	50.8	32.6
Republicans	49.0	29.3***
(n)	1,223	1,231
NDU CMR Survey, 2018-2020	43.4	52.3
Democrats	42.3	57.7
Independents	35.1	63.2
Republicans	45.9	47.1
(n)	256	256

Source. CMR Time of War Survey (2009) and NDU CMR Survey (2017–2020).
Note. Data reflects responses from active-duty army lieutenant colonels and colonels only. Difference between Democrats and Republicans is statistically significant at *** p < .001.

As table 19 highlights, approximately one-third of senior army officers indicated they "often" or "almost always" felt uncomfortable expressing their political views to coworkers in 2009—a figure that jumped to more than 52 percent between 2018 and 2020. It is hard not to conclude that the particularly divisive nature of partisan politics during both the 2016 presidential election campaign and throughout the Trump administration played at least some role in the increasing level of discomfort felt by senior army officers.

In both surveys, however, Republicans were less likely than Democrats and Independents to indicate discomfort expressing their political views. It could be that a smaller proportion of Republican officers felt uncomfortable expressing their political opinions because they did not feel particularly beholden to the norms of a nonpartisan military. The more likely explanation, however, is that they believed their fellow officers shared their same political views and were therefore unafraid to express them at work. Regardless of what might explain why Republicans are more comfortable talking politics at work, it is not a particularly encouraging finding, especially given that Republicans outnumber Independents and Democrats among senior army officers by a ratio of more than three to one. Recent survey research of nearly 1,500 West Point cadets conducted in December 2019 and January 2020 unearthed complementary findings. Cadets who self-identified as Republicans were almost four times more likely than Democrats to say that most people they knew in the military shared their partisan views.[33] Therefore, the fact that fewer Republican senior army officers felt uncomfortable about expressing their political opinions at work was likely a function of them holding a majority political position in the officer corps and assuming that everyone else shared their beliefs.

As a final measure of testing for how politics manifests itself in the workplace for army officers, the CMR Time of War Survey asked respondents if other army officers had ever encouraged them to vote one way or another since joining the army. As depicted in table 20, approximately 27 percent of officers responded in the affirmative—that at some point other officers had attempted to influence the way they were going to vote. Of note, a higher percentage of Democrats reported this (38 percent) than Republicans (23 percent). Additionally, while 32 percent of lieutenants reported being pressured to vote a particular way, only 16 percent of colonels indicated so, suggesting perhaps that senior officers were attempting to influence junior officers how to vote.

Table 20. Influencing the Vote.

	Since you have been in the Army, have other officers ever encouraged you to vote one way or another?
	percent who answered "yes"
TOTAL (n=4,079)	27.1
Lieutenants	31.5
Captains	30.5
Majors	26.6
Lieutenant Colonels	24.9
Colonels	15.9
Democrats	38.1***
Independents	29.7
Republicans	23.2***

Source. CMR Time of War Survey (2009).
Note. Difference between Democrats and Republicans is statistically significant at *** $p < .001$.

These findings, unfortunately, are in line with a vignette Andrew Exum, former US Army officer and later a deputy assistant secretary of defense in the Obama administration, shared in his memoir of combat in Afghanistan:

> I did learn some valuable lessons at IOBC [Infantry Officer Basic Course], however, such as the one I got after the 2000 presidential election when one of my classmates told an instructor, a captain, that I had voted for Gore. The captain proceeded to lock me up at the position of attention and chew me a new asshole for not voting for Bush. I protested that I had voted for my Republican senator, but that wasn't enough, evidently. All good officers, he told me, voted Republican...[34]

Table 21 displays the results of a logistic regression where the dichotomous dependent variable was whether officers reported having been encouraged to vote a particular way, and the independent variables include rank, affiliation with the Democratic Party, and affiliation with the Republican Party. The model also controls for officers reporting that politics was often talked about at work and officers feeling uncomfortable expressing their political views at work. Rank and affiliation with the Republican Party have a negative and statistically significant effect on being encouraged to vote a particular way by other officers in the army. Reporting that politics is often talked about at work, being uncomfortable expressing political views at work, and affiliation with the Democratic Party have positive, statistically significant effects on the dependent variable, having been encouraged to vote a particular way. In other words, as an officer increases in rank or is a Republican, the less likely they are to report that others tried to influence their vote. The more junior in rank an officer is or is a Democrat, the more likely they are to report that others attempted to influence their voting choice.

This finding, more than any other in this chapter, should cause senior army leaders to take pause: over one-quarter of army officers surveyed in 2009—and nearly one-third of lieutenants—reported having been pressured to vote a particular way by other officers, with Democrats more likely to report this than Republicans. No other finding stands in greater contrast to DoDD 1344.10 or is more suggestive of at least a portion of officer corps willing to conflate service with partisanship.

Table 21. Logistic Regression Analysis of Vote Influence.

	Dependent Variable = Officers Who Were Encouraged to Vote a Particular Way by Other Officers (dummy)
Rank/Grade	-0.18*** (0.03)
Politics Often Talked About at Work	0.58*** (0.07)
Uncomfortable Talking Politics	0.35*** (0.08)
Democrats	0.34*** (0.11)
Republicans	-0.30*** (0.09)
Constant	-0.81*** (0.17)
Pseudo R^2	0.03
Log Likelihood	-2272.22
N	4,030

Source. CMR Time of War Survey (2009).
Note. Unstandardized logit coefficients with standard errors in parentheses. * p <.05, ** p < .01, *** p < .001.

One certainly hopes that if surveyed again today, fewer officers would report such attempts of vote influence, but as discussed in chapter 2, the basic demographics and political variables associated with the officer corps have remained generally constant throughout the All-Volunteer Force era, so there is little to suggest findings today would be any different.

CONCLUSION

This chapter sought to further break down the politicization charge and dissect the level of political participation and interest of army officers and to what extent they truly bring politics into the workplace. First, voting appears to have become almost a sacred obligation within the officer corps, with high percentages of them voting and actively encouraging others in uniform to do the same. Army officers—especially Republicans—reported a noticeable dip in voter turnout in the 2016 election which may be more of a function of candidate dissatisfaction than anything else. Nine out of ten respondents agreed that members of the active-duty military *should* vote, and there appears to be little to no desire for having service members abstain from voting to preserve an image of nonpartisanship. The military at all levels has placed command emphasis on affording all service members the opportunity to vote, especially because the law has directed them to do so. The example set by George Marshall, while perhaps a noble commitment to nonpartisanship, appears to be an artifact that holds little sway among officers serving today.

Other than voting, most other measures of political participation by army officers are fairly muted. Only a handful of officers admitted to having participated in all six of the political activities that were measured here. The proportion of senior officers who admitted to donating money to a campaign was surprisingly high—over a quarter—and is fundamentally a partisan act. It is also at odds with most findings that show senior officers are more apt to adhere to professional norms than junior officers and that norms, such as the norm of nonpartisanship, take firmer root over the course of one's career. Of note, while Republicans outnumber Democrats among senior officers by roughly six to one, there is no evidence to suggest that Republican-leaning officers were more politically active than Democrats or Independents.

Party affiliation does matter, however, in other measurable categories of political behavior, including the level of discomfort officers had in talking about politics at work and the pressure within the army to vote a particular way. In both cases, officers who were Democrats were more likely to report feeling uncomfortable expressing their political views with their colleagues and having been pressured to vote a particular way by others in the army. While this is likely a reflection of Democrats having the minority political viewpoint in the army—and while it is unclear from the survey alone how much pressure or intimidation is real or perceived —normatively speaking, it is an area to which senior army leaders must devote attention. It points to an unhealthy degree of politicization within the officer corps and that affiliation with the Republican Party for some is at least perceived to be conflated with service in the officer corps.

This chapter also uncovered possible evidence of partisan rationalization or motivated reasoning, whereby some army officers temper their attitudes on professional norms based on their own partisan leanings. It is encouraging that the vast majority of senior army officers feel those on active duty should have constraints on publicly expressing their political views or criticizing senior civilians in government, but possible partisan filtering raises real concerns. A greater proportion of Democrats were more likely to favor lessening those constraints than Independents or Republicans, but arguably because Trump was in office at the time of the survey. It is hard not to imagine that if surveyed again during the Biden administration, such percentages would flip-flop, with Republicans more likely to tolerate active-duty service members publicly expressing their political views and criticizing civilian government leaders. For senior military officers eager to strengthen the norm of nonpartisanship and political neutrality, this is not a reassuring finding because it suggests adherence to norms can be overridden by one's partisanship, depending on the situation. The fact that the TISS Survey and CMR Time of War survey did not show evidence of partisan rationalization or selective norm adherence may indicate these phenomena are not enduring aspects of officership but rather manifest themselves during times of polarization and deep political division.

Is the army politicized? Voting in large numbers, encouraging others to vote, and displaying an interest in politics does not translate into politicization, but this does not mean there is no cause for concern. The fact that a higher percentage of Democratic officers reported feeling uncomfortable expressing their political views or having been pressured to vote a particular way should cause alarm among senior army leaders. Any suggestion that a conflation exists between officership and affiliation with the Republican Party is contrary to the most basic norms of the profession and meets the textbook definition of politicization. Additionally, the apparent recent proclivity of midgrade to senior army officers—those in the army who should demonstrate the strongest commitment to professional norms—to modify their adherence to critical norms of civil-military relations through a partisan lens suggests that more reinforcement of norms is required among all ranks in the military. The well-intentioned missives by the chairman of the Joint Chiefs once every four years do not appear to be enough.

NOTES

1. Huntington, *The Soldier and the State*, 71.
2. Ibid, 84.
3. Inbody, *The Soldier Vote*, 1–12.
4. Uniformed and Overseas Citizens Absentee Voting Act, 52 U.S.C. (1986) § 20301-2-311. See also Garrett, *Absentee Voting for Uniformed Services and Overseas Citizens*.
5. Department of Justice, *Fact Sheet: Move Act*. October 27, 2010. https://www.justice.gov/opa/pr/fact-sheet-move-act.
6. Friend and Golby, "The Military and the Election."
7. Mullen, "From the Chairman: Military Must Stay Apolitical."
8. Martin Dempsey, "From the Chairman: Putting Our Nation First."
9. Dunford, "Upholding Our Oath."
10. Federal Voting Assistance Program, *FVAP 2016 Post-Election Report to Congress*, Washington, DC: U.S. Department of Defense, 2017; Federal Voting Assistance Program, *FVAP 2012 Post-Election Report to Congress*, Washington, DC: U.S. Department of Defense, 2013.
11. The American Presidency Project at the University of California Santa Barbara reported actual voter turnout as 55 percent in 2016; 54 percent in 2012; 57 percent in 2008; 56 percent in 2004; and 51 percent in 2000. Voting statistics cited are turnout as a percentage of the voting age public, as opposed to the Census Bureau, which provides self-reported voter turnout, which is much higher. "Voter Turnout in Presidential Elections," The American Presidency Project, https://www.presidency.ucsb.edu/statistics/data/voter-turnout-in-presidential-elections.
12. Wolfinger and Rosenstone, *Who Votes?*, 14–21, 37–44; Campbell et al., *The American Voter*, 476–478; and Verba and Nie, *Participation in America*, 125.
13. Jason K. Dempsey, *Our Army*, 133.
14. Ordinarily, a projected, self-reported voter turnout rate of 89 percent, even among Army officers, would seem extraordinarily high, if not inflated, but is consistent with the record-high voter turnout levels in the 2020 presidential election. Schaul, Rabinowitz, and Mellnik, "2020 Turnout is on Pace to Break Century-Old Records."
15. Saad, "Trump and Clinton Finish with Historically Poor Images."

16. Jackman and Spahn, "Why Does the American National Election Study Overestimate Voter Turnout?."

17. Burden, "Voter Turnout and the National Election Studies"; and McDonald, "On the Over-Report Bias of the National Election Study."

18. Education remains one of the strongest predictors of voter turnout, which is evident in this survey's findings as well. Officers are required to have a bachelor's degree and 54 percent of respondents in the 2009 survey reported having obtained a graduate degree. This may help explain the seemingly high turnout rate among officers in 2008 and should be kept in mind when comparing against the general public's voter turnout rates.

19. Jason K. Dempsey, *Our Army*, 130.

20. Teigen, "Enduring Effects of the Uniform."

21. Maury et al., *Military Families*.

22. Cavanaugh, "I Fight for Your Right to Vote. But I Won't Do It Myself"; and Toner, "Officers Should Not Vote."

23. Maury et al., *Military Families*, 22.

24. Ham, "Get Out and Vote but Obey Your Oath, General Tells Officers"; and Dunlap, "It's Wrong to Suppress the Military Vote."

25. Chadwick, "Gen. Petraeus Addresses his 'Legacy,'"; and Shelbourne, "'Apolitical' Petraeus Says He Did Not Vote in Election."

26. Jason K. Dempsey, *Our Army*, 133.

27. The Center for Responsive Politics is a 501(c)3 nonprofit that tracks financial donations to federal elections campaigns through its website, www.opensecrets.org.

28. Jason Dempsey, *Our Army*, 128.

29. Shane, "Here are the 181 Veterans Running for Congress This Year"; Hageman, Teigen, and Best, "The Democrats Are Running More Female Veterans for Office."

30. Hageman, Teigen, and Best, "The Democrats Are Running More Female Veterans for Office."

31. Babcock-Lumish, "Uninformed, not Uniformed?,"51; and Risa Brooks, "Paradoxes of Professionalism," 21.

32. Nix, "American Civil-Military Relations," 96.

33. Brooks, Robinson, and Urben, "What Makes a Military Professional? Evaluating Norm Socialization in West Point Cadets."

34. Exum, *This Man's Army*, 28.

CHAPTER 4

The State of the Nonpartisan Ethic in the World of Social Media

> Technology and social media make it seductively easy for us to broadcast our private opinions far beyond the confines of our homes. The lines between the professional, personal—and virtual —are blurring. Now more than ever, we have to be exceptionally thoughtful about what we say and how we say it.[1]
> —General Martin Dempsey, US Army, ret.

This chapter examines the nature and the extent of political expressions by the military in the realm of social media and whether such expressions are consistent with Department of Defense policy and the norms of a nonpartisan military. As highlighted in chapter 3, with the exception of voting in presidential elections, military officers' political participation, at least as measured in traditional forms, is fairly muted. The Department of Defense directives provide guidelines on permissible but traditional forms of political expression for active-duty members of the military, but the directives largely neglect social media as a forum for political activity.

This chapter aims to answer the following questions: What are the nature and the extent of political expressions by members of the military on social media? How do political expressions on social media vary between active-duty and retired members and between members of the military and nonmilitary alike? Do members of the military violate the nonpartisan ethic on social media, and is there a distinction between the political expressions of active-duty and retired members of the military? And finally, what kind of partisan linkages to service members' social media political expressions, if any, can be discerned?

CURRENT DEPARTMENT OF DEFENSE POLICY AND GUIDANCE

As mentioned in chapter 3, the Department of Defense Directive 1344.10 (DoDD 1344.10), *Political Activities by Members of the Armed Forces*, is the primary policy document that addresses political behavior for members of the military.[2] However, the directive is noticeably silent on political behavior within the realm of social media and on the internet more broadly because the directive is more than thirteen years old and does not reflect recent changes in both technology and political behavior. Since at least 2012, however, the Department of Defense has issued supplemental guidance in advance of each presidential election, including a small section on social media, although it is unclear why there have been no efforts to update DoDD 1344.10 since 2008—especially since the supplemental guidance continues to refer back to DoDD 1344.10 as the authoritative source.[3]

In June 2020, shortly after Black Lives Matter protests erupted nationwide following the death of George Floyd, the US Army circulated a flyer entitled, "Share Your Voice / Know Your Limits."[4] The flyer included a section on both public demonstrations and social media, instructing soldiers that while they can "follow, friend, or like a political party or candidate running for partisan office on a personal social media account, when off duty," they face other restrictions.[5] They cannot "post, share, or link to material from a partisan political party, group, or candidate, even when off duty."[6] The bottom of the flyer lists several references, including DoDD 1344.10, the US Army's social media guidance, and the Hatch Act, which limits political activities of federal employees.

The US Army's guidance on social media is an easy-to-navigate website, broken down into different sections that range from best practices for managers of official army social media accounts to training on operational security and warnings regarding frequently observed scams targeting soldiers online.[7] The website also includes a section entitled, "Guidance on Political Activity and DoD Support," which lists several of the same dos and don'ts referenced on its "Share Your Voice / Know Your Limits" poster. But it also contains a few notable errors. First, it invokes DoDD 1344.10 as the source of the social media guidance on political activities, which is inaccurate because DoDD 1344.10 contains no references to social media whatsoever. It would be problematic if units tried to enforce these provisions, which are essentially codified only on an army website and not in any official US Army Regulation or Department of Defense directive.[8] Second, while the social media guidance includes the prohibition of communicating contemptuous words against the president, vice president, and other key officials as specified in Article 88 of the Uniformed Code of Military Justice, it oddly specifies the Secretary of the Navy but omits secretaries of all the military departments, including the army. It is easy to blame US Army public affairs officials for this lack of attention to detail, but this masks the larger issue at hand: this is not simply a public affairs matter, and it showcases the difficulty the services have issuing clear guidance to service members in the absence of a current Department of Defense directive.

While the army's attempt to clarify and provide examples of allowable and forbidden activity on social media is well-intentioned, it raises more questions beyond its factual errors. If a service member "follows" or "likes" a particular party and candidates of that party, and the service member's social media site is adorned with imagery and written material of that party and its candidates, does that not constitute partisan activity, regardless of whether the service member is encouraging others to do the same? Army and DoD officials may have concluded that "liking" a political candidate's Facebook page is the equivalent of putting a bumper sticker on one's car, an allowable act according to DoDD 1344.10. Other examples of political expression that are made outside social media versus those made in social media may be less comparable.

At the very least, there is the question of reach and magnitude. DoDD 1344.10 states up front that service members are allowed to express their personal political opinions. And while DoDD 1344.10 does not explicitly state so, the underlying norm of nonpartisanship implies that such expressions should be in private.[9] In a later section, DoDD 1344.10 prohibits service members from the very public act of speaking before a political gathering or advocating for a political cause on a radio or television program. Yet political expressions on social media, the modern-day town square, raises more questions—questions that are not answered in the Department of Defense's supplemental election guidance or in the US Army's social media guide. If posting a political comment on Facebook or Twitter, where a post can be quickly read by thousands of people, is inherently a public act, is the social media guidance consistent with DoDD 1344.10? Likewise, the army's social media guide compares a political post on social media to a letter to the editor, which DoDD 1344.10 classifies as allowable. A letter to the editor must meet certain journalistic standards, however, and for members of the military, it usually must pass public-affairs and security screenings. It is hard to conceive of a situation where a service member could have one or several letters to the editor published each day—but in social media, there are few, if any, barriers to or editorial reviews of one's own political commentary. The accessibility, volume, and reach of political expressions in social media is far different from the traditional measures identified in DoDD 1344.10. As the next section explores, this is not only a matter of consistent policy guidance but also one of normative implications.

While DoDD 1344.10 attempts to appeal to the better judgment of those in the military, the Department of Defense nonetheless grants considerable latitude to service members when it comes to political expression. However, the two recent chairmen of the Joint Chiefs, retired Admiral Michael Mullen and retired General Martin Dempsey, often argued throughout their tenures for a stricter adherence to the nonpartisan ethic and a more conservative interpretation of DoDD 1344.10. Both suggested the nonpartisan ethic should extend into retirement, and Dempsey, writing in the lead up to the 2012 presidential election argued for greater restraint in service members' political expressions on social media, as highlighted in the quote that began this chapter.[10] Mullen and Dempsey's admonitions are instructive, as they are undoubtedly reactions to what they perceived to be repeated violations in political and partisan activity by members of the military. Both Mullen and Dempsey raise an important question about political expressions by military members that is certainly applicable for social media: even if it is allowable, is it proper?

To avoid potential social-desirability bias, the Politics & Social Media Survey primarily asked respondents questions about their observations of their military and nonmilitary friends' behaviors on social media, as opposed to asking respondents to report details about their own political expressions on social media.[11] While this approach may help reduce the likelihood of respondents to underreport or overreport in an attempt to provide what they believe is the "correct" answer to a somewhat-sensitive question, it is not without its own limitations. Chiefly, it relies upon the respondents to serve as accurate observers of their friends' political expressions on social media, and this of course, entails some bias. Nonetheless, given the dearth of survey research on political attitudes and participation by members of the military and the untapped arena of how such attitudes play out on social media, this sample of convenience is sufficient to draw some initial conclusions about the behaviors and attitudes of members of the military at the intersection of politics and social media.

Findings from the aforementioned surveys are grouped into three main sections. The first section details the extent of social media usage by respondents, noting the significant differences that exist among generational cohorts in social media use, frequency of access, and the extent to which politics intersects with social media. Following that, the subsequent section examines the nature and extent of political discussions on social media. Analysis here centers on relative comparisons among the levels and types of political activity undertaken by nonmilitary, active-duty, and retired military friends on social media. The third and final section begins by assessing the degree of alignment between the political views of respondents and their friends on social media. It then explores to what degree respondents are made uncomfortable by their friends' political posts and whether they sever social media ties with those friends. Finally, it closes with a look at political behavior on social media that is at odds with the military's nonpartisan ethic.

SOCIAL MEDIA USAGE AND CHARACTERISTICS

Findings from the Politics & Social Media Survey depict an officer corps actively engaged on social media, with age or generational cohort signaling predicted but significant differences in the extent to which respondents use social media. As table 22 shows, 71 percent of those surveyed responded that they have multiple social media accounts, and only nine percent reported they have none.[12] More officers reported having a Facebook account than any other type of social media account measured (87 percent), although Facebook use was higher among West Point cadets (94 percent) than among NDU students (77 percent). Age and rank have other expected impacts on social media use. For example, a significant disparity exists between West Point cadets and NDU students' likelihood of having LinkedIn accounts, with only 15 percent of West Point cadets having an account compared to 58 percent of NDU students.

Table 22. Social Media Use by Military Elites.

	Facebook	Twitter	LinkedIn	No Social Media Accounts	Multiple Social Media Accounts
		percent checking each option			
TOTAL (n = 522)	86.8	31.2	33.0	9.4	70.5
West Point Cadets	93.8***	36.8***	15.3***	4.6***	73.6
NDU Students	76.7***	23.3***	58.1***	16.3***	66.1
Democrats	90.2	32.0	26.2	7.4	74.6
Republicans	86.5	34.9	34.9	8.2	71.2

Source. Politics & Social Media Survey (2015–2016).
Note. NDU students include O-4s, O-5s, and O-6s. Difference between West Point cadets and NDU students is statistically significant at *** p < .001.

This is not surprising, as LinkedIn is a professionally geared social media networking site, used predominantly by midcareer professionals looking for new jobs, and it may be the only social media site where the proportion of 50-to-64-year-old users is higher than the proportion of 18-to-24-year-old users nationwide.[13] Likewise, West Point cadets were more likely to report having a Twitter account than their senior officer counterparts. With the exception of LinkedIn, we would expect West Point cadets to be more prolific in their social media use and more diverse in the variety of accounts they have than more senior officers because of their young age or generational cohort, which the findings from this survey confirm.[14]

Differences in social media use based on party affiliation were not statistically significant. It should be noted, however, that the Pew Research Center's 2012 study, "Social Media and Political Engagement," did find statistically significant differences in the use of social media sites, with Democrats reporting higher rates of use than Republicans.[15] Future research involving a larger, nonrandom sample of military officers may find differences in social media usage based on partisanship and ideology that are more meaningful.

The frequency of social media use among respondents is also largely a function of age or generation. As table 23 shows, while 56 percent of respondents indicated they check their social media accounts several times a day, 70 percent of West Point cadets reported doing so, compared to just 32 percent of NDU students. While an argument could be made that college students simply have more time on their hands compared to more senior military officers at work all day, West Point cadets, with their famously packed schedules, are also not your typical college students. This is more likely a generational effect; relative to their more senior counterparts, West Point cadets are more comfortable and more prolific on social media because they grew up with it.

Table 23. Frequency of Social Media Usage by Military Elites.

| | How Often Military Elites Access Their Social Media Accounts | | | | | |
| | percent checking each option | | | | | |
	Several Times a Day	About Once a Day	A Few Days a Week	Every Few Weeks	Less Often	I'm Not Sure
TOTAL (n = 472)	55.5	23.7	13.6	4.2	2.8	0.2
West Point Cadets	70.2***	20.6*	7.5***	1.0***	0.3***	0.3***
NDU Students	31.7***	28.9*	23.3***	9.4***	6.7***	0.0***
Democrats	65.5	20.4	11.5	0.9	0.9	0.9
Republicans	55.6	21.4	14.0	5.1	3.9	0.0

Source. Politics & Social Media Survey (2015–2016).
Note. NDU students include O-4s, O-5s, and O-6s. Difference between West Point cadets and NDU students significant at * p < .05 and *** p < .001.

The impact of partisanship is a bit more evident when examining the degree to which military officers enjoy talking about politics and the extent to which they get their news about politics from social media. As depicted in table 24, 64 percent of respondents indicated they enjoy talking about government and politics with friends and family, a figure that did not vary substantially based on rank or party affiliation. What is more evident than partisan identification, however, is the impact of partisan strength, with a larger proportion of strong partisans (75 percent) indicating they enjoyed talking about politics than weak partisans (63 percent). This latter finding is consistent with past research that has shown strong partisans having a greater interest and involvement in politics, better knowledge about politics, and higher voter-turnout levels than weak partisans and pure Independents.[16]

The respondents' degree of interest in politics is an important factor because much of the analysis of political participation on social media is based on respondents' observations of their military friends' political activity on social media sites. Respondents who are generally interested in politics are likely to be cognizant of their friends' political behavior, as opposed to those who might have a disinterest in politics altogether. Another gauge of political awareness important to this study is whether respondents consume news about politics through their social media networking sites. As portrayed in table 25, 68 percent of those surveyed indicated they get some news from Facebook, which is by far the top source of news in social media among respondents surveyed in 2015–2016.

As with overall social media use, the impact of age or generational cohort is again evident: 80 percent of West Point cadets versus only 50 percent of NDU students indicated they get some of their political news from Facebook.[17] This observation is expected and consistent with past research. For example, a 2014 Pew Research Center study found that 61 percent of Millennials reported consuming political news on Facebook, compared to 51 percent of Generation X and only 39 percent of Baby Boomers.[18] Younger digital natives are more active and more comfortable on social media than older digital natives, and certainly more so than digital immigrants.[19]

Table 24. Military Elites' Interest in Talking About Politics.

	percent checking "a lot" or "some" How much do you enjoy talking about government and politics with friends and family?
TOTAL (n = 516)	63.6
West Point Cadets	65.3
NDU Students	61.1
Democrats	64.7
Republicans	66.3
Strong Partisans	74.7*
Weak Partisans	63.2*

Source. Politics & Social Media Survey (2015–2016).
Note. NDU students include O-4s, O-5s, and O-6s. Strong Partisans are respondents who self-identified as Strong Democrats or Strong Republicans. Weak Partisans are respondents who self-identified as Weak Democrats, Independents Who Lean Democrat, Independents Who Lean Republican, or Weak Republicans. Difference between Strong Partisans and Weak Partisans is statistically significant at * p < .05.

Although age or generation is the most noteworthy effect here, partisan identification indicates slightly different patterns in news consumption through social media. A slightly higher percentage of Democrats (78 percent) than Republicans (68 percent) reported consuming news through Facebook, but the difference was not statistically significant. It is unclear if similar response rates would be reported today, given the evolution of Facebook and the perception by some that the platform has increasingly become a "right wing echo chamber."[20]

Table 25. Military Elites Who Use Social Media as a News Source.

	Facebook	Twitter	LinkedIn
	percent checking each option		
TOTAL	68.4	16.3	3.2
West Point Cadets	79.9***	18.1	1.4**
NDU Students	49.7***	13.3	6.1**
Democrats	77.9	17.7	3.5
Republicans	67.8	18.2	3.5
Strong Partisans	74.4	22.1	3.5
Weak Partisans	69.8	16.8	3.5
Enjoy Talking Politics	69.8	18.2	3.7
Dislike Talking Politics	65.9	13.1	2.3
(n)	474	473	473

Source. Politics & Social Media Survey (2015–2016).
Note. NDU students include O-4s, O-5s, and O-6s. Difference between West Point cadets and NDU students significant at ** $p < .01$ and *** $p < .001$.

Of note, there were no discernible differences in political news consumption on social media between those who naturally enjoy talking about politics with their friends and family versus those who do not. Nor was strength of partisanship a factor. Again, of the variables measured in this study, age or generational cohort has the strongest association with social media use, in terms of variety of accounts, frequency of access, and propensity to consume news about politics through such sites.

NATURE AND EXTENT OF POLITICAL EXPRESSIONS ON SOCIAL MEDIA BY MILITARY MEMBERS

Much of this chapter's findings regarding political expressions on social media by members of the military rely upon respondents' observations of their social media friends' behavior. To this end, respondents were first asked whether their military friends, both active duty and retired, often talk about politics on social media. As table 26 shows, 45 percent of respondents responded affirmatively, but this figure varied significantly, with 51 percent of West Point cadets indicating their military friends talk about politics, compared to just 35 percent of NDU students.

A similar question was posed again in the NDU CMR Survey that ran from 2017 to 2020, but this time, respondents were only asked whether their active-duty friends talked about politics on social media. The findings from these survey waves are also shown on table 26. In these later waves in 2017–2020, the percentage of NDU and Army War College students who indicated their active-duty friends often discuss politics on social media remained virtually the same compared to responses from NDU students (35 percent) in the 2015–2016 survey. However, the percentage of West Point cadets responding affirmatively dropped dramatically— from 51 percent in 2015–2016, to just 17 percent two years later. Because response rates for NDU students stayed constant, a possible explanation is that West Point cadets underwent increased sensitization to social media etiquette as part of their education and training. As reference, the West Point Admissions Office's website includes an article entitled, "Social Media Tips to Present Your Best Self at West Point and in the Military."[21] Recent survey research also reinforces this notion of a recent change in cadet sensibilities. In a 2019–2020 survey of West Point cadets, only 13 percent thought it was acceptable for members of the military to talk about politics on social media—consistent with the finding here about fewer cadets observing their military friends talk about politics on social media compared to just a few years prior.[22] For those who are concerned about the implications of a politically vocal officer corps, this is an encouraging finding that may reinforce the idea that the consistent teaching of norms can, in fact, lead to an observable change in behavior.

Table 26. US Military Members Talking About Politics on Social Media.

	percent checking "strongly agree" or "agree"	
	My military friends (both active duty and retired) often talk about politics on social media networking sites	My active duty military friends often talk about politics on social media networking sites
	2015-2016	2017-2020
TOTAL	44.9	25.4
West Point Cadets	50.9***	17.1***
NDU Students	35.2***	34.7***
Democrats	46.9	41.1
Republicans	31.3	31.6
Liberals	46.4	45.0*
Conservatives	30.6	30.1*
Enjoy Talking Politics	49.5**	
Dislike Talking Politics	37.1**	
(n)	472	922

Source. Politics & Social Media Survey (2015–2016) and NDU CMR Survey (2017–2020).
Note. Army War College students were also included in the NDU student sample for 2017–2020. NDU students include O-4s, O-5s, and O-6s. Party identification is displayed for NDU students only. Difference between West Point cadets and NDU students is statistically significant at *** p < .001. Difference between those who enjoy talking about politics and those who don't is statistically significant at ** p < .01. Difference between liberals and conservatives is statistically significant at * p < .05.

Because there was such a dramatic shift in responses from West Point cadets in the Politics & Social Media Survey to the NDU CMR Survey, only findings from NDU students' party affiliation and ideology are reported in table 26. Of note, liberals and Democrats were more likely to report their military friends talk about politics on social media than conservatives and Republicans, but the differences were statistically insignificant for party identification, perhaps due to the small sample of Democrats in the NDU sample. In any regard, there are at least two ways to interpret this: liberals and Democrats may be more likely than conservatives and Republicans to indicate that their friends often talk about politics because their friends are politically like-minded, and maybe liberals and Democrats in the military are more outspoken about politics on social media than their conservative and Republican peers. Conversely, and more plausibly given findings in the next section in this chapter, liberals and Democrats may report to a greater extent their friends talking about politics because being a political minority in the officer corps, they are more conscious of political dialogue and their friends share dissimilar political views.

Additionally, respondents who enjoyed talking about politics were more likely to indicate that their military-affiliated social media friends also often talk about politics. Several factors could explain this. First, it could be that people who enjoy talking about politics tend to have friends who also like to talk about politics, just as those who dislike talking about politics tend to associate with like-minded people. Alternatively, even if people who enjoy talking about politics have both friends who actively talk about politics and those who do not, they may be more sensitized to and cognizant of discussions of politics compared to those who have a general dislike of politics.

While the data in table 26 is useful in providing a simple snapshot of political activity by members of the military on social media, a relative comparison is needed to make better sense of the magnitude of this data. For example, do respondents' military friends talk about politics more or less than their civilian friends? And within the category of military friends, are active-duty members more or less politically active than retired military? The results of these questions are displayed in tables 27 and 28.

A few caveats are in order because these relative comparisons have a number of limitations. First, just as the overall survey sample is not intended to be representative of the entire military or officer corps, respondents' civilian friends are by no means representative of the broader civilian populace. Nonetheless, having respondents contrast the political activity of their military and civilian friends provides a baseline comparison that is useful, absent any results from large-scale, random-sample inquiries. Second, while differences between West Point cadets and NDU students have characterized much of the preceding analysis, comparisons between the two subsamples are less useful in this next section due to the low confidence in the data reported by West Point cadets. While West Point cadets had a sufficient sample of military friends on social media to provide valuable insights throughout this study, it is less likely they were able to draw meaningful comparisons between active-duty and retired military, given the likely composition of their social media friend network. Many West Point cadets may have had no retired military friends whatsoever, except those with family members who might have served careers in the military. Thus, while data from West Point cadets is nonetheless reported in tables 27 and 28, the focus of this analysis centers on NDU students, who arguably had a more diverse circle of military friends from which to draw comparisons.

First, as table 27 outlines, 46 percent of respondents indicated that their nonmilitary friends talk about politics on social media more often than their military friends, while 21 percent responded that their military friends talk about politics more. Responses by West Point cadets and NDU students were fairly similar. While not depicted in table 27, the more senior the NDU student, the more likely they were to report their nonmilitary friends talking about politics. Of note, party affiliation elicited no statistically significant differences.

Table 27. Most Active Friends Discussing Politics on Social Media (Military vs. Nonmilitary).

| | Who Is Most Active in Discussing Politics on Social Media? Your Military or Non-Military Friends? *percent checking each option* | | | |
	My Non-Military Friends Talk About Politics More	My Non-military Friends Talk About Politics as Much as My Military Friends Do	My Military Friends Talk About Politics More	I'm Not Sure
TOTAL (n = 471)	45.7	24.4	20.8	9.2
West Point Cadets	43.3	25.4	24.4*	6.9*
NDU Students	49.4	22.8	15.0*	12.8*
Democrats	42.4	24.2	27.3	6.1
Republicans	52.1	20.8	12.5	14.6

Source. Politics & Social Media Survey (2015–2016).
Note. NDU students include O-4s, O-5s, and O-6s. Party identification is displayed for NDU students only. Difference between West Point cadets and NDU students is statistically significant at * p < .05.

Table 28. Most Active Friends Discussing Politics on Social Media (Active Duty vs. Retired).

	Who Is Most Active in Discussing Politics on Social Media? Your Active Duty or Retired Friends? *percent checking each option*			
	My Active Duty Friends Talk About Politics More	My Active Duty Friends Talk About Politics as Much as My Retired Military Friends Do	My Retired Military Friends Talk About Politics More	I'm Not Sure
TOTAL (n = 459)	18.3	10.7	32.9	38.1
West Point Cadets	26.3***	9.3	19.2***	45.2***
NDU Students	5.6***	12.9	54.5***	27.0***
Democrats	9.4	21.9	46.9	21.9
Republicans	5.3	13.7	51.6	29.5

Source. Politics & Social Media Survey (2015–2016).
Note. NDU students include O-4s, O-5s, and O-6s. Party identification is displayed for NDU students only. Difference between West Point cadets and NDU students is statistically significant *** at p < .001.

Table 28 displays the comparison of political expressions on social media by active-duty and retired military. As mentioned earlier, little stock should be put in the responses of West Point cadets, given the low likelihood they had a sufficient sample of retired friends on social media. This is confirmed by the high degree of uncertainty in their responses, with 45 percent of West Point cadets unsure who among their social media friends talked about politics more. For NDU students, however, 55 percent of respondents indicated their retired friends talked about politics more.

Even NDU students exhibited some ambiguity answering this question, with 27 percent indicating they were not sure who talks about politics more. There are at least two possible explanations for this. One reason for this ambiguity may simply be that military respondents do not pay enough attention to the political chatter by their military friends on social media, so they cannot distinguish who discusses politics more actively. Yet this study has already established that the majority of respondents who have social media accounts access them every day, consume news about politics through social media, and have a general interest in discussing politics, so this explanation does not seem adequate. An alternative explanation is that respondents cannot distinguish who talks about politics more because the active-duty and retired distinction, or at least their political opinions, is blurred even in respondents' minds. This carries larger implications for the norm of nonpartisanship because if military respondents tend to blur the opinions of their active and retired friends, civilians are even more likely to do so. Even if retired military are more politically outspoken than their active-duty counterparts, their friends on social media— especially those with little connection to the military—may see no qualitative difference, concluding simply that members of the military in general tend to talk actively about politics on social media.

Table 29. Military Friends' Activity on Social Media Networking Sites.

	Do Your Military Friends Ever Do the Following on Social Media Networking Sites percent checking "Yes"						
	Repost or share links to political stories	Post links to political stories or articles for others to read	"Like" or promote material related to political issues that others have posted	Post their own thoughts/ comments on political issues	"Friend" or follow political figures	Encourage others to vote	Encourage others to take action on political issues
TOTAL	84.7	83.2	77.5	76.4	41.7	32.8	36.8
West Point Cadets	88.0**	88.0***	80.8*	78.4	51.2***	30.3	40.1
NDU Students	79.3**	75.3***	72.1*	73.2	26.3***	36.9	31.5
Democrats	85.0	85.0	78.8	82.1	44.3	34.8	42.5
Republicans	86.0	81.3	76.4	74.8	40.9	30.0	34.2
(n)	471	470	471	471	470	469	470

Source. Politics & Social Media Survey (2015–2016).
Note. NDU students include O-4s, O-5s, and O-6s. Differences between West Point cadets and NDU students are statistically significant at * p < .05, ** p < .01, and *** p < .001.

Table 29 looks at the different political activities undertaken by respondents' military friends, both active duty and retired, on social media. Seven different measures of political participation are listed across the top row, and for the most part, are arrayed in ascending order of political activism from left to right. For example, reposting or sharing a link to a political story is the most restrained form of political expression listed, while encouraging others to take action on a political issue is the most active form. Of note, all forms of political activity are allowable according to DoDD 1344.10 and the army's social media guide, with the exception of the last category: encouraging others to take action on a political issue, which is expressly forbidden.

Well over three-quarters of respondents indicated their military friends participated in the first four measures of political expression. While the percentage of positive responses from West Point cadets was higher than NDU students in all four categories, more than 70 percent of NDU students still responded affirmatively, with reposting or sharing political stories and posting links to articles on politics cited as the most common activities. As table 29 shows, 76 percent of respondents overall indicated their military friends posted their own thoughts or comments on political issues, which is consistent with past research on political participation by army officers, albeit not in the realm of social media. As highlighted in chapter 3, three-quarters of army officers surveyed in 2009 indicated that they had expressed their personal opinions on political candidates or issues to others.[23] Those categories with reported high rates of participation are not only allowable political activities but also relatively benign on the spectrum of political activity.

The next category of political participation has more activist, partisan overtones. Approximately 42 percent of respondents acknowledged that their military friends have "friended" or "followed" political figures on social media, but this statistic varied substantially by subsample with 51 percent of West Point cadets reporting this compared to just 26 percent of NDU students. While this was nonetheless an allowable activity per the Department of Defense's guidelines, it is a more overtly political act than the previously mentioned four activities and carries clear partisan connotations. It is perhaps then unsurprising that only a quarter of NDU respondents indicated their military friends do this compared to roughly half of West Point cadets who had not fully been socialized to the norms of the profession yet.

The last two categories of political activity measured in table 29 are encouraging others to vote and encouraging others to take action on a political issue. Encouraging others to vote, with the obvious caveat that it is not done to influence the vote in a particular direction, is embraced by the all-volunteer military. High voter-turnout rates within the military in recent years are attributed to the Uniformed and Overseas Citizens Absentee Voting Act of 1986, and the CMR Time of War Survey found that 80 percent of respondents acknowledged having encouraged others in the army to vote at some point during their careers.[24] As table 29 shows, roughly one-third of respondents indicated their military friends had encouraged through social media others to vote. Why is there a nearly 50-percentage-point difference? Officers may be more inclined to make direct, in-person appeals to their work colleagues, reflecting adherence to laws and regulations adopted over the past several years aimed at providing voting assistance and education for military service members. Many officers view voting and affording others in the military the opportunity to vote as a duty and obligation of citizenship, and it makes sense that they are more apt to encourage service members with whom they work to vote than their military friends on social media.[25]

The final category measured was whether respondents' military friends encouraged others on social media to take action on a political issue. As table 29 highlights, 37 percent of respondents responded affirmatively, with a higher proportion of West Point cadets (40 percent) indicating that they did so than NDU students (32 percent). This is sensitive ground, given that this activity could violate Department of Defense guidelines that prohibit partisan activity and advocacy. Because respondents were not asked to differentiate between their active-duty and retired military friends, it is entirely possible that the majority of those responding affirmatively were referring to their retired friends, who are not subject to the same constraints as those on active duty. Yet, while that could be true for NDU students, 40 percent of West Point cadets—whose pool of retired friends is likely quite low—indicated their military friends did encourage others to take action on political issues. Regardless, the data point is noteworthy for a couple reasons. First, the data here show that military members, regardless of status, discern differences along the spectrum of political participation. The large proportion of respondents who indicated their military friends share political news stories or comment on political articles stands in sharp contrast to the proportion of those willing to advocate publicly for a political issue. Yet, this last category, which could cross the line in terms of permissibility if the political issues in question are partisan issues, has more than just a small number of outliers: nearly two in five respondents indicated their military friends do this.

CHALLENGES TO THE NORM OF NONPARTISANSHIP

This final section probes the tone and tenor of social media posts by members of the military and the extent to which these posts are consistent with the norm of nonpartisanship. Table 30 shows the degree of alignment in political views between respondents and their military friends on social media. Overall, only 27 percent of those surveyed responded that the political views of their military friends on social media were almost always or often in line with their own views. West Point cadets and NDU students showed remarkable consistency here with nearly identical percentages reported.

The variance among respondents, however, is clearly evident in partisan identification and political ideology. Republican respondents (34 percent) were twice as likely to indicate their military friends on social media shared similar political views than Democrats (16 percent). When strength of partisanship is taken into account, the differences become magnified.

For example, 49 percent of strong Republicans, in contrast to just 6 percent of strong Democrats, indicated they share similar political views with their military friends on social media. One interpretation of this finding is that Republicans in the military may be more likely than Democrats to see social media as their echo chambers, seeking to reinforce their own political beliefs.

Table 30. Alignment in Political Opinions by Military Friends on Social Media.

	Degree of Alignment in Political Opinions By Military Friends on Social Media
	percent checking "almost always" or "often"
	Thinking about the opinions your military friends post about government and politics on social media networking sites, how often are they in line with your own views?
TOTAL (n = 469)	26.7
West Point Cadets	27.2
NDU Students	25.8
Democrats	16.4***
Republicans	33.9***
Strong Democrats	5.9***
Strong Republicans	48.5***
Liberals	15.2***
Conservatives	39.6***

Source. Politics & Social Media Survey (2015–2016).
Note. NDU students include O-4s, O-5s, and O-6s. Differences between Democrats and Republicans, between Strong Democrats and Strong Republicans, and between liberals and conservatives are statistically significant at * $p < .001$.

This interpretation is in line with past research conducted by the Pew Research Center, which found in a 2014 study that "consistent conservatives" were twice as likely as average Facebook users to report that political posts they saw were in line with their own political views. And while "consistent liberals" in the Pew study reported a more diverse range of political opinions on Facebook, 32 percent still reported sharing similar political views—a far larger proportion than liberals (15 percent) and strong liberals (0 percent) who reported their social media friends shared similar views in the Politics & Social Media Survey.[26] The military sample from this study may mirror trends in the broader American public, where Republicans and conservatives are more likely than Democrats and liberals to have military-affiliated social media friends with similar political views. However, the proportion of Democrats and liberals in the officer corps is also significantly underrepresented relative to the broader civilian populace—a finding that not only impacts military elites' friend networks but also shapes respondents' views of online discourse and how they respond to such discourse.

Table 31 delves into this a bit more with a review of the politics of "unfriending," in which respondents were asked whether they had ever severed ties with social media friends and specifically because the politics of their social media friends were to blame. As discussed earlier, West Point cadet responses regarding retired military members should be discounted, given the low likelihood they had a sufficient number of retired military friends from which to draw comparisons. As table 31 indicates, while West Point cadet responses are included, cross tabulations with other variables focus on NDU student responses only. Overall, 68 percent of respondents indicated they unfriended or blocked nonmilitary friends on social media for nonpolitical reasons, compared to 39 percent who unfriended active-duty friends and 30 percent who unfriended retired military friends for nonpolitical reasons. Both West Point cadets and NDU students were far more apt to unfriend nonmilitary friends than military friends.

Table 31. The Politics of Unfriending on Social Media.

| | Have you ever hidden, blocked, unfriended, or stopped following anyone in the following groups on a social media site for nonpolitical reasons? | | | Have you ever hidden, blocked, unfriended, or stopped following anyone in the following media networking site because you did not agree with something they posted about government and politics? | | |
| | *percent checking "yes"* | | | *percent checking "yes"* | | |
	Non-military Friends	Active Duty Friends	Retired Military Friends	Non-military Friends	Active Duty Friends	Retired Military Friends
TOTAL	68.4	38.5	29.7	40.4	25.7	18.4
West Point Cadets	72.7**	41.8	27.2	44.0*	27.8	14.9*
NDU Students	61.5**	33.2	33.3	34.6*	22.4	23.7*
Democrats	69.7	42.4	42.4	42.4	30.3	28.1
Republicans	56.8	29.5	29.0	28.4	15.8	16.0
Those Who Unfriended For Nonpolitical Reasons				50.5***	56.9***	55.2***
Those Who Did Not Unfriend for Nonpolitical Reasons				11.1***	6.4***	8.4***
(n)	468	465	445	470	470	452

Source. Politics & Social Media Survey (2015–2016).

Note. NDU students include O-4s, O-5s, and O-6s. Party identification is displayed for NDU students only. Differences between West Point cadets and NDU students are statistically significant at * p < .05 and ** p < .01. Difference between those who unfriended for nonpolitical reasons and those who have not is statistically significant at *** p < .001.

What is of interest is the degree to which officers unfriend or block their social media contacts, especially other military friends, for political reasons. Generally speaking, more respondents reported unfriending their nonmilitary friends than military friends because of their political positions. Surprisingly, NDU students unfriended their active-duty and retired military friends for political positions roughly at the same rate. This calls into question the oft-cited assumption by many in the officer corps and even some civil-military commentators that political outspokenness is largely a province of those who have taken off the uniform at the end of a career.[27] Whatever it is about the political opinions of their military friends that is turning respondents off is happening equally for their active-duty and retired friends alike.

In addition, party affiliation suggests subtle differences when it comes to unfriending based on politics. Republicans were less likely to report they unfriended due to politics than Democrats. This generally corresponds with findings from past research, most notably the 2014 Pew study that found "consistent liberals" are more likely to unfriend someone because they disagreed with that person's political opinions on social media.[28] This paints a complex picture of how party manifests itself in social media. In the Politics & Social Media Survey sample, Democrats were less likely to have social media friends who share their political views, but they were more apt to unfriend or block friends on social media because they disagreed with something they posted about politics. Republicans were more likely to have social media friends who share their same political views and less likely to unfriend because of politics.

A third and final measure of interaction between respondents and their military social media friends is provided in table 32. When respondents were asked how often they felt uncomfortable about their active-duty military friends' political posts on social media, only a few respondents— just 15 percent—reported "almost always" or "often." While not shown in table 32, another 34 percent of respondents reported they "sometimes" felt uncomfortable, while 42 percent reported they hardly ever felt uncomfortable.

Table 32. Degree of Discomfort with Active-Duty Friends' Political Discussions on Social Media.

	percent checking "almost always" or "often" How often do you feel uncomfortable by the political content your active duty military friends discuss on social media networking sites?
TOTAL (n = 471)	15.4
West Point Cadets	17.7
NDU Students	11.8
Democrats	25.9**
Republicans	13.0**
Those Who Have Similar Political Views as Their Military Social Media Friends	8.8*
Those Who Have Dissimilar Political Views as Their Military Social Media Friends	17.8*

Source. Politics & Social Media Survey (2015–2016).
Note. NDU students include O-4s, O-5s, and O-6s. Difference between Democrats and Republicans is statistically significant at ** p < .01. Difference between those who share similar political views and those who do not is statistically significant at * p < .05.

Responses vary based on party affiliation and the degree to which respondents share similar political views with their social media friends. As table 32 shows, 26 percent of Democrats versus 13 percent of Republicans reported being almost always or often uncomfortable. In addition, respondents who had dissimilar political views from their social media friends (18 percent) were more apt to indicate they often felt uncomfortable, compared to respondents who shared similar political views with their social media friends (9 percent).

What does this all mean? Overall, most respondents were generally not too bothered by the political opinions their active-duty friends share on social media, although Democrats generally tended to feel more uncomfortable more often. This is consistent with the findings highlighted in chapter 2, where Democrats felt more uncomfortable talking about politics in the workplace than their Republican peers. This raises a number of important questions: Do Democrats feel more uncomfortable because they disagree with the politics being discussed by their Republican peers who outnumber them? Or do Democrats feel uncomfortable because the nature of the political discussions is normatively contrary to the military's spirit of nonpartisanship, and Republicans are somehow less sensitive to such violations? In other words, is discomfort a function of being a political minority, or is discomfort a function of sensitivity to normatively inappropriate political behavior? From this data alone, it is unclear, but it is likely that the answer lies somewhere in being a political minority, not sensitivity to inappropriate behavior. Data from the next three tables sheds more light on the influence of partisanship, ideology, and normatively inappropriate behavior.

Thus far, this chapter has focused on the extent to which military friends discuss politics on social media, comparisons in the political discourse among social media friend groups, the types of political activity observed on social media, and the degree of alignment in the political views between respondents and their friends. As the data in table 32 showed, few respondents felt uncomfortable by the political opinions their active-duty friends post on social media, which suggests if normative violations of the nonpartisan ethic exist on social media, they might be infrequent. Yet, a quarter of respondents admitted to unfriending active-duty friends because of something they posted about politics, so it is unclear to what extent normatively inappropriate behavior is prevalent among members of the military, whether active duty or retired, on social media. Tables 33, 34, and 35 more acutely probe whether the political content on social media expressly violates the military's nonpartisan ethic and, even worse, could be labeled as insulting, rude, or disdainful towards certain elected officials and politicians.

Tables 33, 34, and 35 summarize respondents' observations of their social media friends' political activity that clearly crossed the line. Respondents were asked if they ever observed their nonmilitary, active-duty, or retired military friends use or share insulting, rude, or disdainful comments directed at specific elected officials, politicians running for office, or the president of the United States. This question is especially delicate because it touches upon expressly prohibited activities and punishable offenses under the Uniformed Code of Military Justice. Under Article 88, contemptuous words by a commissioned officer against the president, vice president, members of Congress, the secretary of defense or secretaries of military departments, secretary of homeland security, governor, or state legislatures is an offense punishable by court martial.[29] As with the majority of this survey's questions about political behavior, respondents were asked for their observations of their friends' social media activity, not their own, in order to avoid putting respondents in a compromising position.

First, a large majority of those surveyed—over three-quarters— responded that their nonmilitary friends had posted or shared rude comments about elected officials, politicians running for office, and the president. This finding alone is revealing because it attests to broad incivility throughout social media. Yet, this study's primary interest is in whether active-duty and retired military exhibit the same lack of civility in political discourse. As tables 33, 34, and 35 show, albeit not at the same scale, active-duty and retired military members followed suit in such behavior—an alarming finding.

Table 33. Rude Comments Against Specific Elected Officials on Social Media.

| | Have you ever observed the following friends use or share insulting, rude, or disdainful comments directed against specific elected officials on a social media networking site? | | |
| | percent checking "yes" | | |
	Non-military Friends	Active Duty Friends	Retired Military Friends
TOTAL	76.3	34.8	44.0
West Point Cadets	78.0	39.9**	37.6***
NDU Students	73.6	26.6**	54.0***
Democrats	81.8	39.4*	60.6
Republicans	71.6	21.1*	52.1
(n)	469	468	450

Source. Politics & Social Media Survey (2015–2016).

Note. NDU students include O-4s, O-5s, and O-6s. Party identification is displayed for NDU students only. Differences between West Point cadets and NDU students are statistically significant at * p < .01 and ** p < .001. Difference between Democrats and Republicans is statistically significant at * p < .05.

Table 34. Rude Comments on Social Media About Politicians Running for Office.

	Have you ever observed the following friends use or share insulting, rude, or disdainful comments directed against politicians running for office on a social media networking site? *percent checking "yes"*		
	Non-military Friends	Active Duty Friends	Retired Military Friends
TOTAL	80.9	50.6	51.0
West Point Cadets	84.3*	58.9***	46.3*
NDU Students	75.3*	36.9***	58.3*
Democrats	84.9	48.5	63.6
Republicans	72.6	33.7	54.3
(n)	471	468	445

Source. Politics & Social Media Survey (2015–2016).

Note. NDU students include O-4s, O-5s, and O-6s. Party identification is displayed for NDU students only. Differences between West Point cadets and NDU students are statistically significant at * p < .05 and *** p < .001.

Table 35. Rude Comments on Social Media About the President of the United States.

| | Have you ever observed the following friends use or share insulting, rude, or disdainful comments directed against the President of the United States on a social media networking site? *percent checking "yes"* | | |
	Non-military Friends	Active Duty Friends	Retired Military Friends
TOTAL	77.8	34.0	47.3
West Point Cadets	81.4*	39.5**	41.4**
NDU Students	71.6*	24.9**	56.6**
Democrats	75.8	39.4*	65.6
Republicans	72.6	21.1*	54.3
(n)	468	468	448

Source. Politics & Social Media Survey (2015–2016).

Note. NDU students include O-4s, O-5s, and O-6s. Party identification is displayed for NDU students only. Differences between West Point cadets and NDU students are statistically significant at * p < .05 and ** p < .01. Difference between Democrats and Republicans is statistically significant at * p < .05.

More than half of NDU students reported that their retired military friends posted or shared rude comments about elected officials, politicians, and the president and that active-duty members were equally guilty, with well over one-third of all those surveyed indicating their active-duty friends did the same. Thus, while retired members of the military may be less constrained to make or share such controversial statements, active-duty members are by no means silent.

For all three categories—elected officials, politicians, and the president—responses varied by rank, indicating varying degrees of professionalism on social media by respondents' active-duty friends. West Point cadets were far more likely to report normatively inappropriate behavior by their active-duty friends than NDU students in each category. The largest gap between West Point cadets and NDU students is in the category of politicians running for office, where 59 percent of cadets reported observing their active-duty friends directing inappropriate comments towards politicians running for office compared to just 37 percent of NDU students. Again, this reinforces the assumption that the longer one serves in the military, the more they are exposed to and adopt the norms of the profession.

Within the three categories, respondents' active-duty and retired military friends were most vocal towards politicians running for office, with 51 percent of those surveyed indicating their active-duty friends posted rude comments, and 58 percent of NDU students indicating their retired friends did the same. It is also instructive to note that the active-duty friends of both West Point cadets and NDU students seemed to draw a distinction among the three categories as to who was most "fair game" for rude comments and criticism, and this was even evident within the NDU student sample. While 37 percent of NDU students indicated their active-duty military friends posted or shared rude comments about politicians, that figure dropped to 25 and 27 percent for the president and other elected officials, respectively. This is important, because despite the clear normative violations, it shows that at least some active-duty members recognized the tenets of the nonpartisan ethic and, more acutely, provisions of the Uniformed Code of Military Justice and other pertinent regulations. Whether it is appropriate for active-duty members to be engaging in such behavior towards politicians is another matter, but the difference in response rates among NDU students nonetheless indicates some degree of understanding of applicable policies, regulations, and norms.

Relatively speaking, respondents were less likely to report that their active-duty friends were guilty of posting rude or inappropriate comments about individuals in the three measured categories; this is in contrast to the strong majorities of respondents who reported that their nonmilitary friends and retired military friends made such comments. Yet, the proportion of active-duty friends engaging in such behavior can by no means be written off as a mere outlier. Admittedly, there are the caveats that the question asked respondents if *they had ever observed* their friends in engaging in such behavior and that we do not have a true sense of how often such inappropriate behavior is occurring on social media. Nonetheless, even if the offenders formed a small proportion of a respondent's overall active-duty friend group, the fact that a sizeable minority of respondents attested that this was occurring—or 50 percent of respondents in the case of politicians running for office—is extraordinary.

As with previous analysis regarding the politics of unfriending, the degree of alignment in political views between respondents and friends as well as the extent to which respondents felt uncomfortable by their friends' politics, the responses to questions as shown in tables 33, 34, and 35 also vary based party identification. Democrats were more likely than Republicans to report that their active-duty friends posted or shared inappropriate content against specific elected officials and the president. More research is required, but inferences can be made that Democrats were suggesting Republicans were the source of the offending behavior —especially given that Barack Obama was president at the time of the survey.

Table 36. Rude Comments Made by Active-Duty Military Against Elected Officials and the President – A Comparison Over Time.

	Have you ever observed your active duty friends use or share insulting, rude, or disdainful comments directed against specific elected officials on a social media networking site?	Have you ever observed your active duty friends use or share insulting, rude, or disdainful comments directed against the President of the United States on a social media networking site?	Have you ever observed your active duty friends use or share insulting, rude, or disdainful comments directed against specific elected officials or the President of the United States on a social media networking site?
	2015-2016	2015-2016	2017-2020
		percent checking "yes"	
TOTAL	34.8	34.0	31.1
West Point Cadets	39.9**	39.5**	27.7*
NDU Students	26.6**	24.9**	34.8*
Democrats	39.4*	39.4*	49.3**
Republicans	21.1*	21.1*	30.2**
(n)	468	468	890

Source. Politics & Social Media Survey (2015–2016) and NDU CMR Survey (2017–2020).
Note. NDU students include O-4s, O-5s, and O-6s. Army War College students were also included in the NDU student sample for 2017–2020. Differences between West Point cadets and NDU students are statistically significant at * p < .05 and ** p < .01. Differences between Democrats and Republicans are statistically significant at * p < .05 and ** p < .01.

To further probe the degree to which these responses could be a case of partisan rationalization or motivated reasoning (a topic that will be explored in greater depth in chapter 6), a similar question was included in the NDU CMR Survey (2017–2020), thereby allowing a comparison of responses between the Obama and Trump administrations. If the responses were a function of partisan rationalization—where partisans attempt to fit their responses to match their partisan loyalties—Democrats might report higher levels of normatively inappropriate behavior, especially geared towards the president during the Obama administration, while Republicans might be more apt to do so during the Trump administration.

First, from the Politics & Social Media Survey conducted in 2015–2016 to the NDU CMR Survey conducted from 2017 to 2020, there was a 12-point decrease in the percentage of West Point cadets who indicated that their active-duty friends shared insulting comments directed against the president or elected leaders. This corresponds with the findings reported in table 26, where cadets were three times less likely during the 2017–2018 wave, compared to the 2015–2016 survey, to report their active-duty friends talking politics on social media. Because of the sharp drop-off for West Point cadets only, findings for party affiliation are reported for only NDU students in table 36 to ensure a more accurate test for possible partisan rationalization.

In looking just at the results for party affiliation among NDU students, it is possible to interpret how respondents observe criticism of the president and elected leaders on social media as partisan rationalization, insofar as a greater percentage of Republicans indicated they observed rude comments on social media during the Trump administration than during the Obama administration. However, there was also in increase in the percentage of Democrats who reported observing rude comments, and the percentage of Democrats observing such behavior was higher than that for Republicans, so it may not be a perfect case of partisan rationalization. It could be that President Trump simply inspired more rude comments by active-duty members of the military compared to President Obama, and this was observed by both Democrats and Republicans alike. In any regard, while this does not conclusively prove that Republicans exhibited partisan rationalization or motivated reasoning, it remains a possible explanation for the higher percentage of Republican respondents who observed such normative violations occurring during the Trump administration compared to the Obama administration.

The findings about rude comments toward the president, whether occurring in the Obama or Trump administration, should be especially startling to senior military leaders and interested observers of civil-military relations. While attitudes towards the president generally mirrored attitudes towards other elected officials, the military has but one commander in chief. This observation carries the most significant implications for civil-military relations of any in this study because it not only suggests a lack of respect and decorum among active-duty military, but it also questions the military's overall deference to civilian authority. How well assured is subordination to the commander in chief if members of the active-duty military engage in sarcasm or vitriol against the president in a public forum?

This is not the first time in which members of the military have been seen to be harboring resentment towards their commander in chief. In recent history, the Clinton administration stands out as a period of strained civil-military relations, during which disrespect within the ranks made headlines on more than one occasion, including the time when a US Air Force major general was reprimanded and forced to retire after referring to President Bill Clinton as a "pot-smoking," "womanizing" and "draft-dodging" commander in chief during a speech at a military banquet.[30] Resistance to President Clinton's policies, such as his attempt to integrate gays in the military or intervention in Bosnia, was viewed as further manifestations of this disrespect. But the policy resistance debate centers largely on a handful of senior military leaders at the highest levels of the military and their interactions with the executive branch.

What makes today different, and involves a much larger segment of the military, is the accessible, public outlet available for such disrespect. Even if normatively inappropriate behavior is somewhat limited to a small proportion of the military, which this study does contest at times, such behavior is being publicly broadcast to wider audiences than ever before, and this challenges the principle of subordination to civilian authority.

The last set of findings in this study relate to the very public nature of social media, the debate over what constitutes private and public expression, and the perception that one's personal political views implies official endorsement by the military. To get at these issues, respondents were asked if they had ever observed their active-duty friends on social media use a disclaimer to note that their personal political views do not reflect the official position of the Department of Defense.

Table 37. Use of Disclaimers by Active-Duty Friends on Social Media.

	percent checking "yes"
	Have you ever observed an active duty military friend post a disclaimer on a social media networking site that his/her political views are those of the individual only and not those of the Department of Defense?
TOTAL (n = 474)	22.8
West Point Cadets	29.8***
NDU Students	11.7***
Democrats	19.3
Republicans	24.5

Source. Politics & Social Media Survey (2015–2016).
Note. NDU students include O-4s, O-5s, and O-6s. Difference between West Point cadets and NDU students is statistically significant at *** $p < .001$.

As table 37 shows, only 23 percent of respondents indicated they observed their active-duty friends on social media complying with this, with West Point cadets (30 percent) more likely to indicate that their active-duty friends used disclaimers than NDU students (12 percent). At first blush, this seems counter to the professionalization argument, where the longer one serves in the military and is exposed to its norms and regulations, the more likely one is to adhere to and adopt them. However, it again suggests that West Point cadets probably received particular emphasis about this, along with other social media etiquette as part of their general instruction at West Point.

Table 38. Photos in Uniform on Social Media.

	percent checking "all," "most," or "some" Among your military friends, how many have photos of themselves in uniform on their social media networking sites?
TOTAL (n = 364)	92.0
West Point Cadets	96.6***
National War College Students	74.0***

Source. Politics & Social Media Survey (2015–2016).
Note. Difference between West Point cadets and NDU students is statistically significant at *** p < .001.

Lastly, even if respondents lack the requisite Department of Defense disclaimer, it could be that military members' affiliation with the military is not widely visible on their social media accounts. Clearly, the overwhelming majority of their friends must know they are or were in the military, but how well would the general public be able to discern military affiliation from a social media account alone? A simple shortcut is whether military members include photos of themselves in uniform. Table 38 displays the findings for responses by West Point cadets and

National War College students, where 92 percent indicated that some, most, or all of their military friends had photos of themselves in uniform. Of note, this varied somewhat by age or cohort, with 97 percent of West Point cadets reporting this, compared to 74 percent of National War College students. Regardless of the difference in subsamples, strong majorities indicate their military friends do post photos in uniform, further blurring the lines between the perception of public and private personas on social media.

CONCLUSION

This chapter advances our understanding of political activity by uniformed military beyond traditional, if not outdated, measures of political partic-ipation. It also adds to the debate on whether the military is politicized by examining the impact partisanship and political ideology have on political expression in social media. Military elites actively use social media, although younger elites are more prolific in their use, including the extent to which they consume political news on social media and how much their friends discuss politics on social media. Furthermore, while respondents' nonmilitary friends were more politically active than their military friends, both active-duty and retired military actively participate in a number of forms of political and partisan expression.

Responses vary by party affiliation, evident by the variance in the political heterogeneity of military friend networks on social media, the degree to which military elites feel uncomfortable by their active-duty friends' political posts, and the willingness of military elites to sever social media ties with their military friends for political reasons. While some of the differences are subtle, military elites who identify as liberals and Democrats are more likely to have more politically diverse military friends on social media but are also more likely to report feeling uncomfortable by their friends' politics. Finally, a striking percentage of those surveyed indicated their military friends, both active and retired, have engaged in insulting, rude, or disdainful comments directed at politicians, elected officials, and the president. Again, differences are evident in party affiliation, with Democrats more likely to report they observed such normative violations. These findings suggest Republican military elites might see social media as their echo chambers and raise further questions about the politicization of the force. This study notes several significant differences between age or generational cohorts, as well as ideology and party identification but stops short of suggesting clear causal relationships exist between those variables and levels of political activity. Relationships, nonetheless, do exist, and future research is needed to probe more acutely for the real impact that these have in determining political behavior.

This chapter also identifies gaps and inconsistencies in regulations and policies about political behavior, which should be quickly rectified given how prolific social media usage is among members of the military today. The guidance by the Department of Defense on political activity, including political expression on social media turns out to be fairly permissive, erring on the side of the service member's right to free speech rather than erring on the side of caution and the norms of a nonpartisan military. The policy guidance is also ambiguous and inconsistent at times, assuming a clear distinction exists between political and partisan and that the rank and file can clearly discriminate between the two. In a time of intense partisan polarization, most political discussions carry partisan undertones. Regardless, according to this chapter's findings, members of the military who are active on social media are largely ignoring Department of Defense guidance, as reflected by the small minority who reported ever having seen their friends use disclaimers accompanying their political opinions on social media. Moreover, the sizeable percentage of respondents who reported that their active-duty military friends have posted or shared inappropriate comments about political figures, including elected officials and even the president, suggests that enforcement of such policies might be lacking.

At the root of the debate over political expression on social media is the distinction between public and private spheres. While unstated in DoDD 1344.10, implicit in the norms of being apolitical and nonpartisan is the idea that a service member's political opinions and activity should be private. This is why DoDD 1344.10 goes to great lengths to distinguish activity that could be construed as implying official endorsement from the relatively private acts associated with "the obligations of citizenship."[31] Social media, despite its veneer of security through closed-friend networks, is fundamentally a public sphere, a fact the Department of Defense fully acknowledges through the services' respective social media guidelines.[32] Unlike a discussion with colleagues or friends, political commentary on social media becomes a written, lasting record with an exponentially public reach, as friends of friends continue to share or pass on an original post or comment.

Here, the Department of Defense seems to have missed an opportunity to emphasize the unique implications of political expression in social media and how this varies from more traditional means of political activity. Instead, the Department of Defense has chosen to split hairs, arguing that service members cannot use their military affiliations on social media to promote their partisan views, but can do so as long as they caveat that their opinions do not reflect those of the Department of Defense. In doing so, it sidesteps the issue of whether such public, partisan commentary by the military is appropriate and whether it contributes to the charges outlined at the beginning of this chapter—that the military is too partisan and too vocal. It also seems to suggest that as long as a disclaimer accompanies service members' partisan political posts, then "no harm, no foul"—regardless of the tone or content of the political commentary. Yet, each time service members post their political opinions, especially those with unmistakable partisan connections, they publicly reveal their politics, even if disclaimers are used. Given the historically strong affiliation of military elites with one particular political party, this raises questions about the aggregate effect a steady stream of political commentary by members of the military has towards gradually eroding the nonpartisan ethic.

Notes

1. Martin Dempsey, "From the Chairman: Putting Our Nation First," 4.
2. Department of Defense, *Political Activities by Members of the Armed Forces*, DoD Directive 1344.10 (Washington, DC: 2008). Often updated prior to a presidential election year, the current version was last published in February 2008.
3. Cronk, "Service Members, Civilians Bound By DOD Rules During Election Campaigns.".
4. Hill, "Hatch Act, DOD Regulations Govern Political Activities on Social Media."
5. Ibid.
6. Ibid.
7. The U.S. Army Social Media Guide was formerly a handbook but converted to a website in 2016. https://www.army.mil/socialmedia/
8. Army Regulation 600-20, *Army Command Policy,* is the service counterpart to Department of Defense Directive 1344.10, recapping a list of political activity dos and don'ts for soldiers in its Appendix B. It, like DoDD 1344.10, makes no mention of political activity on social media.
9. Retired General Martin Dempsey seems to make this point in his quote that leads off this chapter. By contrasting the far reach of social media against "the confines of our homes," his implicit assertion is that while service members have the right to express their personal opinions on politics, such views should be made in private, not in a public forum.
10. Mullen, "From the Chairman: Military Must Stay Apolitical," 2–3; Mullen, "Speech Delivered at National Defense University Commencement"; Martin Dempsey, "Civil-Military Relations and the Profession of Arms."
11. This chapter relies upon the observations of a sample of military officers attending the National Defense University (n=230) and cadets attending the United States Military Academy at West Point (n=307) from 2015 to 2016 and is supplemented with additional survey data collected from 2017 to 2020 of Army officers attending the National Defense University and Army War College (n=287) and cadets attending the United States Military Academy (n=597). Survey data of National Defense University students in 2015–2016 included officers from each of the branches of the

armed forces, and that data is reported throughout this chapter, although the attitudes of army officers are specifically highlighted as well.

12. Further underscoring the changing nature of social media, the social media platforms measured in the Politics & Social Media Survey in 2015–2016 now seem outdated: in addition to Facebook, Twitter, and LinkedIn, the survey also asked about those who had Google+, which is now defunct, and YouTube accounts. A similar survey conducted today would likely find members of the military who have Instagram, Snap Chat, Tik-Tok, WhatsApp, and many other social media accounts.

13. Duggan, "The Demographics of Social Media Users.".

14. The correlation between a binary variable representing the 18–24-year-old demographic and having a Facebook account is weak but positive (r = 0.24, p < .001), while the correlation between the 18–24 year-old age bracket and having a LinkedIn account is moderate and negative (r = -0.45, p < .001).

15. Brady et al., "Social Media and Political Engagement."

16. See generally Keith et al., *The Myth of the Independent Voter*; Westlye, "The Myth of the Independent Voter Revisited"; and Lewis-Beck, Jacoby, and Norpoth, *The American Voter Revisited.*

17. A positive correlation exists between the 18–24-year-old cohort and getting news from Facebook (r = 0.32, p < .001).

18. Mitchell, Gottfried, and Matsa, "Millennials and Political News."

19. Marc Prensky was among the first to use the term digital natives to describe those who have grown up in the digital world of new technology. In contrast, digital immigrants were not born into this world but try to embrace most aspects of it. See Prensky, "Digital Natives, Digital Immigrants."

20. Timberg, "How Conservatives Learned to Wield Power Inside Facebook"; and Thompson, "Why the Right Wing Has a Massive Advantage on Facebook."

21. See the West Point Admissions website, https://www.blog.westpointadmissions.com/single-post/USMA-Social-Media-Tips.

22. Brooks, Robinson, and Urben, "What Makes a Military Professional? Evaluating Norm Socialization in West Point Cadets."

23. Urben, "Wearing Politics on Their Sleeves?," 577.

24. Urben, "Wearing Politics on Their Sleeves?," 573–576.

25. Past research into Army officers' attitudes found that 93 percent of Army officers agreed with the statement that members of the military should vote, and 81 percent of Army officers stated they voted in the 2008 pres-

idential election—far outpacing voter turnout levels for the general public. See Urben, "Wearing Politics on Their Sleeves? Levels of Political
Activism of Active Duty Army Officers," 575.

26. Mitchell et al., "Political Polarization and Media Habits."
27. See generally, Kohn, "General Elections: The Brass Shouldn't Do
Endorsements;" Golby et al., "Brass Politics"; Swain, "Reflection on an
Ethic of Officership"; Kohn, "The Erosion of Civilian Control of the Military"; Cook, "Revolt of the Generals"; and Nielsen and Snider, *American
Civil-Military Relations.*
28. Mitchell et al., "Political Polarization and Media Habits."
29. 10 U.S. Code § 888 - Article 88, Contempt toward officials.
30. Schmitt, "General to Be Disciplined for Disparaging President." See also
Bacevich, "Tradition Abandoned"; Kohn, "Out of Control"; and Kohn,
"The Erosion of Civilian Control of the Military." Some of the military's
apparent aversion to President Clinton can be traced to the revelation
during the 1992 campaign that he avoided the draft through multiple
educational deferments and by joining the Reserve Officer Training
Corps (ROTC) but never serving in it, along with the fact he joined in
protests of the Vietnam War while overseas. A letter he wrote to the head
of the University of Arkansas' ROTC Department, in which he admitted
having loathed the military probably did not help. *Associated Press*, "The
1992 Campaign; A Letter by Clinton on His Draft Deferment."
31. *Department of Defense Directive 1344.10*, 2.
32. Department of the Army, "Army Social Media: Policies and Resources,"
https://www.army.mil/socialmedia/; Department of the Navy, *Navy
Social Media Handbook*, March 2019, https://www.csp.navy.mil/
Portals/2/documents/downloads/navy-social-media-handbook-2019.pdf;
Department of the Air Force, "Air Force Social Media Guidelines," *https://
www.publicaffairs.af.mil/Programs/Air-Force-Social-Media/*; Department
of the Air Force, Air Force Instruction 35-107, *Public Web and Social
Information*, March 15, 2017, https://static.e-publishing.af.mil/production/
1/saf_pa/publication/afi35-107/afi35-107.pdf; Headquarters, U.S. Marine
Corps *The Social Corps: U.S.M.C. Social Media Principles* (Washington,
DC: Marine Corps Production Directorate, 2017), https://www.marines.
mil/Portals/1/Docs/Social-Media-Handbook20170308.pdf.

CHAPTER 5

"PRINCES OF THE CHURCH"

THE MUCH-DEBATED ROLE OF
RETIRED OFFICERS IN POLITICS

I am convinced that the best service a retired general can perform
is to turn in his tongue along with his suit and to mothball his
opinions.

—General Omar Bradley, US Army, ret.[1]

When someone says, "You're a general, so you have to shut up,"
I say, "Do I have to stop being an American?"

—Lieutenant General Michael Flynn, US Army, ret.[2]

Richard Kohn famously argued that, like "princes of the church," retired
four-stars never truly retire but continue to speak for the institution
after they have left uniformed service.[3] Since at least 1992, however, an
increasing number of retired general and flag officers, henceforth referred
to simply as retired flag officers, have endorsed presidential candidates
on both sides of the aisles, and in several high-profile instances they
have publicly criticized the sitting president, secretary of defense, and
chairman of the Joint Chiefs of Staff. While the norm of nonpartisanship
for the active-duty force is well agreed upon within the ranks, if not
always adhered to, there is little unanimity on the role retired officers—

especially retired flag officers—should or should not play in politics. This chapter examines why that is the case, drawing upon active-duty officers' views of the role that retired officers, especially retired flag officers, should play in the public sphere.

ARE THEY REALLY RETIRED?

Before examining the various ways in which retired flag officers engage in politics and to what extent those serving today think such behavior is appropriate, it is worth posing the question—are retired officers still considered part of the armed forces? Richard Swain, former professor of officership at the US Military Academy minces no words:

> Still, it is at least a false proposition that upon retirement officers revert to full civilian status in so far as the obligations they undertook at their commissioning. Retirement is not resignation. It is a matter of fact, not interpretation, that retired officers remain members of the armed forces by law and regulation. They receive a salary, in the case of senior officers a generous salary, and may be recalled to active duty under provisions of Section 64.4 of Title 32—National Defense of the Code of Federal Regulations.[4]

In fact, Article 2 of the Uniformed Code of Military Justice (UCMJ) specifies that "retired members of a regular component of the armed forces who are entitled to pay" are indeed subject to the UCMJ.[5] Former US Air Force Deputy Judge Advocate General retired Major General Charles J. Dunlap, Jr. has argued that retired service members receiving pay should be subject to court-martial jurisdiction, citing *Barker v. Kansas* (1992), where the Supreme Court ruled that "military retirees unquestionably remain in the service and are subject to restrictions and recall."[6] Dunlap went on to argue that, "in the case of retired personnel voluntarily collecting retired pay...they have *chosen* to keep a relationship with the military."[7]

Despite the fairly clear language in the US Code, the likelihood that retired flag officers would be tried under Article 88, which prohibits commissioned officers from using "contemptuous words" against the president and certain other elected and appointed officials, is next to nil.[8] Thus, the question of whether retired flag officers should be subject to the rules and norms that governed their conduct while on active duty remains a normative question and one that is up for debate. The particular norm on which this book and this chapter focuses is the norm of nonpartisanship and the ongoing debate within military circles and among the American public on whether retired officers, namely retired flag officers, *should* adhere to it.

Those who argue the norm of nonpartisanship should extend to retired members of the military tend to focus almost exclusively on retired flag officers—the "princes of the church" to whom Kohn referred. Peter Feaver has observed, "it is telling that we have a strong custom in our country of referring to retired generals and admirals by their rank, even long after they have left uniformed service—their first name, even in retirement, continues to be general or admiral."[9] The implication any time a retired flag-officer speaks out is that they tacitly speak for the institution they served for decades. Moreover, the idea that the American public can easily distinguish between active-duty and retired members of the military does not hold up to greater scrutiny. For example, in a June 2019 poll conducted by the nonpartisan and objective research organization (NORC) at the University of Chicago, only 31 percent of Americans could correctly identify Secretary Jim Mattis's military status as retired.[10]

Those who support retired flag officers speaking out on political, including partisan, issues tend to do so from two main points: they remain unconvinced by any legal argument that retired officers remain part of the military and argue that retired flag officers should be able to exercise their First Amendment rights just like any other citizen —especially because these officers spent their careers defending such constitutional rights. Second, they argue that retired flag officers offer a particular expertise based on their long careers, and the American public should benefit from hearing their voices.[11]

It is, as many civil-military relations scholars conclude, an unsettled norm, and as this chapter will go on to argue, the norm is not well-inculcated within the ranks. In fact, most advocates for the norm tend to be civil-military relations scholars and practitioners, although retired Major General Charles J. Dunlap, Jr. points out that the vast majority of the more than 7,500 retired flag officers are not politically active and refrain from making partisan endorsements.[12] It is reasonable to assume, then, that most retired flag officers do support the idea of the norm extending into retirement, at least where endorsements are concerned. Retired Admiral Michael Mullen and retired General Martin Dempsey both advocated for an extension of the nonpartisan ethic into retirement when they served as chairmen of the Joint Chiefs of Staff.[13] Dempsey's successor, retired General Joseph Dunford, however, refrained from taking this step and explicitly couched his public statements on the nonpartisan ethic to pertain only to active-duty service members, declining to address the issue of politically vocal retired flag officers.[14] Dunford has also been the least vocal of the three in retirement.[15] If there is little unanimity on the issue among the select group of officers to hold the position of the nation's senior ranking member of the armed forces, it should be unsurprising there is tepid support for it among the rank and file and the broader American public.

POLITICAL ENDORSEMENTS BY RETIRED FLAG OFFICERS

The political act that civil-military scholars—and retired leaders like Dempsey—zero in on as damaging to the military's nonpartisan stature is a relatively recent phenomenon—when a retired flag-officer makes a partisan endorsement for a presidential candidate running for office. The crux of the argument against endorsements, best articulated again by Feaver goes like this: "What is corrosive is claiming that the authority that comes from nonpartisan military service but then deploying that authority in pursuit of a quintessentially partisan mission—electing one candidate over another."[16] Endorsements aim to cash in on the prestige associated with the military in general, and high-ranking officers in particular, in an attempt to further a partisan cause. Partisan endorsements differ markedly from veterans running for political office, yet they are often conflated by those who point out there has been a strong tradition of politically active retired flag officers in the United States.[17] True, career soldiers such as George Washington, Ulysses S. Grant, and Dwight D. Eisenhower have been elected president, and the nineteenth century witnessed several non-career officers, even including some on active duty, running for president.[18] However, as others have argued, when candidates run for office, they fully embrace a partisan role and subject themselves to the full scrutiny of the electorate.[19] Endorsements offer no such accountability.

Scholars and pundits alike point to the 1988 and 1992 presidential elections as the start of partisan endorsements by retired flag officers. In 1988, former Marine Corps Commandant retired General P.X. Kelley co-chaired "Veterans for Bush," publicly proclaiming on the campaign trail, "Michael Dukakis is anti-military."[20] Four years later, Admiral William J. Crowe, Jr. endorsed Bill Clinton for president and was later appointed ambassador to the United Kingdom during Clinton's first term. From there, endorsements by retired flag officers have been featured in every presidential election campaign and have increased in number, despite consistent condemnation by civil-military-relations scholars as well as current and former members of the military.[21] While the 2012 presidential campaign witnessed the largest number of retired flag-officer endorsements to date—more than 500 for Republican nominee Mitt Romney—many thought the 2016 campaign crossed a line with the over-the-top convention speeches by retired Lieutenant General Michael Flynn and retired General John Allen.[22] Flynn's caustic chants of "lock her up" against Hillary Clinton at the Republican National Convention and Allen's call for active-duty military to join him in his partisan cause to help elect Clinton at the Democratic National Convention drew swift condemnation from many, including Dempsey and Mullen.[23]

Despite the prolific endorsements by retired flag officers, our understanding of both their motivations and the impact they have on the public's attitudes is limited to a handful of studies. Zachary Griffiths and Olivia Simon examined more than 1,300 endorsements by retired flag officers between 2004 and 2016 and found that the primary motivation for such endorsements were personal entreaties from close friends and colleagues—not necessarily purely partisan or ideological reasons.[24] Nonetheless, Griffiths and Simon also found that retired flag officers endorse Republican candidates over Democrats by a ratio of 8 to 1 and that retired Navy admirals and Marine Corps generals accounted for 62 percent of total flag-officer endorsers but made up just 25 percent of living retired flag officers. Retired army generals were the least likely to make partisan endorsements, suggesting that something about service culture or socialization to professional norms may explain such differences in endorsements across the services.

A report by the Center for New American Security prior to the 2012 election found that endorsements from retired flag officers have little, if any effect, on partisans' overall support for candidates and only a modest effect on Independents' attitudes.[25] Thus, the issue of endorsements by retired flag-officer is a bit of a puzzle: endorsements generally fail to sway voters, but they can damage the credibility of the military, especially as a nonpartisan institution, in the minds of the public, depending on one's partisanship. Despite this, endorsements show no sign of abating. Political candidates running for office, especially those without military experience, continue to seek endorsements as validation from a sought-after interest group; and each election cycle shows a cohort of retired flag officers who are all too eager to oblige.[26]

REVOLTS OF THE GENERALS: TAKING ON THE COMMANDER IN CHIEF

Endorsements for political office are by no means the only way retired flag officers wade into partisan politics. Pointed criticism of the president by retired flag officers has been prominent in the post-9/11 era, raising more questions on the appropriateness of such activity and whether retired generals still speak for the institution once retired. The 2006 "revolt of the generals," as popularly referred, in which six recently retired army and Marine Corps generals called for the resignation of Secretary of Defense Donald Rumsfeld over his handling of the Iraq War was described by one commentator as both a "cultural milestone" and "political watershed" moment.[27] While the criticism may not have been explicitly directed at President George W. Bush, by implication it was, since it amounted to condemnation of both Bush's decision to invade Iraq and his subsequent mismanagement of the conflict. Predictably, this prompted debate on professional ethics and the precedent set by these recently retired generals with their high-profile, public dissent.[28]

Fourteen years later, the widespread condemnation by scores of retired flag officers against President Trump dwarfed the 2006 revolt of the generals. Researchers at New America catalogued 230 individual statements and signatures to letters by retired three- and four-star flag officers criticizing Trump during his presidency.[29] These included cosigned letters by retired flag officers who urged Trump to oppose the use of torture after he endorsed it on the campaign trail, who denounced Trump for revoking former Central Intelligence Agency Director John Brennan's security clearance, and who opposed Trump's ban on transgender troops.[30] Others, such as retired Admiral William McRaven—who signed two of the aforementioned letters—penned several op-eds squarely taking on Trump over his efforts to undermine the press, the intelligence community, and the armed forces. In one *New York Times* op-ed in which he called for Trump to be voted out of office, McRaven intimated that he spoke for many still in uniform and quoted an unnamed retired four-star general who said, "I don't like the Democrats, but Trump is destroying the Republic!"[31]

The civil rights protests in the summer of 2020, following the murder of George Floyd and Trump's heavy-handedness in quelling protests, provoked great backlash among retired flag officers. Following Secretary of Defense Mark Esper's call to "dominate the battlespace," Trump's threats to invoke the Insurrection Act, and the ignominious photo-op in Lafayette Square that later prompted an apology from General Mark Milley, the chairman of the Joint Chiefs of Staff, New America recorded 63 statements by active-duty and retired flag officers—including four former chairmen of the Joint Chiefs of Staff—condemning the president's words or actions or calling out the pernicious effects of systemic racism within the ranks.[32]

It would be easy to dismiss the recent wave of criticism by retired flag officers as unique and solely a reaction to Donald Trump, but the precedent established by the 2006 revolt of the generals and the trend of partisan endorsements over the past 30 years point to an increasingly vocal cohort of retired flag officers. The question remains, as it did with endorsements, is how the public responds to political, especially partisan, statements made by retired flag officers. The most compelling analysis on the topic comes from the recent survey experiments Michael Robinson conducted.[33] Robinson found that retired flag officers who were politically outspoken and easily identifiable as partisan were seen to be less credible by respondents who shared opposing political views and more credible by respondents who shared the same partisan attitudes. Additionally, exposure to partisan retired flag officers negatively impacted participants' perception of the military's overall trustworthiness. Whether it was criticizing Rumsfeld's management of the Iraq War or Trump's many inflammatory statements, retired flag officers who spoke out in each instance undoubtedly had the courage of their convictions and believed that they were applying their hard-earned expertise to inform the public at a time of heightened political salience. Robinson, however, warns that when the public discerns a retired flag-officer's partisanship, their trust in those officers is conditional on their holding the same partisan views.

It is clear that the issue of retired officers engaging in politics thus presents several paradoxes. Despite not having a real impact on voters' preferences, partisan endorsements by retired flag officers continue to remain a fixture of modern campaigns and elections.[34] And while retired flag officers have been less constrained in recent years in speaking out politically—including criticizing the president directly—they end up losing a broad audience when they are perceived to be partisan and are only seen as credible by ideologically like-minded groups.[35] It is against this backdrop that the views of active-duty officers on the topic of politically vocal retired officers are more closely examined.

ACTIVE-DUTY OFFICERS' VIEWS OF POLITICALLY VOCAL RETIRED OFFICERS

In both the CMR Time of War Survey and the NDU CMR Survey, respondents were asked their views on the propriety of retired officers publicly expressing their political views (see table 39). In each question asked, a majority of officers and cadets supported a permissive view of retired officers publicly airing their political views, although it is clear that attitudes shifted over the decade. There are also few discernible differences in the attitudes of cadets and army lieutenants compared to army lieutenant colonels and colonels. Throughout this book, there have been plenty of instances in which the views of cadets and lieutenants were at odds with their more senior officer counterparts, reflecting that socialization to norms in the officer corps is solidified the longer one stays in the military. In the case of officers' support for retired officers—including retired flag officers—publicly airing their political opinions, the alignment of attitudes among the army's most junior and senior officers suggests that little purposeful norm socialization is actually occurring in the officer corps as far as this is concerned. If this were occurring, we would see more cadets and lieutenants supportive of retired officers publicly expressing their political views and fewer senior officers in favor. But this is not the case—there are virtually identical levels of support in both cohorts.

Table 39. Views of Retired Officers Publicly Expressing Their Political Views.

	percent checking "agree" or "strongly agree"		
	Retired officers should be allowed to publicly express their political views just like any other citizen.	Retired officers should not publicly criticize members of the civilian branch of government.	It is proper for retired generals to publicly express their political views.
CMR Time of War Survey, 2009 (n = 1,866)	81.5	19.4	67.7
Army Lieutenants	81.1	16.4	67.5
Army Lieutenant Colonels & Colonels	81.7	20.9	67.8
Democrats	86.4*	14.9**	81.1***
Republicans	81.7*	21.1**	66.0***
NDU CMR Survey, 2017-2020 (n = 852)	66.1	34.5	48.6
West Point Cadets	66.8	35.1	47.5
Army Lieutenant Colonels & Colonels	64.5	33.2	51.2
Democrats	69.0	33.3	52.3
Republicans	68.0	34.9	50.7

Source. CMR Time of War Survey (2009) and NDU CMR Survey (2018–2020).

Note. Data reflects responses from US Army lieutenants, lieutenant colonels, and colonels in the CMR Time of War Survey and West Point cadets and US Army lieutenant colonels and colonels in the NDU CMR Survey. Differences between Democrats and Republicans are statistically significant at * p < .05, ** p < .01, *** p < .001.

As table 39 shows, in the CMR Time of War Survey, 82 percent of respondents agreed with the notion that just like any other citizen, retired officers should be able to publicly express their political views. Similarly, few respondents—less than one-fifth—indicated support for the idea that retired officers should not publicly criticize civilian members of government. In both of these measures, active-duty army officers strongly supported the belief that once retired, officers should no longer be beholden to the norms that govern behavior for those on active duty.

Despite a clear preference for retired officers being able to exercise their First Amendment rights, the difference in respondents' attitudes towards retired flag officers is noteworthy. Although most respondents in the CMR Time of War Survey (68 percent) thought it was fine for retired flag officers to speak out publicly on political issues, it is lower than respondents' support for retired officers—no ranks specified—speaking out. This is instructive because it suggests some officers differentiate between retired officers and retired flag officers and concede that the nonpartisan ethic should be extended into retirement for flag officers specifically. It is noteworthy that Democrats were more apt than Republicans to support retired flag officers speaking out. A potential explanation is that respondents associated retired flag officers speaking out with the "revolt of the generals" just three years prior when retired flag officers criticized the Bush administration's handling of the Iraq War, but it is unclear from the data here alone.

Even more noteworthy is the change in attitudes which the officer corps appears to have undergone in the decade between the CMR Time of War Survey and the NDU CMR Survey. While majorities of respondents in the NDU CMR Survey continued to endorse free political expression by retired military officers, they were considerably smaller majorities than a decade prior: 82 percent advocated public political expression by retired officers, compared to just 66 percent who did nearly a decade later. A larger minority also argued against retired officers from publicly criticizing civilian government leaders, moving from 20 percent up to

35 percent. However, the most significant change in attitudes among army officers was in their declining level of support for retired generals publicly expressing their political opinions: dropping from 68 percent to 49 percent. Additionally, in the CMR Time of War Survey, Democrats were more likely than Republicans to favor fewer restrictions on retired officers speaking out publicly on politics, but there were few partisan differences in the NDU CMR Survey.

Throughout this book, a persistent theme emerges—that for most of the All-Volunteer Force era, the officer corps seems to have taken its nonpartisan stance for granted. This neutral position has ceased to be a prominent feature in professional military education, and many officers have arguably failed to reflect on the importance of civil-military norms until they are under attack or making front-page news. It is in this context that the change in officers' attitudes towards retired generals who are politically vocal should be viewed. It is hard not to think that these declining levels of support are rooted at least partially in the over-the-top performances of retired general officers at the 2016 presidential-nominating conventions and the relatively recent but increasing trend of endorsements by retired flag officers.

Another gauge of active-duty officers' comfort with retired flag officers—in this case, retired four-stars, specifically—playing visible, partisan roles is displayed in table 40. The question of whether more retired four-stars should serve as political appointees is far more specific than the previous battery of questions on the question of the appropriateness of retired officers speaking about politics publicly. It also directly tests officers' attitudes regarding Trump's proclivity early in his administration to fill his cabinet with retired four-star generals, and in the case of the position of National Security Advisor, a retired three-star general followed by an active-duty three-star general.

Table 40. Support for More Retired Four-Stars Serving as Political Appointees.

	percent checking "agree" or "strongly agree" More retired four-star generals/admirals should be encouraged to serve as political appointees
TOTAL (n = 1,218)	43.4
West Point Cadets	45.8
NDU/AWC Students	41.2
Democrats	34.9***
Republicans	50.2***

Source. NDU CMR Survey (2018–2020).
Note. Data reflects responses West Point cadets and officers of all branches of service attending the National Defense University and Army War College in the grades of O-4, O-5, and O-6. Differences between Democrats and Republicans are statistically significant at ***p < .001.

As table 40 indicates, a strong minority of respondents (43 percent) agreed that more retired four-stars should be encouraged to serve as political appointees. Only 17 percent of respondents disagreed, while 39 percent were neutral, indicating some ambivalence among respondents. What is most noteworthy, however, is the breakdown of responses by partisanship. Republicans (50 percent) were far more likely than Democrats (35 percent) to advocate for more retired four-stars serving as political appointees. It is probable that Republican respondents were either defending the Trump administration or Trump's generals themselves.

Noteworthy is the respondents' support for retired four-stars serving as political appointees standing in sharp contrast to the views of most civil-military relations scholars, who have widely commented on the further politicization of the military that results from such appointments.[36] The strong level of support among active-duty military officers for retired flag officers serving in exclusively political (and partisan) roles during the Trump administration is likely rooted in at least three issues: first, an overarching belief by some that success in senior leadership positions within the military somehow translates to success in other unrelated lines of work, including partisan politics, after retirement; second, a factor unique to the Trump presidency, where some preferred for him to be surrounded by a bunch of serious former generals in the hopes they would mediate his worst tendencies—the "adults in the room" thesis; or third, the overwhelming popularity of Secretary Jim Mattis within the uniformed military.

At the core, all three issues are rooted in the extraordinarily high trust and confidence levels which the American public has in the uniformed military—especially at a time when public confidence in other institutions is declining. The US military has either topped every Gallup poll or tied for the top on confidence in institutions going back to 1986, while other measured categories, such as Congress, big business, and television news continue to report declining levels of trust.[37] As Americans' trust in institutions other than military has declined, elected leaders who hope to capitalize on those high trust and confidence levels have increasingly turned to the military for help on matters that have little to do with the military.[38] For example, until he withdrew his name from consideration, Dunford, was the leading candidate to serve as the chair of the Congressional Oversight Commission charged with supervising relief spending for the coronavirus pandemic.[39]

While a retired four-star could certainly excel in a political-appointee position such as White House Chief of Staff, there is nothing to suggest retired generals by virtue of their military experience would do so or would be better than other civilian candidates, and there are plenty of reasons to be circumspect about placing retired four-stars in top civilian political positions. Few have extensive political experience, let alone savvy with the legislative process, which can occupy a significant portion of a cabinet secretary's portfolio. And for those occupying national security positions, some have argued that an individual with an exclusively military background could be predisposed to view all security and foreign policy challenges through the lens of the military instrument, thereby creating blind spots.[40] Regardless, the majority of respondents in the NDU CMR Survey appeared willing to overlook these concerns or were inclined to believe that success as a four-star general meant they would excel in other demanding civilian, political positions.

Some of respondents' choice on the question of four-stars serving as appointees could also be a function of subscribing to the "adults in the room" thesis, which surfaced early in the Trump administration as justification for supporting his picks to top positions.[41] People such as Mattis, retired General John Kelly, retired Lieutenant General H.R. McMaster, and former Secretary of State Rex Tillerson—one of the few nonmilitary "adults" in the circle—would bring discipline to national security discussions in the Oval Office, or so the notion went. Whether they truly served as "adults in the room" was moot by the end of 2018 when Mattis resigned as secretary of defense—the last of the ostensible adults to leave the administration. Nonetheless, it remains a plausible explanation for at least some of respondents' support for more retired four-stars serving as political appointees during the time of the NDU CMR Survey.

A third possible explanation for the high level of support among active-duty military officers for seeing more retired four-stars in political positions could be in response to one four-star in particular: Trump's choice of Mattis for secretary of defense. Mattis had long been a favorite among the rank and file, especially for some of his quotes while on active duty, such as "Be polite, be professional, but have a plan to kill everybody you meet."[42] Shortly after Trump announced Mattis as his choice for secretary of defense, Marine Special Operations Command (MARSOC) posted—and then removed—a meme that portrayed the former Marine four-star as "Saint Mattis of Quantico, Patron Saint of Chaos."[43] According to a 2017 *Military Times* poll, 84 percent of active-duty troops had a favorable view of Mattis.[44] While officers surveyed in the NDU CMR

Survey were not queried explicitly on their views on it, they likely had little reservations over the fact Mattis required a waiver from Congress that stipulates that former members of the military must have been out of the military for seven years in order to serve as secretary of defense.[45]

Support from active-duty military members for Mattis as secretary of defense as well as for veterans in general to hold this position has been documented in recent research. A survey of nearly 1,500 cadets at the US Military Academy in late 2019 and early 2020 found that 57 percent of cadet respondents believed that in order to be respected, the secretary of defense should have served in uniform.[46] This particular finding—more than the desire among active-duty officers to see more retired flag officers in political positions—is especially concerning as it presumes optimal form of civilian control of the military only comes from one who has served in uniform. By implication, one could assume that the 57 percent of West Point cadets referenced earlier would not respect a secretary of defense who had not served in uniform—or at least, would respect such an individual less than someone who had served.

Just as the Constitution does not require the president to have served in uniform to carry out the duties of commander in chief, nowhere is it specified that the secretary of defense must have served in the armed forces. In fact, the exact opposite, as already discussed regarding the waiver Mattis required, was prescribed in the National Security Act of 1947; 10 U.S. Code § 113 explicitly states that the secretary of defense is "appointed from *civilian* life by the president." Regardless of what is written into law, a majority of West Point cadets embarking on their careers as army officers believe military experience is required to serve as secretary of defense.[47]

Lastly, President Joe Biden's appointment of retired General Lloyd Austin to be his secretary of defense demonstrates that both political parties aim to capitalize on the prestige and popularity of the uniformed military and are willing to sidestep norms in order to do so. As with the discarded norm that retired flag officers should abstain from partisan endorsements, the norm that recently retired flag officers should not serve as secretary of defense—which held for nearly 70 years—must now be looked upon as a defunct norm that no longer holds sway with elected leaders, the public, or members of the military, both active and retired.

Conclusion

There is no other issue that muddies the nonpartisan ethic more than the issue of retired flag officers' involvement in partisan politics. While the vast majority of those in the military profession acknowledge the need for those on active duty to remain nonpartisan, there is simply no consensus on the issue of the norm extending to those in retirement. If anything, as the findings from the CMR Time of War Survey and NDU CMR Survey show, most active-duty officers are supportive of retired officers—flag officers included—speaking out politically. However, the reduction in support over the past decade for retired generals talking about politics— which could be a response to the rise of partisan endorsements or the now-infamous 2016 convention speeches by Flynn and Allen—suggests that not everyone is on board and that a portion of the officer corps is open to influence.

The healthy level of support by active-duty officers for more retired four-stars serving in political positions—which breaks on party lines— further demonstrates how adherence to the norm of nonpartisanship can quickly be set aside in favor of partisan loyalties. It remains to be seen how much of this effect is attributed to specific factors associated with the Trump presidency. The fact that over 40 percent of active-duty officers surveyed think *more* retired four-stars should embrace purely partisan roles demonstrates a significant portion of the officer corps is unswayed by the argument that such moves could damage the military's credibility as a nonpartisan institution in the eyes of the American public.

Absent some form of intervention, partisan campaign endorsements, impassioned op-eds, and retired four-stars serving as political appointees may already be establishing a new set of norms for retired flag officers in the minds of those in and out of uniform as well as the broader public. Senior military leaders who are troubled by these trends would be well advised to focus their efforts on the narrow issue of curbing partisan endorsements because of the particular damage they do to the institution's reputation as a nonpartisan actor. Moreover, today's cohort of retired flag officers may not be persuaded, but a concerted campaign condemning the impact of partisan endorsements aimed at those serving in uniform today—the next generation of flag officers—may pay dividends on down the road. To be sure, when senior military leaders say nothing after each presidential candidate releases a list of retired flag-officer endorsements, it amounts to tacit approval or indifference at the very least. Either way, this is not how norms take root—or perhaps more accurately in this case —it is the textbook way that norms die.

NOTES

1. MacQuarrie, "Last Year, He Was the Country's Top Military Officer."
2. Priest and Miller, "He Was One of the Most Respected Intel Officers of His Generation."
3. Kohn, "General Elections: The Brass Shouldn't Do Endorsements."
4. Swain, "Reflection on an Ethic of Officership."
5. Houghton, "The Law of Retired Military Officers and Political Endorsements."
6. Dunlap, "Should Retired Servicemembers Be Subject to Military Jurisdiction?."
7. Ibid.
8. Houghton, "The Law of Retired Military Officers and Political Endorsements;" and Corbett and Davidson, "The Role of the Military in Presidential Politics." Corbett and Davidson note one reported court-martial for a retired officer using contemptuous speech—a retired Army musician who did so against President Woodrow Wilson in 1918.
9. Feaver, "We Don't Need Generals to Become Cheerleaders at Political Conventions."
10. Urben, "Generals Shouldn't Be Welcome at These Parties." Golby and Feaver, "Former Military Leaders Criticized the Election and the Administration. That Hurts the Military's Reputation."
11. Griffiths and Simon found only one academic or professional journal article—by Richard D. Hooker, Jr.—that was ambivalent about the normative implications of retired flag officer endorsements. Griffiths and Simon, "Not Putting Their Money Where Their Mouth Is"; Hooker, "Reconsidering American Civil-Military Relations," 9. Other examples of commentary advocating for retired officers speaking out politically include Bucella, "No, Retired Military Officers Don't Check Their Free Speech at the Door"; Kilmeade, "General Michael Flynn Sounds Off on Generals Allen and Dempsey, Khizr Khan"; Gelpi, "Retired Generals are People Too!"; and O'Hanlon, "Civil-Military Relations and the 2016 Presidential Race.".
12. Hicks et al., "Civil-Military Relations, Part 1: The 2020 Legacy." According to the Department of Defense's Fiscal Year 2019 Statistical Report on the Military Retirement System, there were 7,514 living retired flag officers as of 30 September 2019. Department of Defense, *Statistical*

Report on the Military Retirement System, Washington, DC: Department of
Defense, Office of the Actuary, May 2020, https://media.defense.gov/2020
/Aug/12/2002475697/-1/-1/0/MRS_STATRPT_2019_FINAL.PDF. Zachary
Griffiths and Olivia Simon estimate that 1,041 retired flag officers made
endorsements between 2004 and 2016. As of 2016, there were 7,442 living
retired flag officers; see Griffiths and Simon, "Not Putting Their Money
Where Their Mouth Is."

13. Mullen, "National Defense University Commencement;" and Martin
Dempsey, "Civil-Military Relations and the Profession of Arms."
14. Garamone, "Active Duty Personnel Must Remain Apolitical."
15. MacQuarrie, "Last Year, He Was the Country's Top Military Officer."
16. Feaver, "We Don't Need Generals to Become Cheerleaders at Political
Conventions."
17. Corbett and Davidson, "The Role of the Military in Presidential Politics,"
59.
18. Ibid., 59–61; and Canter, "Generals Are People Too."
19. Feaver, "We Don't Need Generals to Become Cheerleaders"; Martin
Dempsey, "Keep Your Politics Private."
20. Moreland, Baker, and Steed, *The 1988 Presidential Election in the South,*
206; and Kohn, "Military Endorsements Harm National Interest."
21. Kohn, "General Elections;" Kohn, "The Erosion of Civilian Control of
the Military," 28; Kaplan, "Officer Politics"; Golby et al., "Brass Politics";
Barno and Bensahel, "How to Get Generals Out of Politics"; Griffiths,
"Let's Use Peer Pressure to End Political Endorsements by Retired Generals"; and Urben, "Generals Shouldn't Be Welcome at These Parties."
22. Dinan, "Retired Top Military Brass Push for Romney."
23. Feaver, "We Don't Need Generals to Become Cheerleaders"; Martin
Dempsey, "Military Leaders Do Not Belong at Political Conventions";
and Priest and Miller, "He Was One of the Most Respected Intel Officers
of His Generation."
24. Griffiths and Simon, "Not Putting Their Money Where Their Mouth Is."
25. Golby, Dropp, and Feaver, *Military Campaigns.*
26. Hutzler, "Over 200 Retired Senior Military Leaders Endorse Donald
Trump"; DeYoung, "Nearly 500 Former Senior Military, Civilian Leaders
Signal Support for Biden"; and Berube, "Presidential Military Service."
27. Cloud, Schmitt, and Shanker, "Rumsfeld Faces Growing Revolt by
Retired Generals;" and Margolik, "The Night of the Generals."
28. Cook, "Revolt of the Generals," 7; Binkley, "Revisiting the 2006 Revolt of
the Generals"; Feaver, "The Right to Be Right," 118; Owens, "Rumsfeld,

the Generals, and the State of U.S. Civil-Military Relations"; and Robinson, "Danger Close" (dissertation), 60–63.

29. Kablack et al., "The Military Speaks Out."
30. Ibid.
31. McRaven, "Our Republic Is Under Attack from the President."
32. Ibid.; Ryan and Lamothe, "Trump Administration to Significantly Expand Military Response."
33. Robinson, "Danger Close" (article).
34. Golby, Dropp, and Feaver, *Military Campaigns.*
35. Robinson, "Danger Close" (article).
36. Barno and Bensahel, "Why No General Should Serve as White House Chief of Staff"; Simpson, "I Love Mattis, But I Don't Love Him as SECDEF"; Carter and Schulman, "Trump is Surrounding Himself with Generals"; Schulman and Schafer, "Too Many Generals in the Situation Room?"
37. Brenan, "Amid Pandemic, Confidence in Key U.S. Institutions Surges."
38. See generally Rosa Brooks, *How Everything Became War and the Military Became Everything.*
39. While Dunford was universally respected during his 42-year career in the Marine Corps, he had limited, if any, experience in fiscal policy and oversight. Both Speaker of the House Nancy Pelosi and Senate Majority Leader Mitch McConnell's reported preference for Dunford was likely rooted in the public and other elected leaders' trust in the military, the perception that the military is nonpartisan, and the lack of candidates who were widely perceived to be unbiased and had bipartisan support or were willing to serve. Werner, "Dunford Signals He Won't Chair Coronavirus Panel."
40. Schulman and Schafer, "Too Many Generals in the Situation Room?"
41. Kitfield, "Trump's Generals Are Trying to Save the World"; and Mann, "The Adults in the Room."
42. Conway, "9 Unforgettable Quotes by James Mattis."
43. Schogol, "MARSOC Facebook Page Takes Down Meme of 'Saint Mattis,'"; and Friend, "Mattis is Outstanding, So What's the Problem?."
44. Shane, "Military Times Poll."
45. Chesney, "Trump Will Need a New Law to Put Mattis Back in the Pentagon."
46. Robinson, Brooks, and Urben, "How Biden's Pick for Defense Secretary Might Shake Up Civil-Military Relations."
47. Friend, "A Military Litmus Test?."

CHAPTER 6

PARTY IDENTIFICATION, POLITICAL ATTITUDES, AND NORMS OF CIVIL- MILITARY RELATIONS —DO THEY MATTER?

> In fact, one senior officer on the Joint Staff…said that what he had learned under [former Secretary of Defense Donald] Rumsfeld was that it's best to distrust Republicans as much as they had historically distrusted Democrats.
>
> —Thom Shanker[1]

Thus far, this book has examined the partisan identification and political ideology of army officers over time, the nature of political behavior and level of political activism within the officer corps, how active-duty military members engage in political expression on social media, and the role retired officers play in politics. The three preceding chapters found that officers' partisan affiliation shapes their political discourse in the workplace, their behavior and perception of others' political behavior online, and the degree to which they are comfortable with retired flag officers occupying political roles. While those are all important factors—and while this book's findings do point to some concerning trends—they do not necessarily provide evidence of threats to civilian control.

This chapter examines US Army officers' opinions of interactions between senior military leaders and civilian policy-makers in order to uncover how officers' partisanship and political views shape their views of these civil-military interactions. From decisions on the use of force to the role of senior military leaders during wartime, this chapter reports on the attitudes of army officers towards their civilian superiors. It also examines to what degree military elite opinions on these issues has changed over the past twenty years, comparing survey data from Feaver and Kohn's TISS project with data from the CMR Time of War Survey from 2009 and the NDU CMR Survey from 2018 to 2020. In short, this chapter seeks to answer the question, Does any of this really matter? Do the officer corps' partisan political leanings impact their views of critical civil-military norms and ultimately their views of civilian control of the military?

Officers' Understanding of and Adherence to Civil-Military Norms

Samuel Huntington's *The Soldier and the State*, written in 1957, remains the dominant theory of civil-military relations for officers serving in the U.S. military, even more than 60 years after it was written.[2] Retired Major General William Rapp, former Commandant of the U.S. Army War College has reflected, "Soldiers have been raised on Huntingtonian logic and the separation of spheres of influence since their time as lieutenants."[3] Many officers accept Huntingtonian logic, even if they have never read the book, with Eliot Cohen observing that Huntington "is more cited than read, and many of its subtleties have been lost on those who have admired it most."[4] It is understandable why generations of officers have been attracted to Huntington's model of objective control, which Cohen terms the "normal" theory because it is so widely accepted within military circles.[5] The "normal" theory, or objective control, stresses separate spheres between the military and its overseers. In return for remaining apolitical, civilian leaders grant the military professional autonomy; and with such autonomy, military professionals are able to develop their expertise in matters of tactics and operations.[6] Michael Desch takes this a step further, arguing that "the best system is one that allows for substantial military autonomy in the military, technical, and tactical realms (how to fight wars) in return for complete subordination to civilian authority in the political realm (when and if to fight them)."[7]

Peter Feaver contends that most academics and practitioners accept the basic aspects of Huntington's objective control: civilians should guard the guardians, and the military should cultivate professional expertise relating to the management of violence. But he posits that two camps—professional supremacists and civilian supremacists—vary considerably on "who should be giving more and taking less" in this give-and-take relationship.[8] Professional supremacists speak "candidly and forcefully to their civilian superiors," while civilian supremacists empower "civilian leaders to involve themselves more forcefully and directly in the business of war making."[9] Feaver also introduces an extreme variant of professional supremacists—"McMasterism," drawing inspiration for the name from those who misread H.R. McMaster's classic, *Dereliction of Duty*.[10] Professional supremacists who adhere to McMasterism not only think civilians should largely defer to military advice during wartime, but they also favor taking "dramatic action to ensure that the military voice is heard and heeded."[11] This chapter examines not only whether army officers subscribe to the notions of civilian supremacy, professional supremacy, or even McMasterism but also how their embrace of these particular civil-military relations models may vary based on party affiliation.

THE ROLE OF PARTY IN SHAPING ATTITUDES

A substantial body of work has documented how partisanship shapes identity and how partisans consume information and make judgments about unfolding political events.[12] Campbell et al. likened party affiliation to a "perceptual screen" that makes it difficult for people with strong partisan loyalties and well-developed political attitudes to process information that does not adhere to their preexisting partisan loyalties.[13] The concept of partisan rationalization or motivated reasoning further explains how individuals adjust their opinions on certain issues to fit with and maintain their preexisting partisan attachments or "unconscious affective biases."[14] Benjamin Lauderdale describes this phenomenon as "rationalizing backwards from their partisan preferences to beliefs about political facts and processes that would justify those preferences."[15] Pertinent to this chapter's focus on senior military officers' attitudes, Milton Lodge and Charles S. Taber conclude in *The Rationalizing Voter* that "people find it very difficult to escape the pull of their prior attitudes and beliefs, which guide the processing of new information in predictable and sometimes insidious ways."[16]

Several civil-military relations scholars have found the American public's attitudes towards the military and on decisions surrounding the use of force are heavily shaped by their partisan attachments. Through survey experiments, Jim Golby, Kyle Dropp, and Peter Feaver found that Republicans were more apt to be swayed by public statements made by senior military officials regarding potential interventions abroad than Democrats and Independents.[17] Michael Robinson's survey experiments found that the public regarded politically outspoken retired flag officers to be less credible if those officers were from the opposing political party.[18] Robinson also found that when presented with negative or derogatory information about behavior by members of the military, Republicans were far less likely than Democrats and Independents to reduce their approval ratings of the military.[19]

In their 2019 survey of nearly 2,000 Americans, Ronald R. Krebs, Robert Ralston, and Aaron Rapport found the degree to which the public was comfortable deferring major decisions on the use of force to senior military officers over the president was conditioned on their partisanship and approval ratings of the president. Those who disapproved of Trump were 60 to 80 percent more likely to favor deferring such decisions to the military.[20] They also found that Republicans became less deferential to the military during the Trump presidency, in contrast to their attitudes during the Obama administration, when a greater percentage of Republican respondents supported the idea of the president following the advice of the generals during wartime.[21]

Despite its socialization to professional norms and general embrace of the nonpartisan ethic, the officer corps tends to exhibit similarities to the broader American public from time to time, as highlighted in the previous four chapters and in past research.[22] Moreover, as recent survey research of West Point cadets has noted, partisanship is often a deeply ingrained sense of identity that can outweigh fidelity to professional norms.[23] Survey research in this chapter aims to determine if officers' views of civil-military norms and their civilian superiors are also shaped by their partisan affiliation.

ARMY OFFICERS' VIEWS OF CIVILIAN LEADERS

Table 41 displays the findings for midgrade to senior US Army officers' views of civilian leaders in the context of civilian oversight of the military. The first question, which asked respondents whether they agreed that when civilians tell the military what to do, domestic politics, rather than national security requirements, are often the primary motivation; this also doubles as a measure of army officers' trust in government. Responses from midgrade army officers were fairly consistent across the TISS, CMR Time of War, and NDU CMR surveys.

166 PARTY, POLITICS, AND THE POST-9/11 ARMY

Table 41. US Army Officers' Views of Civilian Leaders Over Time.

	Views of Civilian Leaders percent checking "agree" or "strongly agree"		
	When civilians tell the military what to do, domestic partisan politics, rather than national security requirements are often the primary motivation	In wartime, civilian government leaders should let the military take over running the war	To be respected as Commander-in-Chief, the president should have served in uniform
TISS Survey, 1998-1999 (n=211)	55.7	56.5	43.5
Democrats	45.5	63.6	63.6*
Republicans	55.3	56.7	41.8*
CMR Time of War Survey, 2009 (n=2,220)	55.0	33.1	31.1
Democrats	51.9*	27.8**	14.4***
Republicans	57.7*	36.1**	38.2***
NDU CMR Survey, 2018-2020 (n=288)	49.0	16.7	11.5
Democrats	62.2	13.5	21.6*
Republicans	47.7	15.9	10.6*

Source. TISS Survey (1998–1999), CMR Time of War Survey (2009) and NDU CMR Survey (2018–2020).
Note. Data reflects responses from army majors, lieutenant colonels, and colonels. Differences between Democrats and Republicans are statistically significant at * p < .10, ** p <.01, *** p <.001.

Roughly half of respondents agreed with the statement, indicating a fair degree of skepticism, if not cynicism, towards those exercising civilian control of the military—reminiscent of the quote from the unnamed flag-officer that led off this chapter.

Due to the small number of Democrats among midgrade to senior officers in the TISS and NDU CMR survey samples in table 41—there were 11 out of 211 and 37 out of 288, respectively—it is difficult to draw meaningful conclusions on the role party identification might have in shaping army officers' views of civilian leaders' motivations. However, the much larger sample size of midgrade to senior officers in the CMR Time of War Survey allows for more robust comparisons. In 2009, 52 percent of Democrats, compared to 58 percent of Republicans, agreed with the statement that civilian leaders' motivations are based more on domestic partisan politics than national security.[24] Similarly, in the TISS Survey a decade prior, 45 percent of Democrats agreed with the statement, compared to 55 percent of Republicans, although a difference of proportions test was not statistically significant—again, likely due to the small subsample of Democrats. The NDU CMR Survey tells a different story, however, with 62 percent of Democrats agreeing with the statement compared to just 48 percent of Republicans. This "flip-flop" in attitudes, where a greater proportion of Republicans exhibited skepticism towards their civilian overseers when surveyed during Democratic presidential administrations, but a smaller proportion of Republicans did so during a Republican presidential administration, may again provide some evidence of partisan rationalization or motivated reasoning. In other words, officers may be more likely to attribute domestic partisan politics as the primary motivator behind civilian leaders' national security decision-making when the president happens to be from the opposing party. Regardless of the effect partisanship might have, that half of midgrade to senior army officers consistently agreed with this statement points to a fair degree of skepticism towards civilian authority in the context of civilian control of the military.

Table 41 reports an encouraging finding regarding army officers' commitment to civil-military norms, likely an outgrowth of nearly two decades at war. The percentage of midgrade to senior army officers who responded that civilian leaders should essentially let the military take over running the war has declined dramatically since TISS respondents were first posed the question in the late 1990s. In the TISS Survey, 57 percent of midgrade to senior army officers agreed with this statement— an astonishing rebuke of civilian control of the military and disregard for the most basic civil-military norms. By 2009, only 33 percent of army officers agreed that in wartime, civilians should let the military take over running the war, and by 2018–2020, only 17 percent of army officers responded this way. In some ways, this may seem a counterintuitive finding. The post-9/11 wars have been anything but conclusive, and at times, some in the officer corps have shown support for the "stabbed-in-the-back" narrative—faulting civilian leaders for failures in Iraq, Afghanistan, or Syria but failing to take accountability themselves.[25] In other words, the effects of the difficult, protracted, and often unpopular wars have not caused officers serving today to believe that the military should be in charge of all aspects of running wars but rather the opposite.

This finding is especially noteworthy given other recent survey research. During, Krebs, Ralston, and Rapport's 2019 survey of 2,000 Americans, 40 percent agreed that if senior military leaders favor a proposed military mission, the president should approve it, even if he does not think the mission is worthwhile.[26] Even more startling, in the 2013 YouGov survey featured in Kori Schake and Secretary Jim Mattis's book, *Warriors and Citizens*, 76 percent of respondents overall and 83 percent of veteran respondents agreed that during wartime, the president should basically follow the advice of the generals.[27] In other words, while midgrade to senior army officers surveyed in the NDU CMR Survey (2018–2020) largely provided the "normatively correct" response to the question of whether civilian leaders should let the military run the war, large percentages of the American public did not.[28] While it is encouraging that attitudes have shifted among midgrade to senior army officers over the past 20 years, the fact that the American public is largely unpersuaded by (or uninformed of) long-established civil-military norms is concerning.

This shift in attitudes among midgrade to senior officers could be a function of these particular respondents' experiences fighting in the post-9/11 wars. It is probable that the TISS respondents included some veterans from the Persian Gulf War or Panama invasion, and 78 percent of midgrade to senior officers surveyed in the CMR Time of War Survey had deployed to Iraq or Afghanistan. In contrast, 98 percent of army majors, lieutenant colonels, and colonels surveyed in the NDU CMR Survey reported they had deployed to combat. In addition to the variable of combat deployment experience, rank or time in service also has an impact. While not pictured in table 41, the more senior the respondent, the more likely they were to provide the normatively appropriate response to this question. For example, 34 percent of West Point cadets surveyed in the NDU CMR Survey agreed that civilians should let the military take over running the war during wartime, as did 46 percent of lieutenants surveyed in the CMR Time of War Survey—much higher percentages than what midgrade to senior officers reported in both surveys. Additionally, during a survey of nearly 1,500 cadets at the U.S. Military Academy conducted in December 2019 and January 2020, 36 percent of respondents agreed with the statement that when at war, leaders should follow the advice of the generals—a close proxy for the question shown in table 41.[29] In some ways, even this, too, is encouraging. The longer officers stay in the army and are exposed to the professional ethic, the more likely they are to demonstrate adherence to critical civil-military norms.

As mentioned earlier, Krebs, Ralston, and Rapport found that the public's deference towards the military is conditioned on respondents' party affiliation and the party affiliation of the president at the time. Democrats and respondents who disapproved of Trump were more apt to favor deferring to senior military officials than Republicans and those who approved of Trump.[30] The findings in table 41 about letting the military take over running the war are not inconsistent with Krebs, Ralston, and Rapport's findings, although they do not present as clear cut of a case of partisan rationalization as Krebs, Ralston, and Rapport do. Republican officers surveyed in the TISS and CMR Time of War surveys during the Clinton and Obama administrations were more apt to advocate deference to the military than they were in the NDU CMR Survey during the Trump administration, but Democrats and Republicans' responses were fairly similar in all three surveys. Again, the small number of Democrats in the TISS and NDU CMR Survey could be skewing results, and there may be a stronger case of partisan rationalization than the data suggests. Should a similar cohort be surveyed in the Biden administration and a larger percentage of Republicans return to preferring deference towards military leaders in wartime again, this may provide stronger evidence of partisan rationalization and explain the shift in officer attitudes on this question over time.

Lastly, table 41 also displays the results from a question that further probes attitudes on norms surrounding civilian control by asking if in order to be respected as the commander in chief, the president should have served in uniform. As with the previous question about letting the military take over running the war, the percentage of midgrade to senior officers who agreed with this notion has steadily declined since the late 1990s. In the TISS Survey, 44 percent of army officers agreed that the commander in chief should have served in uniform, compared to 31 percent in 2009 and just 12 percent from 2018 to 2020. On the surface, this appears to be another good news story on adherence to civil-military norms. Upon closer examination, however, this looks to be a more significant case of partisan rationalization.

When surveyed during the Clinton and Obama administrations, 42 percent and 38 percent, respectively, of army majors, lieutenant colonels, and colonels who self-identified as Republican agreed with the notion that, in order to be respected as commander in chief, the president should have served in uniform. Yet just 12 percent of Republican army officers agreed when surveyed during the Trump administration, suggesting again that Republicans might adjust their views on important norms of civil-military relations to fit their preexisting partisan leanings. Army officers who identified as Democrats do not appear to exhibit the same degree of partisan rationalization, although the percentage in agreement that the president should have served in the military increased from 14 percent in the Obama administration to 22 percent during the Trump administration. This swing in attitudes is not trivial. It is also worth recalling that the question asked respondents if their *respect* for the commander in chief hinged on whether the president had served in uniform. In other words, at least for a significant portion of Republican officers, and perhaps for some Democrats, their views on whether the president should have served in uniform is conditioned on whether the president is their co-partisan.

ARMY OFFICERS' VIEWS OF SENIOR MILITARY LEADERS' ROLES IN WARTIME

The previous section provides insights into how US Army officers view their civilian overseers. This section highlights how officers think senior military leaders should execute their duties during wartime, providing insights on which norms in civil-military-relations that army officers buy into: civilian supremacy, professional supremacy, or McMasterism. The CMR Time of War Survey and NDU CMR Survey replicated a battery of questions first posed in the TISS study, asking respondents whether they thought the proper role of senior military leaders was to be neutral, to advise, to advocate, or to insist on their way in various wartime decisions. The seven different decisions posed were deciding whether to intervene, setting rules of engagement, ensuring that clear political and military goals exist, deciding what goals or policy should be, generating public support for the intervention, developing an exit strategy, and deciding what military units will be used (tables 42a–b).

Civilian supremacists would argue that the only appropriate response to any of these seven wartime decisions is to be neutral or to advise, whereas those who Feaver says subscribe to "McMasterism" would likely feel the appropriate response for senior military leaders is to insist on their way in any scenario. But any suggestions that Huntingtonian purists (if such people exist) would also feel it proper for senior military leaders to insist on having their way should read Huntington more closely:

> Loyalty and obedience are the highest military virtues....When the military man receives a legal order from an authorized superior, he does not argue, he does not hesitate, he does not substitute his own views; he obeys instantly. He is judged not by the policies he implements, but rather by the promptness and efficiency with which he carries them out.[31]

Even if senior military leaders have grounds to question the validity of their civilian superiors' decisions, they still must salute and execute— a view best captured by Feaver's oft-quoted phrase that "civilians have the right to be wrong."[32] Huntington's assessment here stands in sharp contrast to those who would find it acceptable for senior military officials to be insistent with civilian leaders:

> The superior political wisdom of the statesman must be accepted as a fact. If the statesman decides upon war which the soldier knows can lead to national catastrophe, then the soldier, after presenting his opinion, must fall to and make the best of a bad situation.[33]

Given this, it is hard to envision Huntington ever finding it acceptable for senior military officers to insist on having their way in discussions with their civilian superiors over the use of force. Professional supremacists are not pure Huntingtonians, as Feaver notes, so they may find it more acceptable for senior military leaders to advocate or insist on their way in certain wartime decisions but not as consistently as those who subscribe to McMasterism.

Table 42a. US Army Officers' Views of the Proper Role of Senior Military Leaders.

This question asks you to specify the proper role of senior military leaders in decisions to commit U.S. armed forces abroad. Please specify the proper role of the military for each element.

percent checking each option

	Be Neutral			Advise			Advocate			Insist		
	1998-1999	2009	2018-2020	1998-1999	2009	2018-2020	1998-1999	2009	2018-2020	1998-1999	2009	2018-2020
Deciding whether to intervene	2.9	5.4	4.3	87.0	76.8	86.3	6.3	11.5	6.1	3.9	5.2	1.8
Democrats	20.0	7.4	8.6	70.0	76.5	77.1	0.0	10.6	11.4	10.0	4.8	2.9
Republicans	2.1	4.7	1.8	86.5	77.2	88.4	7.1	11.8	6.7	4.3	5.5	2.4
Setting rules of engagement	0.0	0.8	0.7	19.1	24.6	43.3	33.5	33.0	37.6	47.4	40.9	17.3
Democrats	0.0	1.0	2.9	18.2	31.9	31.4	45.5	33.2	42.9	36.4	32.9	22.9
Republicans	0.0	0.5	0.6	20.6	22.4	47.0	36.9	33.7	37.8	42.6	42.9	14.6
Ensuring clear political and military goals exist	0.0	0.9	0.4	12.4	18.7	22.4	23.0	22.6	26.0	64.6	56.9	50.5
Democrats	9.1	1.0	0.0	0.0	23.2	17.1	27.3	21.6	22.9	63.6	53.6	60.0
Republicans	0.0	0.9	0.6	14.2	17.4	22.6	22.0	23.8	28.0	63.8	57.3	48.8

Source. TISS Survey, 1998–1999 (n=208), CMR Time of War Survey, 2009 (n=2,219) and NDU CMR Survey, 2018–2020, (n=277).
Note. Data reflects responses from army majors, lieutenant colonels, and colonels. Responses of "no opinion" are not included in this table.

Table 42b. US Army Officers' Views of the Proper Role of Senior Military Leaders (*Cont'd*).

	Be Neutral			Advise			Advocate			Insist		
	1998-1999	2009	2018-2020	1998-1999	2009	2018-2020	1998	2009	2018-2020	1998-1999	2009	2018-2020
Deciding what goals or policy should be	6.7	8.2	10.5	70.3	58.8	70.8	19.1	22.8	12.3	3.8	9.0	4.7
Democrats	18.2	10.3	8.6	45.5	58.1	65.7	27.3	19.7	11.4	9.1	10.0	14.3
Republicans	7.8	7.8	11.6	70.9	59.1	72.0	17.7	23.6	12.2	3.6	8.6	3.7
Generating public support for intervention	49.8	60.5	67.5	20.8	22.0	18.1	20.8	10.6	6.5	6.8	3.9	1.4
Democrats	63.6	60.1	62.9	9.1	19.91	14.3	9.1	11.3	14.3	18.2	5.1	2.9
Republicans	48.9	60.7	70.1	21.6	22.4	18.9	23.0	10.6	6.1	5.0	3.8	0.6
Developing an exit strategy	0.5	1.0	0.4	19.6	25.7	38.6	26.8	26.4	30.3	53.1	45.9	30.0
Democrats	9.1	1.6	0.0	18.2	27.5	34.3	27.3	25.9	31.4	45.5	44.3	34.3
Republicans	0.0	1.1	0.6	19.2	24.8	35.4	23.4	27.3	34.2	57.5	46.1	29.9
Deciding what military units will be used	0.0	0.9	0.0	13.4	19.7	28.9	23.4	21.1	29.6	63.2	57.6	40.1
Democrats	0.0	1.6	0.0	27.3	25.8	28.6	18.9	18.7	22.9	54.6	53.6	42.9
Republicans	0.0	0.8	0.0	12.8	17.3	31.1	24.1	21.4	29.3	63.1	60.0	39.6

The responses from army majors, lieutenant colonels, and colonels for each of the seven wartime decisions across the three referenced surveys are shown in tables 42a–b. When first surveyed in the TISS study in the late 1990s, a majority of midgrade to senior army officers responded that the proper role of senior military leaders was to insist on their way in four of the seven wartime decisions: setting rules of engagement, ensuring clear political and military goals exist, developing an exit strategy, and deciding what military units will be used. Most officers indicated the proper role of senior military leaders was to advise on deciding whether to intervene and deciding what the political and military goals should be —recognizing that those are decisions for democratically elected leaders and their politically appointed civilian representatives to make. Moreover, when it came to generating public support for an intervention—a political task clearly outside the realm of military officers to perform—most officers rightly responded that the proper role was to be neutral. Still, that army officers felt it was proper for senior military officials to insist on their way in a majority of the wartime decisions is telling.

By 2009, when a comparable sample of army officers was surveyed in the CMR Time of War Survey, the same general pattern held true, although smaller majorities of officers chose senior military officers insisting on their way than in the TISS Survey. Smaller majorities also supported an advisory role for deciding whether to intervene and deciding what the political and military goals should be, although a larger percentage of respondents indicated senior officers should be neutral where generating public support for an intervention was concerned. In general, though, responses to this battery of questions remained fairly constant among respondents in the TISS Survey and CMR Time of War Survey a decade later.

Responses in the NDU CMR Survey (2018–2020) varied considerably from the previous two surveys, however. This time, army officers surveyed indicated that the proper role for senior military leaders in four of the seven wartime decisions was to advise, and the only category in which they thought it appropriate for senior officers to insist on having their way was ensuring that clear goals exist. The change in attitudes is stark. During the TISS Survey, 47 percent of army majors, lieutenant colonels, and colonels felt that senior military officers should insist on setting rules of engagement, compared to 41 percent in the CMR Time of War Survey and just 17 percent in the NDU CMR Survey. Similarly, 53 percent of army officers in the TISS sample thought senior officers should insist on their way when developing an exit strategy, compared to 46 percent in the CMR Time of War Survey and just 30 percent in the NDU CMR Survey. Even in the one category where a majority of respondents thought senior officers should insist on having their way—ensuring clear goals exist—there was a 14-percentage point drop from the TISS Survey to the NDU CMR Survey. Additionally, the one category where a majority of respondents consistently felt the proper role was to be neutral—generating public support for the intervention—the majorities only solidified over time: from 50 percent in the TISS Survey to 61 percent in the CMR Time of War Survey to 68 percent in the NDU CMR Survey.

There are several competing explanations behind the change in army officers' attitudes over time. The first possibility is that army officers' attitudes have been shaped by nearly two decades at war. What army officers serving in peacetime in the late 1990s may have deemed as appropriate roles for senior military leaders to play during wartime may have less support among a cohort of officers who fought in the post-9/11 wars. In other words, the officers' experience in fighting the protracted wars of the twenty-first century may have given them a better appreciation for the political roles civilian leaders play in wartime—responsibilities that fall outside the purview of those in uniform. This is evident in the declining percentage of army officers who felt it was proper to insist on ensuring clear goals exist and developing an exit strategy—two responsibilities that fall squarely in the laps of civilian leaders, not the military. In all, a larger percentage of army officers surveyed in the NDU CMR Survey selected "advise" in six of seven wartime decisions compared to officers surveyed in the CMR Time of War Survey. And in the seventh category—generating public support for the intervention—a larger percentage of respondents in the NDU CMR Survey selected "be neutral" than those surveyed in the previous two surveys. In short, respondents in the NDU CMR Survey were less likely to insist and more likely to advise than respondents surveyed ten and twenty years prior.

In this interpretation, respondents were more apt to exhibit professional supremacist or McMasterism tendencies during the TISS and CMR Time of War surveys but more prone to reflect civilian supremacist tenets in the NDU CMR Survey. It is certainly plausible that the experience of respondents waging the post-9/11 wars proved decisive in shaping attitudes. Officers surveyed in the NDU CMR Survey may have more of an appreciation for the complexities of civil-military interaction during wartime; they may believe that military expertise is best focused on matters pertaining to the military instrument of power and that civilian elected leaders are ultimately responsible for the major decisions surrounding the commitment of US forces abroad. However, the sample of army officers in the CMR Time of War Survey also included a significant number who had deployed to Iraq and Afghanistan, and yet their attitudes generally mirrored the attitudes of the TISS sample. So, experience fighting the post-9/11 wars may not fully explain the significant change in officers' attitudes over time.

A second possibility that may explain the change in attitudes is rooted in the partisan affiliation of respondents and who was president at the time each survey was conducted. Bill Clinton was president during the TISS Survey when respondents were most apt to indicate senior military leaders should insist on their way in various wartime-decision scenarios. Another Democrat, Barack Obama, was in office during the CMR Time of War Survey, and these responses generally mirrored those of the TISS Survey a decade prior. But in the NDU CMR Survey that found fewer officers inclined to suggest senior military leaders should be insistent on decisions regarding the use of force, Donald Trump—a Republican—was president then. Could it be that the major changes in attitudes had nothing to do with respondents' experience fighting the post-9/11 wars and everything to do with their partisanship instead?

First, it is worth recalling that the majority of US Army majors, lieutenant colonels, and colonels surveyed in each of these three surveys identified as Republicans: 65 percent in the TISS and CMR Time of War surveys and 59 percent in the NDU CMR Survey. When examining the breakdown of responses by party affiliation in tables 42a–b, it is clear that responses by Republican officers exhibited the most dramatic change across the three surveys. For example, the percentage of Democrats who thought senior military leaders should insist on decisions pertaining to rules of engagement declined by 13 percentage points between the TISS and NDU CMR surveys, but the percentage of Republicans indicating the same declined by 28 points. This pattern was repeated in the other three scenarios where a majority of respondents had indicated senior officers should insist: ensuring clear political and military goals exist, developing an exit strategy, and deciding what military units will be used. While the percentage of Democrats answering "insist" for each of those questions declined by four, 11, and 12 percentage points from the TISS Survey to the NDU CMR Survey, the percentage of Republicans answering "insist" declined by 15, 27, and 23 points, respectively.

Given this fairly dramatic shift in attitudes among Republicans, it is fair to question the degree to which this can be attributed to partisanship, considering a noteworthy variable that distinguishes the TISS and CMR Time of War surveys from the NDU CMR Survey is that a Democrat occupied the White House in the former and a Republican in the latter. In the former two surveys, Republican respondents thought it was appropriate for senior military leaders to insist on having their way on decisions surrounding the use of force—perhaps because a Democrat was the commander in chief at the time and they did not trust Democrats' decision-making on matters of national security. Only when a Republican was commander in chief did Republican respondents think it was more appropriate for senior military leaders to advise. If partisanship is the main driver behind Republicans' responses to this battery of civil-military integration questions, it demonstrates that adherence to professional norms and the principle of civilian control is fairly tenuous and shaped by one's partisanship. The fact that respondents in each of these surveys were majors, lieutenant colonels, and colonels is even more surprising. It might be more understandable if young lieutenants—those still undergoing socialization to professional norms—demonstrated conflicted loyalties and a weak adherence to norms. But that midgrade to senior officers, who have spent ten to twenty-plus years in uniform, show indications of partisan rationalization or motivated reasoning in how they assess civil-military integration on decisions surrounding the use of force is worrisome.

CONCLUSION

The survey data of US Army officers over the past twenty years featured in this chapter found a strong degree of skepticism, if not outright cynicism, directed against their civilian leaders. Notably, this is not a new phenomenon; nor is the intensified officers' distrust of their elected leaders because of fighting protracted wars with inconclusive results —roughly half of midgrade to senior army officers have felt this way consistently over the past two decades. What is new, however, is the degree to which army officers' civil-military attitudes seem to rationalize their partisan preferences—as opposed to the sentiment behind quote that led off this chapter, which insinuated that senior officers are skeptical of all civilian officials, regardless of party. Evidence uncovered here suggests Republicans may be more skeptical of civilian leaders when a Democrat is in the White House as opposed to when a Republican is president, and the converse may also hold true with Democrats. Signs of partisan rationalization can also be found in shifting sentiments among army officers about whether they think the president should have served in uniform to be respected as commander in chief. The dramatic shift in attitudes among Republican officers surveyed during two Democratic administrations compared to when queried during a Republican administration is noteworthy, considering none of the presidents in office during these three surveys served in the military. Certainly, there could be something about the makeup of each cohort of officers surveyed, but given the durability of attitudes in other areas, it is unlikely this is anything other than officers trying to adjust their views on civilian control to fit their partisan preferences.

It also appears that partisan rationalization is evident in how officers view civilian control and critical civil-military norms regarding decision-making over the use of force. Republican officers were more apt to "insist" when surveyed during two Democratic administrations and more apt to "advise" during a Republican administration. The evidence presented in this chapter finds that partisan rationalization is strongest among Republicans, but Republicans also constitute the majority of the officer corps and the majority of respondents in each of the surveys referenced here. Slight evidence of partisan rationalization can be seen among Democrats in these surveys, but they constitute such a small number of the TISS and NDU CMR surveys, it is difficult to say for certain.

Nonetheless, this is worth exploring further. Similar survey research of the officer corps in the Biden administration may uncover further evidence of partisan rationalization. Given the research presented here, it would be unsurprising to find Republicans more apt to say the president should have served in uniform to be respected and more likely to think the proper role of senior military officials in wartime is to insist on having their way. Meanwhile, it follows that Democrats would be less cynical towards civilian leaders and more inclined to indicate the proper role of senior military leaders is to advise rather than insist. But more survey research is required.

It should be noted that the findings in this chapter do not necessarily suggest that Republicans and Democrats engage in partisan rationalization in the same fashion or to the same extent. For example, a 2019–2020 survey of West Point cadets found that Republicans were four times more likely to believe that one party makes better decisions about national security (54 percent of Republicans compared to 14 percent of Democrats).[34] This suggests that partisan rationalization might be stronger and occur more frequently among Republicans than Democrats in the officer corps. Again, more large-scale survey research within the officer corps is merited.

While these surveys uncovered modest evidence of partisan rationalization, the findings here cannot sufficiently explain why exactly respondents rationalize their attitudes on civilian leaders and professional norms. Is it because army officers' partisan attachments are so strong—that their "perceptual screens" are so effective—they end up distorting their views of civilian control? That seems unlikely, given the findings in chapter 2 that point towards smaller percentages of strong partisans today compared to a decade ago. Or is it that officers' socialization to key professional norms is so weak, the conditions are ripe for their partisan attachments to win out when the two come into conflict? It may be a combination of both factors. Senior military leaders cannot affect the strength of partisan loyalties of their officers, but they can do a better job in ensuring a stronger, more consistent socialization process in the officer corps that rests on a firm understanding of and commitment to professional norms.

This chapter demonstrates that party affiliation does indeed matter on real matters of civil-military relations substance, including how officers conceive of civilian control. That a significant portion of the officer corps may be willing to filter their attitudes on such an important topic through their party identification should concern both civilian elected leaders and senior military officers alike. At the very least, it calls into question the durability of professional norms and the extent to which they are constantly taught and reinforced throughout officers' careers. Moreover, if army officers believe that leaders in the opposing political party cannot be trusted to make sound decisions on the use of force or merit their respect simply by virtue of their position, civilian control of the armed forces is far more tenuous than previously thought.

NOTES

1. Shanker, "The Wars on Three Fronts."
2. Huntington, *The Soldier and the State*.
3. Rapp, "Civil-Military Relations," 1. For an assessment of how Huntington has shaped civil-military relations scholarship and theory, see also Nielsen and Snider, *American Civil-Military*; Risa Brooks, "Paradoxes of Professionalism"; and Beehner, Brooks, and Maurer, *Reconsidering American Civil-Military Relations*.
4. Cohen, *Supreme Command*, 226.
5. Ibid.
6. Huntington, *The Soldier and the State*, 11–13, 62–64, 83–85.
7. Desch, "Bush and the Generals"; Myers et al., "Salute and Disobey?."
8. Feaver, "The Right to Be Right," 93.
9. Ibid., 94.
10. McMaster, *Dereliction of Duty*.
11. Ibid. See also Myers et al., "Salute and Disobey?."
12. Campbell et al., *The American Voter*; Bartels, "Beyond the Running Tally"; Abramowitz and Webster, "Negative Partisanship"; Abramowitz and Webster, "The Rise of Negative Partisanship"; and Iyengar, Sood, and Lelkes, "Affect, Not Ideology."
13. Campbell et al., *The American Voter*, 133.
14. Lodge and Taber, *The Rationalizing Voter*, 22; Taber and Lodge, "Motivated Skepticism in the Evaluation of Political Beliefs."
15. Lauderdale, "Partisan Disagreements Arising from Rationalization of Common Information," 478.
16. Lodge and Taber, *The Rationalizing Voter*, 169.
17. Golby, Feaver, and Dropp, "Elite Military Cues and Public Opinion About the Use of Military Force."
18. Robinson, "Danger Close" (dissertation), 178–252.
19. Ibid., 127–135.
20. Krebs, Ralston, and Rapport, "No Right to Be Wrong.".
21. Ibid.; Schake and Mattis, *Warriors and Citizens*.
22. Brooks, Robinson, and Urben, "What Makes a Military Professional? Evaluating Norm Socialization in West Point Cadets."
23. Ibid.; Robinson, Brooks, and Urben, "How Biden's Pick for Defense Secretary Might Shake Up Civil-Military Relations."

24. While not pictured in table 41, the partisan gap on this question for the full CMR Time of War Survey sample—lieutenants through colonels, not just majors, lieutenant colonels, and colonels, as depicted in Table 41 —was even larger: 53 percent of Democrats compared to 62 percent of Republicans.
25. Ricks, "Can the Military Learn From Its Mistakes?."; Hoffman, "Dereliction of Duty *Redux*?."
26. Krebs, Ralston, and Rapport, "No Right to Be Wrong."
27. Golby, Cohn, and Feaver, "Thanks For Your Service," 117.
28. Ibid.; Krebs, Ralston, and Rapport, "No Right to Be Wrong."
29. Brooks, Robinson, and Urben, "What Makes a Military Professional? Evaluating Norm Socialization in West Point Cadets."
30. Krebs, Ralston, and Rapport, "No Right to Be Wrong."
31. Huntington, *The Soldier and the State*, 73.
32. Feaver, *Armed Servants*.
33. Huntington, *The Soldier and the State*, 76–77.
34. Brooks, Robinson, and Urben, "What Makes a Military Professional? Evaluating Norm Socialization in West Point Cadets."

Chapter 7

Conclusion

The story of the military's culpability in its politicization is not one punctuated by dramatic, egregious lapses in professionalism, blatant partisanship, or outright rejection of civilian control; rather, it is one marked by the much quieter, subtler form of erosion.[1] Civil-military relations scholars often feel like scientists trying to warn elected leaders and the general public about the pernicious effects of climate change—and how difficult it is to reverse years' worth of slow but steady damage. Perhaps because the erosion of the nonpartisan ethic has been gradual, it has been especially challenging to grab the attention of lawmakers, senior military leaders, or the American people. It is difficult to point to a single breaking point, seismic event, or culpable actor. The stage is thus set for inaction and rationalization.

Those who thought that the fraying of civil-military norms was unique or isolated to the Trump administration are mistaken. As demonstrated throughout this book, the erosion of civil-military norms predates the Trump administration. Moreover, civil-military relations have not suddenly ameliorated with the change in presidential administration, but rather they continue to be shaped by partisan polarization. With regard to the fraying of the norm of nonpartisanship within the military, there

seems to have been little abatement in the first year of the Biden administration. In January 2021, an airman stationed in Europe made headlines
after posting on social media, "Beijing Biden is not my president."[2] In
May 2021, a group of 124 retired flag officers calling themselves, "Flag
Officers 4 America" published an open letter that questioned, among
other allegations, the legitimacy of the 2020 presidential election and
the mental and physical fitness of President Biden.[3] And in August
2021, a Marine battalion commander was relieved after posting a video
of himself in uniform to social media in which he criticized his chain
of command for the botched withdrawal from Afghanistan, and in a
subsequent video, encouraged other service members to join with him
to "bring the whole [expletive] system down."[4] Instances such as these
garner plenty of media attention because they are aberrant actions that
deviate from the established norm. However, these incidents, no matter
how few and far between they might be characterized, demonstrate to
leaders in the military profession that norms require constant teaching
and sensitization across the force.

Further complicating matters, if the only focus is to apportion blame
for politicizing the military, civilian politicians would surely garner far
more of it than those in uniform. From using the military as a political
prop to engaging in partisan commentary in front of military audiences
and eliciting partisan endorsements from retired flag officers, politicians
have been trying to capitalize on the military's prestige and popularity for
decades. However, adopting a "civilians are the real problem" approach,
allows the uniformed military to avoid introspection and accountability
for its role in the institution's politicization.

Revisiting the issue of being too partisan, too politically vocal, and
too resistant to civilian control, which was presented in this book's
introduction, allows for an evaluation of where exactly the military—the
army, to be precise—is on the spectrum of politicization. On the "too-
partisan" charge, twenty years after 9/11, the officer corps of America's
army remains as consistently conservative and reliably Republican than

at any other point measured during the All-Volunteer Force era. Yet, despite partisan polarization in both the electorate and in government, army officers' partisanship is also weaker today than it was a decade ago—this is an encouraging sign that cannot be overstated. At a time of intense partisan polarization in this country, senior army officers are weaker partisans—specifically, weaker Republicans—than they were a decade ago. It remains to be seen if the tumultuous year that was 2020, the final year of the Trump presidency, and the January 6th insurrection created an inflection point among Republicans in the officer corps. Future research will determine if the trend of decreasing partisan strength among Republican officers will continue, including whether more will relabel themselves as Independents, or if party affiliation will normalize and reflect the same long-standing patterns that have characterized the officer corps since the 1990s. Much in that regard also depends on the future trajectory of the Republican Party.

Lest there be a misreading of this book's findings, there is nothing normatively wrong with officers predominantly affiliating with one party over another. The real concerns about "too partisan" are not that a majority of officers continue to identify as Republicans but rather the consequences of the officer corps being less representative of the American public, albeit it long has been less representative of the broader public in various important demographic variables, such as race, gender, and region of origin. The concerns are thus how partisanship manifests itself within the ranks and whether affiliation with the Republican Party is conflated with officership in general—a concern that Jason Dempsey first sounded the alarm on over a decade ago.[5]

Findings from this book's research do point to a number of areas of concern that merit further investigation. While there remains no evidence that service in the army somehow causes its officers to become conservative Republicans over time, it remains unclear why its senior ranks have consistently been populated by staunch Republicans compared to junior officers who have historically been more balanced in their partisan affiliation. Coupled with the finding that junior officer attrition is characterized by a higher affiliation with the Democratic Party than for those who make the army a career, this raises the question whether Democrats leave the army as junior officers because, at least in part, they are a political minority. This concern is not simply relegated to matters of partisanship; the army has long faced similar criticism about attrition of non-whites and women in the officer corps. This forces the obvious questions: what is it about service in the officer corps that causes whites, men, and Republicans to be more apt to make the army a career than non-whites, women, and Democrats? Are minorities made to feel unwelcome in the institution? Is their path to success in the institution limited because of their minority status? More research is clearly needed.

Retired flag officers—the "princes of the Church" who ostensibly guard the institution's reputation, even into their retirement—contribute to the perception that the military is a partisan actor and that its service members are partisans. They do so, most notably, through partisan campaign endorsements, the number of which have risen dramatically since the early 1990s. Beyond endorsements, retired flag officers' continued participation in partisan politics—through commentary, public criticism of elected leaders, and serving as high-profile political appointees—at the very least, blurs the dividing line between the uniformed military and partisan politics for the public, elected leaders, and even those currently serving. Notably, while most active-duty army officers are comfortable with retired flag officers speaking out politically, they are less comfortable than they were a decade ago—perhaps a response to some of the more notorious recent examples, such as retired Lieutenant General Mike Flynn. Despite this, there is little to suggest these trends regarding retired flag officers' involvement in partisan politics will reverse themselves anytime soon, absent some form of intervention.

On the charge of being too vocal, again, the army has considerable work to do. First, the good news: most army officers view voting as a sacred duty; they vote in high numbers and encourage their fellow service members to vote. Moreover, their participation in traditional forms of political expression tends to be fairly muted. However, there are ample indications that service members talk freely about partisan politics in the workplace. To be clear, this means service members in uniform talking about partisan politics with other service members in uniform while on duty. What else can explain how army officers have been able to pinpoint the officer corps' politics so accurately over time? Furthermore, officers' political expressions have partisan implications, with Democrats more apt to indicate they are uncomfortable expressing their political views and more likely to report that other officers in the military have tried to sway their votes.

Of greatest concern regarding the issue of being too vocal is the extent to which active-duty members of the military engage in partisan commentary, including vitriol against elected leaders and politicians, on social media. The combination of vague or outdated regulations, coupled with an increasingly polarized American public and an institution loathe to talk about politics—let alone confront partisan behavior—makes this the single greatest threat to the military's nonpartisan ethic today. That over a third of senior officers have observed active-duty service members engage in behavior that could constitute a violation of Article 88 of the Uniformed Code of Military Justice is nothing short of alarming.

Finally, with regard to the charge of being too resistant to civilian control, there is ample evidence that a non-trivial portion of army officers meet that criterion today, but more importantly, their commitment to civilian control may be conditioned on their partisanship and which party controls the White House at the time. Survey data presented here suggests partisan rationalization may be occurring on several matters pertaining to civilian control: the appropriateness of active-duty service members publicly expressing their political views and criticizing civilian leaders, their beliefs on whether the president should have served in uniform in order to be respected as commander in chief, and the degree of cynicism directed against civilian national security leaders. Equally worrisome, army officers show signs that their views of how senior military leaders should interact with their civilian superiors on decisions surrounding the use of force may also be conditioned on their partisanship. In short, the answer to one of this book's guiding questions is that party does indeed matter for officers in the post-9/11 army. The remaining question is what can be done to dampen the effects of partisanship within the officer corps and to recommit all officers to a fuller commitment to the nonpartisan ethic.

RECOMMENDATIONS

This book concludes by offering five recommendations aimed at reinvigorating the nonpartisan ethic within the uniformed military, especially its officer corps. Many of these are not new, and that alone should send an important signal to leaders in the Department of Defense (DoD). Failing to address these issues will all but guarantee that the nonpartisan ethic will remain tenuous and continue to erode. At a time when public trust and confidence in institutions continues to plummet, assuming the military can retain the American public's trust and confidence by continuing business as usual is short-sighted.

The intent here is not to admonish service members on where they have fallen short but rather to encourage them, especially senior military leaders, to reexamine why the nonpartisan ethic has been assumed but not well-examined for decades. In a recent critique of Huntington, Risa Brooks argues Huntington's objective control model—widely embraced by the officer corps—paradoxically enables political behavior by officers. Moreover, the near-universal embrace of Huntingtonian norms by the officer corps—especially the notion that the military is and must be apolitical—alleviates the officer corps from real introspection about their politics:

> First, the reflexive self-identification of military officers as apolitical can encourage blind spots such that they fail to recognize

the political content or impact of their actions. Tautological and ambiguous aspects of Huntington's argument contribute to this dynamic. Huntington measured the outcome (professionalism) with reference to its purported cause (the absence of political behavior). Thus, by definition, those who see themselves as professionals define away the possibility that their actions might be political. An officer socialized to Huntingtonian norms potentially assumes that, because he is a professional, he is by definition apolitical. He cannot be the former if he is the latter.[6]

The purpose behind these recommendations (along with the prescriptions in Appendix A) is to spur *more* thinking about politics and the military in the officer corps—especially the nonpartisan ethic—and to identify where officers' political blind spots are, as Brooks terms them, that might be degrading their professionalism. Both norms and rules govern the behavior of members of a profession. Ideally, norms should help regulate individuals' behavior, but when norms alone are insufficient or routinely ignored, they must be buttressed with appropriate rules. These recommendations reflect a mix of both normative and regulatory steps to bolster nonpartisanship in the military over the next decade.

1. Update and Clarify DoD Guidance on Political Activity to Match the Realities of Today

Leaders in each of the services and in DoD should acknowledge that DoDD 1344.10 in its current form has not served as a sufficient guidepost in promoting the importance of the nonpartisan ethic among service members today, nor has it aged well. It has failed, in large part, because it tries to split hairs—actively encouraging service members to participate in politics as private citizens but avoiding partisan politics while in uniform.[7] The regulation should be amended to first explain in greater detail *why* it is important for members of the military to be nonpartisan, lest the document simply be a catalogue of prohibited activities, devoid of any normative language. It should unambiguously advise service members to proceed with great caution when it comes to participating in any form of political activity, even those activities that are allowed.

The regulation should also clearly articulate the differences between political and partisan activities and provide examples to eliminate as much ambiguity as possible.

In addition to infusing the directive with normative language that better ties the nonpartisan ethic to a broader sense of military professionalism, DoD leaders also need to account for the tremendous changes in technology and patterns of human behavior that have occurred since the directive was last updated over 13 years ago. DoDD 1344.10 is now obsolete and fails to acknowledge the preponderance of partisan political commentary, especially among service members, that now occurs in social media. DoDD 1344.10 must be updated to include clearer, more consistent language about political activity on social media and make clear the real harm that service members' partisan commentaries, especially when laced with vitriol, does to the profession. Moreover, the services likely will not update their respective regulations until DoD updates its directive; the net effect for several years has been institutional paralysis and a set of guidelines that no longer addresses the realities of political behavior, communication, and human interaction today. This puts an undue burden on unit commanders who must adjudicate when there are violations in their formations because they cannot glean relevant guidance from current regulations. DoD and service leaders owe them a directive that meets the realities of today.

2. Congress Should Reexamine Article 88 of the Uniformed Code of Military Justice

Since the Uniformed Code of Military Justice was enacted in 1950, only officers have been subject to Article 88 of the UCMJ, which prohibits the use of contemptuous words against the president and other civilian leaders. This is outdated and should be amended to apply to noncommissioned officers as well. Is it acceptable for a senior noncommissioned officer to refer to the president or the Speaker of the House in a derogatory manner on Facebook? If not, there is no reason why Article 88 should not be expanded to include noncommissioned officers. Some critics might offer that Article 134—a catch-all provision that covers any behavior counter to good order and discipline and brings discredit to the force —is sufficient, as it was in former Marine Corps Sergeant Gary Stein's case, when he received an other than honorable (OTH) discharge for disparaging President Obama in 2012 on Facebook.[8] Others contend that Article 88 applies only to officers because of early fears that officers could lead a coup.[9] One observer noted, however, that Article 88 violations also "threaten the hierarchical systems within the military," in addition to eroding civilian control, which would make it logical to extend Article 88 to apply to noncommissioned officers.[10]

Since 1950, there have only been two courts martial involving Article 88.[11] While an increase in courts martial pursuant to Article 88 remains unlikely—and while Article 88 certainly has not deterred retired officers (who are subject to its provisions) from using contemptuous words—it may serve as an effective deterrent to those on active duty, regardless of rank. More importantly, expanding Article 88 has a symbolic effect and sends a strong message that not only unequivocally condemns insulting language against civilian leaders but also reinforces civilian control during a time when it has arguably been weakened.

3. Commit to Purposeful Inculcation of the Norm Across Professional Military Education

Criticizing the limitations of professional military education (PME) has become a parlor game of late, and there is no shortage of commentaries calling for some form of PME reform today.[12] As Appendix A of this book notes, an improved and more consistent teaching of both the regulations and norms that govern the traditions of nonpartisanship within the military is needed, but that alone will not fix the problem. If nothing else, the uniformed military has to come to grips with the fact that this topic, let alone the broader theme of civil-military relations, is barely addressed in formal PME settings throughout an officer's career. Instead, leaders of all ranks simply assume it is being taught, rather than examining the extent to which it is actually addressed.

As it turns out, the most comprehensive instruction on the nonpartisan ethic currently takes place at the service academies—when nineteen-year-olds are first getting socialized to the profession—and nearly thirty years later for the minute fraction of the officer corps who makes it to the rank of general officer.[13] That the vast majority of the officer corps gets little or no formal classroom exposure to the nonpartisan ethic is troubling. Moreover, while professors at the service academies and senior service colleges are well-equipped to teach and guide discussions on partisan politics and the military, service school instructors who teach basic and advanced level courses to junior officers—and perhaps even at the staff college level—will need a grounding in how to adequately teach this material and foster constructive dialogue.

4. Senior Military Leaders Must Address the Importance of Nonpartisanship More Consistently

Senior military leaders should be more vocal and consistent in talking about the importance of being nonpartisan and how violations of this norm threaten the American public's trust and confidence in the military. Rather than focusing on what is allowable and not, discussions should center on whether such political activity is appropriate—even, and perhaps especially, those activities that are allowable. By doing so, senior leaders will strengthen the nonpartisan ethic and reignite discussions about what it means to be part of a profession. Both retired Admiral Mullen and retired General Dempsey were strong advocates of the nonpartisan ethic, but it should not solely be the responsibility of the chairman of the Joint Chiefs of Staff to initiate such discussions, nor should they only occur on the eve of a presidential election. Service chiefs and all general and flag officers should be more vocal in stressing to their subordinates on why it so important to remain nonpartisan. The normative violations revealed in this book suggest more attention, not less, is required.

Senior military leaders must also demonstrate more interest in examining the political blind spots that Brooks warns has plagued the military for decades—if, as General Milley contends, remaining apolitical is the most important thing service members do.[14] This means inviting more studies, more research, and more accountability regarding the political behavior of active-duty service members—and not being afraid of talking about the topic candidly to service members, elected leaders, and the public. The services, especially the army, pride themselves on being learning organizations. However, being a learning organization is predicated on valuing introspection and welcoming unpleasant news to improve the profession. Professions cannot effectively self-regulate or strengthen their ethics if they cannot "see themselves" and the potential fault lines that exist in the ranks. The only way this can happen meaningfully is for senior leaders in the profession to stress consistently and publicly the importance of greater awareness to nonpartisanship in the ranks and its ongoing erosion. This has to occur more than once every presidential election cycle. Leaders can do this the way they tackle any other challenge they face and prioritize: by constantly talking about the issue; devoting top-tier, professional symposiums to tackle the issue; inviting outside scholars and think tanks to research the nature of the challenge across the services; incentivizing those on active duty to research and study the issue in PME settings; and forcefully showcasing how violations of the nonpartisan ethic are damaging to the institution and are met with swift accountability.

Finally, given some of the violations on social media by military members, the services should exercise greater enforcement of the policies already in existence. An institution that is subordinate to civilian authority cannot tolerate rude, disparaging comments made by its members towards the president and other elected leaders under the veil that it constitutes free speech made in a personal capacity. Moreover, the insurrection against the Capitol, and the role social media played leading to that moment, should create a greater sense of urgency for senior military leaders. This is not a call to establish a police state, where every political post must be reviewed and scrutinized, but rather to deter inappropriate political activity from ever occurring in the first place through increased sensitization. Unit commanders are already charged with maintaining the good order and discipline of their units, and the extension of that framework to include modeling prudent political behavior on social media is consistent with the scope and nature of their authority. Consistent sensitization to the bounds of appropriate political discourse on social media by leaders at all levels—backstopped by current regulations that are easier to enforce—should better regulate the political expressions of those on active duty while reinforcing the norm of nonpartisanship.

5. Address the Harmful Impacts of Retired Flag Officers' Partisan Campaign Endorsements

If past performance is any indicator, the vast majority of active-duty flag officers are loath to call out the partisan fouls of their retired flag-officer peers—this has to change. Active-duty flag officers, especially the chairman and the service chiefs, must become comfortable with publicly disavowing retired flag officers who use their ranks for purely partisan purposes, such as campaign endorsements. Again, endorsements differ from retired flag officers running for political office and most forms of political commentary. Several civil-military relations scholars have already provided good recommendations that senior military leaders could immediately implement or endorse. First, as Nora Bensahel and retired Lieutenant General David Barno have argued, the chairman of the Joint Chiefs of Staff and each service chief should send all newly selected flag officers a letter outlining clear expectations about their roles in upholding the norm of nonpartisanship, including when they are out of uniform.[15] Such expectations include refraining entirely from partisan endorsements, especially the use of one's rank and service in such endorsements.

Second, if norms alone and strong peer pressure from active-duty flag officers cannot persuade retired flag officers to refrain from endorsements, Congress should carefully consider implementing a "cooling off" period for retired flag officers before they can engage in partisan politics.[16] DoD Instruction 1000.32, *Prohibition of Lobbying Activity by Former DoD Senior Officials*, prohibits retired flag officers from lobbying DoD for one to two years after retiring from the military.[17] The same could apply for retired flag officers and partisan politics: officers in grades O7 and O8 would be prohibited from participating in partisan politics (with the exception of voting) for two years, and officers in grades O9 and O10 would be subject to a four-year prohibition. Doing so would also safeguard recently retired flag officers from speaking out against the presidential administration under which they served.

Third, senior military leaders must be unafraid to call out bad behavior when they see it, no matter the repercussions or friction this might cause in the relationships with their mentors and colleagues. When retired flag-officers make partisan endorsements, the chairman and that particular service chief should publicly deride it. And while the four-stars atop the institution carry the most responsibility for doing so, it will carry more weight if an overwhelming number of active-duty and retired flag officers are also on board. Griffiths' call for "counter-mobilization," whereby a large number of retired officers cosign a letter denouncing flag-officer endorsements at the outset of a presidential election campaign, may also serve as a further peer deterrent.[18] The chairman of the Joint Chiefs of Staff and the service chiefs could enact all of these measures. Even though a sizeable number of retired flag officers might still make partisan endorsements in spite of these measures, senior leaders should not lose sight of the fact that by not taking action, endorsements are sure to continue.

One additional proviso, tangentially related to the issue of partisan endorsements, is that senior military leaders, such as the chairman of the Joint Chiefs of Staff and the service chiefs, should lead a campaign to correctly refer to retired flag officers who have crossed over into explicitly partisan roles and positions—and correct those who continue to misuse the terms. Despite serving as a cabinet official, Jim Mattis was routinely referred to by the president, other politicians, and uniformed members of the military as "General," as was John Kelly, who served as the Secretary of the Department of Homeland Security and later as White House Chief of Staff.[19] In fact, nearly two years after Mattis stepped down as secretary of defense, chairman of the Joint Chiefs of Staff General Mark Milley repeatedly referred to Secretary Mattis as "General Mattis" during a talk at the Brookings Institution, even when highlighting Mattis's authorship of the National Defense Strategy as secretary of defense.[20] This only muddies the waters even more for the American public, who have a tough time acknowledging distinctions between active-duty and retired flag officers in the first place. In addition, further confusing the public are retired flag officers who assume partisan, political roles in retirement and then use the cloak of the military's vow of nonpartisanship to shield them from having to answer political questions over which they had purview.[21] It also degrades the norm of nonpartisanship itself, turning it into a convenient excuse when it best suits the general-turned-political figure.

FINAL THOUGHTS

There are a host of additional laws, rules, and regulations that could also be explored to further strengthen the nonpartisan ethic, since many might conclude that norms alone cannot sufficiently restore the military's commitment to partisan neutrality today. Doing so, however, would all but admit the profession can no longer adequately regulate the behavior of its members. Rules and regulations certainly play a role, and the few adjustments called for here will remedy some existing loopholes. But before sweeping calls are made for new legislation or DoD directives, senior members of the profession would be well-served to take ownership of the deficiencies outlined here and recommit their respective organizations to the concept of loyal subordination and what all it entails.[22] Appendix A offers some thoughts for unit commanders on how to best implement a professional development program on the nonpartisan ethic in their organizations. The tumultuous events of the past few years—which propelled civil-military relations, and more acutely, the allegation of the military's politicization, into Americans' households as a topic of nightly dinner conversation—suggests they cannot wait.

NOTES

1. Civil-military relations scholars have long used this metaphor to describe the deterioration of civil-military relations and civilian control of the military. See Kohn, "The Erosion of Civilian Control of the Military."
2. Kime and Pawlyk, "'Beijing Biden is Not My President:' Troops' Social Media Posts in Spotlight After Capitol Riots."
3. Bryan Bender, "'Disturbing and Reckless': Retired Brass Spread Election Lie in Attack on Biden, Democrats."
4. Hohmann, "The Kabul Evacuation Illuminated a Dangerous Strain of Thought in the Military About Civilian Control."
5. Jason K. Dempsey, *Our Army*, 152–176.
6. Risa Brooks, "Paradoxes of Professionalism," 17.
7. Liebert and Golby "Midlife Crisis?," 128.
8. James and Taylor, "Marine Sgt. Gary Stein Gets 'Other Than Honorable' Discharge Over Anti-Obama Facebook Comment."
9. Sherill, *Military Justice Is to Justice as Military Music Is to Music*, 180. For a good overview on the issue, see Davidson, "Contemptuous Speech Against the President."
10. Fidell, "Free Speech v. Article 88."
11. United States v. Howe, 17 C.M.A. 165, 37 C.M.R. 429, 17 USCMA 165 (1967); and Davis, "'Accountability' Marine gets light sentence; judge blasts command."
12. Lacey, "Finally Getting Serious About Professional Military Education"; Lowther and Mitchell, "Professional Military Education Needs More Creativity, Not More History."; Garamone, "Joint Chiefs Vision Changes Military Education Philosophy."
13. Brooks, Robinson, and Urben, "What Makes a Military Professional? Evaluating Norm Socialization in West Point Cadets."
14. Macias and Mangan, "Joint Chiefs of Staff Chairman Milley Apologizes for Appearing with Trump at Church Photo-Op."
15. Barno and Bensahel, "How to Get Generals Out of Politics."
16. Golby, et al, "Brass Politics: How Retired Military Officers Are Shaping Elections;" and Miller, "Generals & General Elections.".

17. U.S. Department of Defense, *Department of Defense Instruction 1000.32, Prohibition of Lobbying Activity by Former DoD Senior Officials* (Washington, DC: March 26, 2020).
18. Griffiths, "Let's Use Peer Pressure to End Political Endorsements by Retired Generals."
19. Wagner, "White House Press Secretary: It's 'Highly Inappropriate' to Question a 4-star Marine General."
20. Milley, "A Conversation with Chairman of the Joint Chiefs of Staff General Mark A. Milley."
21. Jason K. Dempsey, "John Kelly Lent His Military Credibility to Trump."
22. Feaver and Kohn, *Soldiers and Civilians*, 473.

Appendix A

A Guide to Instilling the Nonpartisan Ethic at the Unit Level

> We must hold dear the principle of an apolitical military that is so deeply rooted in the very essence of our Republic. And this is not easy. It takes time and work and effort. But it may be the most important thing each and every one of us does every single day.[1]
> —General Mark A. Milley

The relative durability of the nonpartisan ethic in the officer corps is impressive, given the limited extent to which it is formally taught and reinforced throughout an officer's career. Moreover, measuring compliance or noncompliance with the nonpartisan ethic is not only a subjective endeavor, but a difficult one. There is no such thing as a service-wide database of violations of the nonpartisan ethic. And yet, assuming the nonpartisan ethic remains healthy and intact in the armed forces may inhibit introspection and self-assessments among service members. As highlighted by General Milley's public apology following his appearance in the Lafayette Square photo-op referenced in the quote above, it may be that officers do not reflect deeply upon the nonpartisan ethic until the issue has become so salient that the officer corps then finds itself in a civil-military relations crisis or worse yet, its credibility as a nonpartisan institution has already been damaged.

Calls for reinvigorated professional military education to better address fundamental principles of civil-military relations are necessary but insufficient to bolster the officer corps' understanding of and commitment to civil-military norms. Focusing only on reforming professional military education lets commanders off the hook for failing to promote what should be a core aspect of professionalism throughout their formations.

It also reinforces the fallacy that professional military education can and should solve all sorts of professionalism deficiencies within the ranks. As the army's abysmal record in combatting sexual harassment and sexual assault demonstrates, commanders should be more—not less—engaged when it comes to demonstrating personal leadership on core matters pertaining to the profession.[2] Outsourcing such matters to others outside the chain of command generally reflects leader disinterest and therefore signals to service members of all ranks that these issues just aren't that important. Certainly, professional military education, especially at the staff-college and senior-service-college levels, should be reformed to include purposeful instruction on civil-military relations and the nonpartisan ethic. More must be done at the unit level, however, to ensure officers of all ranks have a foundational understanding of what it means to be apolitical and nonpartisan. Commanders and leaders in the armed forces are charged with promoting all sorts of aspects associated with professionalism—teaching and modeling the nonpartisan ethic should be no different than any other discussion of professional ethics.

This brief guide is intended to assist leaders, especially unit commanders at the O-5 and O-6 level, in establishing professional development programs on the nonpartisan ethic with their officers, although it can and should be adapted for noncommissioned officer development as well. Additionally, while it is geared towards army officers, the content is universal and can easily be tailored for the other services. As with all aspects of leader development, senior officers and commanders should take ownership of this program and resist the temptation to delegate the responsibility of leading such discussions to their Judge Advocate General (JAG) officers. Certainly, JAG officers play a critical advisory role and must be included in such professional development sessions; however, allowing JAG officers to lead them runs the risk that discussions will center primarily on debates of what is and is not permissible.

Rules and regulations typically outline the formal minimum require-ments for standards of conduct, while norms are informal mechanisms that govern behavior. Although understanding service and DoD directives is necessary, a deeper understanding of professional norms must center on how officers *should* behave—even when certain activities may technically be allowable. Some commanders might be intimidated about or feel uncomfortable leading discussions with their officers that fundamentally point back towards politics, especially domestic politics. This might explain why commanders often default to their JAG officers to spearhead such discussions, figuring that JAG officers are best poised to answer tough questions and provide clear interpretations of regulations—this is a mistake. Unit commanders are not only responsible for maintaining good order and discipline in their formations, but they must also guard their unit's reputation and, by extension, the reputation of the profession of arms. Topics pertaining to professionalism rarely offer black and white prescriptions but instead depend on candid discussion and debate, which commanders are best suited to lead.

This guide includes recommended professional readings, broken down by foundational lessons on military professionalism and the roots of civilian control, the intersection of partisan politics and social media, the much-debated role of retired flag officers in partisan politics, and finally the overarching debate regarding politicization of the military. It is by no means an exhaustive treatment of all civil-military relations dynamics, nor is intended to cover all aspects of how the military as an institution intersects with politics. It solely addresses how leaders might attempt to talk about the importance of nonpartisanship within the ranks. Commanders could envision this as a four-part series; each section builds on the next and concludes by offering follow-on discussion questions that can be employed in group settings. With the exception of a few of the readings, most are readily accessible through the internet. This appendix also includes hypothetical partisan scenarios that officers are likely to encounter throughout their careers, along with considerations officers should weigh when they do inevitably confront these situations.[3]

ROOTS OF CIVILIAN CONTROL AND PROFESSIONALISM

Any discussion of politics and the officer corps should first be grounded in a broader discussion of the foundations of civilian control and the military as a profession. All officers should understand the constitutional roots that subordinate the armed forces to civilian authority, as outlined in Article I, Section 8, and Article II as well as the democratic traditions that have shaped and reinforced civilian control in the United States. During the Newburgh Conspiracy in 1783, a group of officers in the Continental Army came close to mutiny over Congress's inability to consistently pay Continental soldiers during the Revolutionary War. George Washington put a stop to the plotting in an eloquent speech about the importance of civilian control of the armed forces that appealed to the officers' sense of duty and selfless service. He encouraged them to trust Congress and not to do anything that would tarnish their dignity and honor, and he made it clear that anyone who would do otherwise would "overturn the liberties of our country," and "open the flood gates of civil discord."[4]

Few have done more to advance an understanding of the army as a profession than Don Snider, emeritus professor in West Point's Department of Social Sciences and former Professor of the Army Profession at the U.S. Army War College. His writings on the army as a profession, as Nathan Finney highlights well, help ground any discussion of the importance of nonpartisanship into a broader examination of the professional ethic and the characteristics of the army profession.[5] Lastly, in addition to contemplating the difference between partisan and political as well as the difference between nonpartisan and apolitical, officers should also reflect upon why the norm of nonpartisanship is a critical aspect of professionalism.

Recommended Readings

Washington, George. Newburgh Address: George Washington to Officers of the Army, March 15, 1783. https://www.mountvernon.

org/education/primary-sources-2/article/newburgh-address-george-washington-to-officers-of-the-army-march-15-1783/#.

Hattem, Michael. "Newburgh Conspiracy." The Digital Encyclopedia of George Washington at the Fred W. Smith National Library for the Study of George Washington at Mount Vernon, https://www.mountvernon.org/library/digitalhistory/digital-encyclopedia/article/newburgh-conspiracy/.

U.S. Constitution

Finney, Nathan K. "Views on the #Profession from the Professional," The Strategy Bridge, January 28, 2015, https://thestrategybridge.org/the-bridge/2016/1/28/views-on-the-profession-from-the-professional.

Department of the Army. *Army Leadership and the Profession.* Army Doctrine Publication 6-22.

Washington, DC: 2019. https://armypubs.army.mil/epubs/DR_pubs/DR_a/ARN20039-ADP_6-22-001-WEB-0.pdf. See specifically 1-1 to 1-13.

Babcock-Lumish, Brian. "Uninformed, not Uniformed? The Apolitical Myth." *Military Review,* September-October 2013, 48-56. https://www.armyupress.army.mil/Portals/7/military-review/Archives/English/MilitaryReview_20131031_art009.pdf.

Brooks, Risa. "The Real Threat to Civilian Control of the Military: The Officer Corps Can No Longer Simply Ignore Politics." *Foreign Affairs,* January 18, 2021, https://www.foreignaffairs.com/articles/united-states/2021-01-18/real-threat-civilian-control-military.

Discussion Questions

- What does civilian control of the armed forces mean, and how is it specified in the Constitution? Why is civilian control of the military an important feature of democracies? What are some of the democratic ideals in the Constitution that military members swear an oath to support and defend?

- What does it mean to be part of a profession? What marks professions as different from other jobs or occupations? As officers, what are your responsibilities as custodians of a professional ethic?

- When reflecting on why the American public ranks the military as the most trusted institution, retired General Martin Dempsey once remarked, "Maybe if I knew what it would take to screw it up, I could avoid it."[6] Why is trust such an integral component to the profession of arms? What do you think could cause the public to lose trust in the military? Why?

- Harold Lasswell once defined politics as, "who gets what, when, and how?" Despite this value-neutral, matter-of-fact definition, the word "political" has taken on a negative connotation in the military —why?

- What is the difference between political and partisan? Why is nonpartisanship a critical aspect of military professionalism?

Figure 2. Scenario #1: Watercooler Talk Just Among Friends.

Scenario: A brigade commander, battalion commander, and company commander are having lunch together at a dining facility. A large screen television in the dining facility is replaying last night's presidential primary debate, where 10 candidates are vying for their party's nomination. The brigade commander looks up at the television and remarks, "What a bunch of [expletive] morons." The battalion commander and company commander look at each other and laugh.

Is this a foul? Most certainly. It is inappropriate for any officer, let alone a brigade commander, to make disparaging comments—especially about a potential future commander-in-chief. The officer's comment also may be a violation of Article 88 of the Uniformed Code of Military Justice (UCMJ), which prohibits officers from making contemptuous words against the president and other elected leaders, assuming some of the individuals running for president on that debate stage were already sitting elected officials.

Discussion: More than that, however, the comment reflects exceedingly poor judgment on the part of the brigade commander, who made an implied partisan comment in front of his subordinate officers and probably assumed the other two officers shared his partisan leanings. The subordinate officers are now in an uncomfortable position. If the battalion commander fails to correct or admonish the brigade commander, the young captain will have now witnessed two failures in judgment by senior officers and will conclude that publicly criticizing politicians and elected leaders is fine for officers to do. Even if the brigade commander might try to rationalize his comments by arguing he was just expressing his personal opinion and was not making a public pronouncement or that perhaps he knew the other two officers shared his political views, the fact that he did so on duty, in uniform, and in front of his subordinates reflects poor judgment.

PARTISAN POLITICS AND THE PROFESSION: ON SOCIAL MEDIA AND BEYOND

While the point of officer professional development is to move beyond a simple retelling of dos and don'ts, all officers must at least be familiar with the few regulations or directives that guide political behavior within the uniformed military. Some of these regulations are outdated, like DoD Directive 1344.10, *Political Activities by Members of the Armed Forces on Active Duty*, which has not been updated in over 13 years and fails to address social media considerations. Others, such as the U.S. Army's official social media website are vague in outlining what is and is not allowable. While there are a few exceptions, these regulations provide a fair amount of latitude to service members, allowing them to express their First Amendment rights like other citizens.

Recommended Readings

Department of Defense. Political Activities by Members of the Armed Forces. DoD Directive 1344.10. Washington, DC: Department of Defense, 2008. https://www.esd.whs.mil/Portals/54/Documents/DD/issuances/dodd/134410p.pdf.

Department of the Army. Army Command Policy. Army Regulation 600-20. Washington, DC: 2020. See Appendix B, Political Activities. https://armypubs.army.mil/epubs/DR_pubs/DR_a/ARN30511-AR_600-20-002-WEB-3.pdf.

10 U.S. Code § 888 - Article 88, Contempt toward officials, https://www.law.cornell.edu/uscode/text/10/888.

Department of the Army. "Army Social Media: Policies and Resources." https://www.army.mil/socialmedia/. See specifically the section entitled, "Guidance on Political Activity and DoD Support."

Urben, Heidi. "Partisan Activity on Social Media Hurts the Military Profession." *Proceedings* 147, no. 9 (September 2021): 64–67.

Discussion Questions

- Department of Defense directives and Department of the Army regulations outline certain restrictions on political activities for active-duty service members. Is compliance with these regulations sufficient to maintain the military's nonpartisan ethic? Department of Defense Directive 1344.10 was last updated in 2008. If you could update it, what else should be included?

- Only officers are subject to the provisions of Article 88 in the Uniformed Code of Military Justice, which prohibits them from using contemptuous words against the president and other elected officials. Since they are not prohibited from doing so, is it appropriate for noncommissioned officers to make disparaging comments about the president and other elected leaders? Why or why not?

- How do service members' social media activity and behavior impact their professionalism in the army? What are the benefits and pitfalls from service members engaging on social media sites?

- What considerations should service members weigh when engaging on social media, especially on matters pertaining to politics?

- Using a disclaimer on your social media sites that your views are yours only and do not reflect the official views of the U.S. Army is always a good practice. If service members use a disclaimer, but it is still clear they are affiliated with the military, is it still okay for them to post partisan material on their social media pages? Why or why not?

Figure 3. Scenario #2: Posting in a Private Capacity.

Scenario: A well-liked field grade officer, who is prolific on social media, shared a meme on his Facebook page that depicts a president in a disparaging manner in a political cartoon. The account is a personal account, although he does not include a disclaimer in his profile or posts, and his profile picture is of him in uniform during one of his deployments to Afghanistan. He has more than 700 "friends" on Facebook, many of whom are current or former members of the military.

Is this a foul? Yes. The officer may contend that he was posting in a personal capacity, and he may also argue that "sharing" someone else's post is more innocuous than posting his own original thoughts, but it nonetheless reflects poor judgment on his part. He may also be in violation of Article 88 of the UCMJ for contempt towards the president. His failure to include a disclaimer that his social media activity does not in any way reflect official positions of the US Army or Department of Defense, and the fact that his page includes multiple photos of him in uniform and many linkages to the US Army is problematic.

Discussion: Even if he had included a disclaimer, his posts—especially if he has a history of posting or sharing partisan content or rude comments towards the president—set a poor example for his fellow service members, demonstrate a lack of professionalism, and normalize criticism of elected leaders. By sharing or posting such material on social media, he made a lasting, written, public commentary that carried undeniable partisan undertones.

THE ROLE OF RETIRED FLAG OFFICERS IN PARTISAN POLITICS

In the movie White Christmas, Bing Crosby croons, "What can you do with a general / When he stops being a general? / Oh, what can you do with a general who retires?" Retired generals and admirals have made headlines for endorsing political candidates for office during election campaigns, speaking at presidential-nominating conventions, serving as high-profile political appointees, and much more in recent years. Yet, the vast majority of the roughly 7,500 living retired general officers choose not to engage in partisan politics. Many who defend retired four-stars' involvement in partisan politics point to the precedent set by George Washington, Ulysses S. Grant, and Dwight Eisenhower when they were elected president following their military service. However, when retired officers run for office, they unambiguously shed their military identity in favor for a partisan one and subject themselves to the full scrutiny of the electorate. Retired flag officers, who mix their military personas with partisan ones through campaign endorsements, face no such accountability. Despite this, survey data of active-duty officers finds many officers serving today are comfortable with the political outspokenness of retired flag officers, indicating more work is required to sensitize officers to the negative impacts partisan politics—even from those who are no longer in uniform—can have on the institution.

Recommended Readings

Dempsey, Martin E. "Keep Your Politics Private, My Fellow Generals and Admirals." *Defense One*, August 1, 2016. https://www.defenseone.com/ideas/2016/08/keep-your-politics-private-my-fellow-generals-and-admirals/130404/.

Feaver, Peter. "We Don't Need Generals to Become Cheerleaders at Political Conventions," *Foreign Policy*, July 29, 2016. https://foreignpolicy.com/2016/07/29/we-dont-need-generals-to-become-cheerleaders-at-political-conventions/.

Gelpi, Chris. "Retired Generals are People Too!" *Duck of Minerva* (blog). August 9, 2016. https://duckofminerva.com/2016/08/retired-generals-are-people-too.html

Griffiths, Zachary. "Let's Use Peer Pressure to End Political Endorsements by Retired Generals." *Defense One*, February 18, 2020. https://

www.defenseone.com/ideas/2020/02/use-peer-pressure-stop-retired-generals-making-political-endorsements/163034/.

Robinson, Michael. "Danger Close: Military Politicization and Elite Credibility." *War on the Rocks*, August 21, 2018. https://warontherocks.com/2018/08/danger-close-military-politicization-and-elite-credibility/.

Discussion Questions

- How might partisan actions and behavior by retired officers negatively affect the military or society?

- Do retired officers—especially retired general officers—still speak for the institution? Should retired general officers be held to a different standard than other retired officers when it comes to partisan political commentary? Why or why not?

- How do partisan political endorsements by retired general officers differ from other types of political commentary? Are there any benefits from retired general officers speaking out on political issues?

- When generals and admirals retire from the military, they are subject to a "cooling off" period, preventing them from engaging in lobbying activities towards the Defense Department for one to two years, depending on their rank. Should retired flag officers face a similar "cooling off" period regarding their involvement in partisan politics? Why or why not?

- Recent survey data suggests most Americans may not distinguish retired flag officers from those on active duty. How does this affect the debate over retired flag officers' role in partisan politics?

Figure 4. Scenario #3: All in the Family.

> Scenario: A lieutenant who just finished a deployment to Iraq is home on block leave. Her family has thrown a party to celebrate her homecoming, and there are close to 50 of her family and friends in attendance. The presidential election is two weeks away, and at some point during the party, the discussion turns to politics. As her friends and family proudly declare who they plan to vote for and why, the lieutenant joins in the conversation and does the same.
>
> Is this a foul? No, she is at home with family and friends, sharing her personal, political opinion.
>
> Discussion: Here's how her actions could become questionable, though. If the lieutenant is wearing her uniform, even though they are in a private setting at the time, she might want to think through the impression some of her distant relatives or friends might draw. An even greater concern would be if she claims—for example, in a public setting while in uniform—that everyone she knows in the military is going to vote for this particular candidate, too. Then she's almost implying official endorsement, which would be inappropriate.

Is The Military Politicized?

Alice Hunt Friend defines a politicized military as one that "exercises loyalty to a single political party and/or consistently advocates for and defends partisan political positions and fortunes."[7]

Politicization of the military does not happen overnight, and both civilians and the uniformed military bear responsibility here. Even if politicians are deemed to be most culpable in politicizing the military—and that is certainly up for debate—members of the military, especially senior leaders, should be accountable and play an important role in preventing and resisting attempts to politicize the military. It is important for officers to reflect on the particular role they have in keeping those in uniform out of the partisan political fray. During times of partisan polarization, this is even more challenging, as virtually every political issue carries partisan connotations. Lastly, service members of all ranks and grades should purposefully reflect on the oath they take to the Constitution and the democratic principles within it that they swear to support and defend. Doing so, at routine intervals in one's career, may serve to remind military professionals about how to navigate times of great political uncertainty and tension.

Recommended Readings

Brooks, Risa. "What Can Military and Civilian Leaders Do to Prevent the Military's Politicization." *War on the Rocks*, April 27, 2020, https://warontherocks.com/2020/04/what-can-military-and-civilian-leaders-do-to-prevent-the-militarys-politicization/.

Foster, Gregory. "The Real Problem With 'Politicizing the Military.'" *Defense One*, July 30, 2020. https://www.defenseone.com/ideas/2020/07/politicizing-military/167361/

Friend, Alice Hunt. "Military Politicization." *Center for Strategic and International Studies*, May 5, 2017. https://www.csis.org/analysis/military-politicization.

Milley, Mark. *Keynote Address to National Defense University Class of 2020 Graduates*. 2020. https://www.youtube.com/watch?v=7AKmmApwi0M.

Thornhill, Paula. "How to Teach Troops About the Constitution." *Defense One*, February 18, 2021, https://www.defenseone.com/ideas/2021/02/how-teach-troops-about-constitution/172117/.

Discussion Questions

- First, what does it mean when we say the military is or could be politicized? Has the military been politicized or are these claims overblown? What evidence can you provide to support your assessment, one way or the other?

- What steps should those in uniform take to ensure the military does not become politicized?

- Like any other citizen, all service members have the right to vote. But why is it important for the uniformed military to play no role in elections and campaigns?

- In General Milley's 2020 commencement address to National Defense University graduates, he tells officers to keep the Constitution close to their hearts. What does it mean to take an oath to the Constitution?

- As a leader in the armed forces, how might you go about teaching your subordinates about the Constitution and the democratic principles they swear to support and defend?

Figure 5. Scenario #4: Get Out the Vote.

Scenario: A captain assigned to the Military District of Washington spends her off-duty time volunteering with a variety of nonprofit organizations committed to gender and racial equality. She often posts photos of herself in civilian attire, volunteering and attending peaceful rallies on social justice matters in Washington, DC, to her Instagram account. In the lead-up to the last election, she was very active on social media, posting reminders directed at her military friends to get out and vote. She often shares links to the Federal Voting Assistance Program and tells her military friends to research their states' voting procedures.

Is this a foul? No, she is exercising her first amendment rights, consistent with Department of Defense (DoD) Directive 1344.10 and participating in various political causes in her capacity as a private citizen. Her calls for her fellow service members to vote in the upcoming election are appropriate and consistent with DoD guidelines.

Discussion: Here's how this scenario could become a partisan foul: If she encouraged her fellow military members to vote for a particular candidate or party, that would clearly cross the line. Similarly, if her involvement with a nonprofit organization crossed over into partisan territory, where she publicly advocated for service members to take a partisan stance on the particular political causes she favors, that would also be out of line.

NOTES

1. Macias and Mangan, "Joint Chiefs of Staff Chairman Milley Apologizes for Appearing with Trump at Church Photo-Op."
2. Fort Hood Independent Review Committee, *Report of the Fort Hood Independent Review Committee,* November 6, 2020, https://www.army.mil/e2/downloads/rv7/forthoodreview/2020-12-03_FHIRC_report_redacted.pdf.
3. For scenarios that distinguish between partisan and political activity, see also Friend, "Navigating Politics in 2020 and Beyond."
4. George Washington, *Newburgh Address: George Washington to Officers of the Army, March 15, 1783,*https://www.mountvernon.org/education/primary-sources-2/article/newburgh-address-george-washington-to-officers-of-the-army-march-15-1783/.
5. Finney, "Views on the #Profession from the Professional."
6. Jim Gourley, "What Is the Tipping Point for America's Trust in the Military?."
7. Friend, "Military Politicization."

Appendix B

Civil Military Relations in a Time of War Survey (2009)

This survey is designed to assess the impact that the wars in Iraq and Afghanistan are having the state of civil-military relations today. Throughout the survey, your anonymity will be preserved. This survey should take approximately 10–15 minutes to complete.

The survey requires your AKO username to log in. Usernames and identification of respondents will not be recorded, and responses are completely anonymous through the secure survey portal.

Thank you again for your time. With your participation, we will be able to better understand the state of civil-military relations in this era of persistent conflict. Please direct any questions to the chief researcher by responding to this email.

Informed Consent
By completing this survey, I consent to participate in this study. I understand my participation is strictly voluntary.

About Your Military Service

1. How would you best describe your specialty/branch?

    ___ Combat Arms (air defense artillery, armor, aviation, engineers, field artillery, infantry)
    ___ Combat Support (chemical, military intelligence, military police, signal)
    ___ Combat Service Support (adjutant general, finance, logistics, medical service)

___ Special Branches (chaplains, judge advocate general, medical/dental/veterinary, nursing)

2. What was your source of commissioning?

    ___ Service Academy
    ___ ROTC
    ___ OCS
    ___ Other

3. Approximately how many years of service do you currently have? ___

4. What is your current rank?

    ___ O-1/O-2
    ___ O-3
    ___ O-4
    ___ O-5
    ___ O-6

5. Are you currently in the process of separating from the Army or do you plan on separating from the Army in the next six months?

    ___ Yes ___ No

6. Has a member of your immediate family (parent, spouse, sibling, child) served, or do they currently serve on active duty in the military?

    ___ Yes ___ No

7. Have you deployed to Iraq?

    ___ Yes ___ No

8. How many cumulative months have you spent deployed to Iraq? ___

9. Have you deployed to Afghanistan?

    ___ Yes ___ No

10. How many cumulative months have you spent deployed to Afghanistan? ___

Civic Participation

11. Do you agree or disagree with this statement: "Politics is something often talked about at work."

    ___ Strongly Disagree
    ___ Disagree
    ___ Neutral
    ___ Agree
    ___ Strongly Agree

12. How often do you feel uncomfortable about expressing your political views with your coworkers?

    ___ Hardly ever
    ___ Sometimes
    ___ Often
    ___ Almost always

13. Did you vote in the 2008 presidential election?

    ___ Yes ___ No

14. Following my career in the military, I would consider the following:

A. Becoming more involved in politics and campaigns

    ___ Strongly Disagree
    ___ Disagree
    ___ Neutral
    ___ Agree
    ___ Strongly Agree

B. Running for political office

    ___ Strongly Disagree
    ___ Disagree

___ Neutral
___ Agree
___ Strongly Agree

C. Joining or working for an interest group

___ Strongly Disagree
___ Disagree
___ Neutral
___ Agree
___ Strongly Agree

15. The following questions all relate to permissible political activities by uniformed members of the military as outlined in Department of Defense Directive 1344.10. As a private individual (not representing the U.S. Army), have you ever done any of the following during an election or campaign?

A. Given money to an individual candidate running for public office or to a political party?

___ Yes ___ No

B. Worn a campaign button or put a campaign sticker on your car?

___ Yes ___ No

C. Encouraged other members in the military to vote?

___ Yes ___ No

D. Joined a partisan or nonpartisan political club and attend its meetings when not in uniform?

___ Yes ___ No

E. Expressed your personal opinion on political candidates or issues to others?

___ Yes ___ No

F. Attended a partisan or nonpartisan political fundraiser, meeting, rally, debate, convention, or any other political activity as a non-uniformed spectator?

___ Yes ___ No

16. Since you have been in the Army, have other officers ever encouraged you to vote one way or another?

___ Yes ___ No

Civil-Military Relations

17. This question asks for your opinion on a number of statements concerning the military's role in civilian society.

A. Members of the active-duty military should not publicly criticize senior members of the civilian branch of the government.

___ Strongly Disagree
___ Disagree
___ Neutral
___ Agree
___ Strongly Agree

B. Members of the active-duty military should be allowed to publicly express their political views just like any other citizen.

___ Strongly Disagree
___ Disagree
___ Neutral
___ Agree
___ Strongly Agree

C. Members of the active-duty military should vote.

___ Strongly Disagree
___ Disagree
___ Neutral
___ Agree
___ Strongly Agree

18. This question asks for your opinion on the role of retired officers' roles in civilian society.

A. Retired officers should not publicly criticize senior members of the civilian branch of the government.

    ___ Strongly Disagree
    ___ Disagree
    ___ Neutral
    ___ Agree
    ___ Strongly Agree

B. Retired officers should be allowed to publicly express their political views just like any other citizen.

    ___ Strongly Disagree
    ___ Disagree
    ___ Neutral
    ___ Agree
    ___ Strongly Agree

C. It is proper for retired generals to publicly express their political views.

    ___ Strongly Disagree
    ___ Disagree
    ___ Neutral
    ___ Agree
    ___ Strongly Agree

19. This question asks you to specify the proper role of the senior military leadership in decisions to commit U.S. Armed Forces abroad.

The following are typical elements of the decisions the President must make. Please specify the proper role of the military for each element.

A. Deciding whether to intervene

___ Be neutral ___ Advise ___ Advocate ___ Insist ___ No opinion

B. Setting rules of engagement

___ Be neutral ___ Advise ___ Advocate ___ Insist ___ No opinion

C. Ensuring that clear political and military goals exist

___ Be neutral ___ Advise ___ Advocate ___ Insist ___ No opinion

D. Deciding what the goals or policy should be

___ Be neutral ___ Advise ___ Advocate ___ Insist ___ No opinion

E. Generating public support for the intervention

___ Be neutral ___ Advise ___ Advocate ___ Insist ___ No opinion

F. Developing an exit strategy

___ Be neutral ___ Advise ___ Advocate ___ Insist ___ No opinion

G. Deciding what kinds of military units (air vs. naval, heavy vs. light) will be used to accomplish all tasks

___ Be neutral ___ Advise ___ Advocate ___ Insist ___ No opinion

20. This question asks for your opinion on a number of statements concerning relations between the military and senior civilian leaders.

A. When civilians tell the military what to do, domestic partisan politics rather than national security requirements are often the primary motivation.

___ Strongly Disagree
___ Disagree
___ Neutral
___ Agree
___ Strongly Agree

B. In wartime, civilian government leaders should let the military take over running the war.

___ Strongly Disagree
___ Disagree
___ Neutral
___ Agree
___ Strongly Agree

C. To be respected as Commander in Chief, the President should have served in uniform.

___ Strongly Disagree
___ Disagree
___ Neutral
___ Agree
___ Strongly Agree

Your Personal Beliefs

21. Generally speaking, do you usually think of yourself as a strong Democrat, a not very strong Democrat, an Independent who leans Democrat, an Independent, an Independent who leans Republican, a not very strong Republican, a strong Republican, or what?

___ Strong Democrat
___ Not very strong Democrat
___ Independent who leans Democrat
___ Independent
___ Independent who leans Republican
___ Not very strong Republican
___ Strong Republican

___ Other

22. Generally speaking, would you call your parents (or guardians) Democrats, Republicans, Independents, or what?

    ___ Democrats
    ___ Independents
    ___ Split Affiliations (one is a Democrat, and one is a Republican, etc.)
    ___ Republicans
    ___ Other

23. Generally speaking, how would you describe the officer corps in general?

    ___ Most are Democrats
    ___ Some are Democrats, and some are Republicans
    ___ Most are Republicans
    ___ Not sure

24. Here is a 7-point scale on which the political views that people might hold are arranged from very liberal to very conservative. Where would you place yourself on this scale?

    ___ Very liberal
    ___ Liberal
    ___ Somewhat liberal
    ___ Moderate
    ___ Somewhat conservative
    ___ Conservative
    ___ Very conservative

25. Where would you place the officer corps in general on this scale?

    ___ Very liberal
    ___ Liberal
    ___ Somewhat liberal
    ___ Moderate

___ Somewhat conservative
___ Conservative
___ Very conservative

26. Since joining the Army, would you say your political views have changed?

___ Yes, I am more liberal
___ Yes, I am less conservative
___ Yes, I am more moderate
___ Yes, I am less liberal
___ Yes, I am more conservative
___ No, my political views have not changed much

27. Since joining the Army, has your party affiliation changed?

___ Yes, I feel more attached to the Democratic Party
___ Yes, I feel less attached to the Democratic Party
___ Yes, I feel less attached to either party
___ Yes, I feel less attached to the Republican Party
___ Yes, I feel more attached to the Republican Party
___ No, my party affiliation has not changed much

Your Background

28. Are you male or female? ___ Male ___ Female

29. What is your age?

___ 20–24 years old
___ 25–29 years old
___ 30–34 years old
___ 35–39 years old
___ 40–44 years old
___ 45–49 years old
___ 50 or older

30. What is the highest level of education you obtained?

___ Some college

___ College graduate
___ Some graduate work
___ Graduate degree

31. Where did you live most of the time growing up?

___ Northeast
___ Mountain states
___ Pacific coast
___ Mid-Atlantic
___ Midwest
___ Southwest
___ Moved around a lot
___ Other

32. What is your religious affiliation? _____

33. Would you call yourself Evangelical or Born Again?

___ Yes ___ No ___ Not sure

34. What is your racial or ethnic identity?

___ White or Caucasian, not Hispanic
___ Hispanic
___ Asian American
___ Black or African American, not Hispanic
___ American Indian, Eskimo, or Aleut
___ Native Hawaiian or Pacific Islander
___ Other

Thank you for taking the time to complete this survey.

Appendix C

Politics, the Military, and Social Media Research Survey (2015–2016)

This survey is part of an approved research fellowship being conducted at the National War College. It seeks to examine the nature and extent of political expression on social media and will help researchers better understand the state of civil-military relations today. Throughout the survey, your anonymity will be preserved, and identification of respondents will not be recorded. This survey should take no more than 5–10 minutes to complete. It is only with the generous help of people like you that such research on the professional military ethic can be successful.

   Thank you for your time and consideration.

Informed Consent

By completing this survey, I consent to participate in this study. I understand my participation is strictly voluntary.

Your Social Media Use

1. Which of the following social media networking sites do you currently have an account with? (Please check all that apply)

   ___ Facebook
   ___ Twitter
   ___ LinkedIn
   ___ Google+
   ___ YouTube
   ___ I do not have any social media networking accounts
   (If you have no social media networking accounts, skip to question 22.)

2. Which social media networking sites did you get news about government and politics from in the past week? (Please check all that apply. If you are unsure, leave it unchecked.)

___ Facebook
___ Twitter
___ LinkedIn
___ Google+
___ YouTube

3. How often do you access your social media networking accounts?

___ Several times a day
___ About once a day
___ A few days a week
___ Every few weeks
___ Less often
___ I'm not sure

4. About how many friends do you currently have on social media networking websites?

Please specify the approximate number _____

5. Approximately what percentage of your friends on social media networking sites are affiliated with the military, either active duty or retired?

___ Less than 20%
___ 20 – 40%
___ 40 – 60%
___ 60 – 80%
___ More than 80%
___ I'm not sure

Social Media Observations

6. To what extent do you agree or disagree with this statement: "My military friends (both active duty and retired) often talk about politics on social media networking sites."

    ___ Strongly Agree
    ___ Agree
    ___ Neutral
    ___ Disagree
    ___ Strongly Disagree

7. Generally speaking, who is more active in discussing politics on social media networking sites, your military friends or nonmilitary friends?

    ___ My nonmilitary friends talk about politics more
    ___ My nonmilitary friends talk about politics as much as my military friends do
    ___ My military friends talk about politics more
    ___ I'm not sure

8. Generally speaking, who is more active in discussing politics on social media networking sites, your active-duty military friends or retired military friends?

    ___ My active-duty friends talk about politics more
    ___ My active-duty friends talk about politics as much as my retired friends do
    ___ My retired friends talk about politics more
    ___ I'm not sure

9. Generally speaking, among all of your military friends, who is more active in discussing politics on social media networking sites, your officer friends or enlisted friends?

    ___ My officer friends talk about politics more
    ___ My officer friends talk about politics as much as my enlisted friends do
    ___ My enlisted friends talk about politics more

___ I'm not sure

10. Do your military friends ever do the following on social media networking sites?

1. Repost or share links to political stories

___ Yes ___ No ___ I'm not sure

2. Post links to political stories or articles for others to read

___ Yes ___ No ___ I'm not sure

3. "Like" or promote material related to political issues that others have posted

___ Yes ___ No ___ I'm not sure

4. Post their own thoughts/comments on political issues

___ Yes ___ No ___ I'm not sure

5. "Friend" or follow political figures

___ Yes ___ No ___ I'm not sure

6. Encourage others to vote

___ Yes ___ No ___ I'm not sure

7. Encourage others to take action on political issues

___ Yes ___ No ___ I'm not sure

11. Of the following list of topics related to government and politics, please check which ones your friends often discuss on social media networking sites (please check all that apply).

1. The 2016 election

___ Your nonmilitary friends
___ Your active-duty military friends
___ Your retired military friends

2. The war in Afghanistan

___ Your nonmilitary friends
___ Your active-duty military friends
___ Your retired military friends

3. Russian President Vladimir Putin

___ Your nonmilitary friends
___ Your active-duty military friends
___ Your retired military friends

4. ISIS

___ Your nonmilitary friends
___ Your active-duty military friends
___ Your retired military friends

5. President Obama

___ Your nonmilitary friends
___ Your active-duty military friends
___ Your retired military friends

6. Congress

___ Your nonmilitary friends
___ Your active-duty military friends
___ Your retired military friends

7. The economy

___ Your nonmilitary friends
___ Your active-duty military friends

___ Your retired military friends

8. Immigration

    ___ Your nonmilitary friends
    ___ Your active-duty military friends
    ___ Your retired military friends

9. Gun control

    ___ Your nonmilitary friends
    ___ Your active-duty military friends
    ___ Your retired military friends

10. Health care

    ___ Your nonmilitary friends
    ___ Your active-duty military friends
    ___ Your retired military friends

11. LGBT issues

    ___ Your nonmilitary friends
    ___ Your active-duty military friends
    ___ Your retired military friends

12. Women in combat

    ___ Your nonmilitary friends
    ___ Your active-duty military friends
    ___ Your retired military friends

13. The federal budget and sequestration

    ___ Your nonmilitary friends
    ___ Your active-duty military friends
    ___ Your retired military friends

14. Veterans' affairs

___ Your nonmilitary friends
___ Your active-duty military friends
___ Your retired military friends

12. Thinking of that same list of topics related to government, which are the top 3 most commented upon topics by your friends? (Check 3 for each grouping of friends)

Your nonmilitary friends
___ 1. The 2016 election
___ 2. The war in Afghanistan
___ 3. Russian President Vladimir Putin
___ 4. ISIS
___ 5. President Obama
___ 6. Congress
___ 7. The economy
___ 8. Immigration
___ 9. Gun control
___ 10. Health care
___ 11. LGBT issues
___ 12. Women in combat
___ 13. The federal budget and sequestration
___ 14. Veterans' affairs

Your active-duty military friends
___ 1. The 2016 election
___ 2. The war in Afghanistan
___ 3. Russian President Vladimir Putin
___ 4. ISIS
___ 5. President Obama
___ 6. Congress
___ 7. The economy
___ 8. Immigration
___ 9. Gun control
___ 10. Health care
___ 11. LGBT issues
___ 12. Women in combat
___ 13. The federal budget and sequestration

___ 14. Veterans' affairs

Your retired military friends
___ 1. The 2016 election
___ 2. The war in Afghanistan
___ 3. Russian President Vladimir Putin
___ 4. ISIS
___ 5. President Obama
___ 6. Congress
___ 7. The economy
___ 8. Immigration
___ 9. Gun control
___ 10. Health care
___ 11. LGBT issues
___ 12. Women in combat
___ 13. The federal budget and sequestration
___ 14. Veterans' affairs

13. Among your military friends, how many have photos of themselves in uniform on their social media networking sites?

___ All have photos of themselves in uniform
___ Most have photos of themselves in uniform
___ Some have photos of themselves in uniform
___ Most do not have photos of themselves in uniform
___ None have photos of themselves in uniform
___ I'm not sure

14. Thinking about the opinions your military friends post about government and politics on social media networking sites, how often are they in line with your own views?

___ Almost Always
___ Often
___ Sometimes
___ Hardly Ever
___ I'm Not Sure

15. Have you ever hidden, blocked, unfriended, or stopped following anyone in the following groups on a social media networking site because you did not agree with something they posted about government and politics?

      Your nonmilitary friends: ___ Yes ___ No ___ I'm not sure
      Your active-duty military friends: ___ Yes ___ No ___ I'm not sure
      Your retired military friends: ___ Yes ___ No ___ I'm not sure

16. Have you ever hidden, blocked, unfriended, or stopped following anyone in the following groups on a social media networking site for nonpolitical reasons?

      Your nonmilitary friends: ___ Yes ___ No ___ I'm not sure
      Your active-duty military friends: ___ Yes ___ No ___ I'm not sure
      Your retired military friends: ___ Yes ___ No ___ I'm not sure

17. How often do you feel uncomfortable by the political content your active-duty military friends discuss on social media networking sites?

      ___ Almost always
      ___ Often
      ___ Sometimes
      ___ Hardly Ever
      ___ I'm not sure

18. Have you ever observed an active-duty military friend post a disclaimer on a social media networking site that his/her political views are those of the individual only and not those of the Department of Defense?

      ___ Yes ___ No ___ I'm not sure

19. Have you ever observed the following friends use or share insulting, rude, or disdainful comments directed against _____ on a social media networking site?

Specific Elected Officials

Your nonmilitary friends: ___ Yes ___ No ___ I'm not sure
Your active-duty military friends: ___ Yes ___ No ___ I'm not sure
Your retired military friends: ___ Yes ___ No ___ I'm not sure

20. Have you ever observed the following friends use or share insulting, rude, or disdainful comments directed against _____ on a social media networking site?

Politicians Running for Office

Your nonmilitary friends: ___ Yes ___ No ___ I'm not sure
Your active-duty military friends: ___ Yes ___ No ___ I'm not sure
Your retired military friends: ___ Yes ___ No ___ I'm not sure

21. Have you ever observed the following friends use or share insulting, rude, or disdainful comments directed against _____ on a social media networking site?

President of the United States

Your nonmilitary friends: ___ Yes ___ No ___ I'm not sure
Your active-duty military friends: ___ Yes ___ No ___ I'm not sure
Your retired military friends: ___ Yes ___ No ___ I'm not sure

22. Below are a number of terms used to describe the overall tone of political discussions on social media networking sites. Please check which terms most accurately represent the tone of political discussions among your different groups of friends (please check all that apply).

Your nonmilitary friends
___ 1. Restrained
___ 2. Active
___ 3. One-sided
___ 4. Diverse
___ 5. Agreeable

___ 6. Confrontational
___ 7. Informative
___ 8. Combative
___ 9. Balanced
___ 10. Polarizing
___ 11. Nonpartisan
___ 12. Partisan

Your active-duty military friends
___ 1. Restrained
___ 2. Active
___ 3. One-sided
___ 4. Diverse
___ 5. Agreeable
___ 6. Confrontational
___ 7. Informative
___ 8. Combative
___ 9. Balanced
___ 10. Polarizing
___ 11. Nonpartisan
___ 12. Partisan

Your retired military friends
___ 1. Restrained
___ 2. Active
___ 3. One-sided
___ 4. Diverse
___ 5. Agreeable
___ 6. Confrontational
___ 7. Informative
___ 8. Combative
___ 9. Balanced
___ 10. Polarizing
___ 11. Nonpartisan
___ 12. Partisan

Your Beliefs and Background

23. How much do you enjoy talking about government and politics with friends and family?

      ___ A lot ___ Some ___ Not much ___ Not at all

24. Generally speaking, do you usually think of yourself as a strong Democrat, a not very strong Democrat, an Independent who leans Democrat, an Independent, an Independent who leans Republican, a not very strong Republican, a strong Republican, or other?

     ___ Strong Democrat
     ___ Not very strong Democrat
     ___ Independent who leans Democrat
     ___ Independent
     ___ Independent who leans Republican
     ___ Not very strong Republican
     ___ Strong Republican
     ___ Other (please specify) _____

25. Here is a 7-point scale on which the political views that people might hold are arranged from very liberal to very conservative. Where would you place yourself on this scale?

     ___ Very liberal
     ___ Liberal
     ___ Somewhat liberal
     ___ Moderate
     ___ Somewhat conservative
     ___ Conservative
     ___ Very conservative

Demographics

26. What is your age group?

     ___ 18–24 years old
     ___ 25–29 years old
     ___ 30–34 years old

___ 35–39 years old
___ 40–44 years old
___ 45–49 years old
___ 50–54 years old
___ 55 or older

27. What is your branch of service?

___ U.S. Air Force
___ U.S. Army
___ U.S. Coast Guard
___ U.S. Marine Corps
___ U.S. Navy
___ Other (please specify) _____

28. What is your current status in the military?

___ Active Duty
___ Reserve
___ National Guard
___ Pre-commissioning
___ Other (please specify) _____

29. What is your current grade?

___ Cadet / Midshipman
___ O-1 / O-2
___ O-3
___ O-4
___ O-5
___ O-6
___ Other (please specify) _____

Thank you for participating in this study.

Appendix D

National Defense University Civil-Military Relations Survey (2017–2020)

This survey is part of approved research being conducted at the National Defense University and will help researchers better understand the state of civil-military relations today.

Throughout the survey, your anonymity will be preserved, and identification of respondents will not be recorded. This survey should take no more than 5–10 minutes to complete. It is only with the generous help of people like you that such research on the professional military ethic can be successful. Thank you for your time and consideration.

Informed Consent

By completing this survey, I consent to participate in this study. I understand my participation is strictly voluntary.

Military Service

1. What is your branch of service?

      ___ U.S. Air Force
      ___ U.S. Army
      ___ U.S. Coast Guard
      ___ U.S. Marine Corps
      ___ U.S. Navy
      ___ Other (please specify) _____

2. What is your current status in the military?

      ___ Active Duty
      ___ Reserve
      ___ National Guard

___ Pre-commissioning
___ Other (please specify) _____

3. What is your current grade?

    ___ Cadet/Midshipman
    ___ O-1/O-2
    ___ O-3
    ___ O-4
    ___ O-5
    ___ O-6

4. What is/was your source of commissioning?

    ___ Service Academy
    ___ ROTC
    ___ OCS/OTS
    ___ Direct
    ___ Other

5. Have you ever deployed to a combat zone?

    ___ No
    ___ Yes (please specify the number of total months you spent deployed in a combat zone in your career) ____

6. Has a member of your immediate family (parent, spouse, sibling, child) served or do they currently serve in the military?

    ___ Yes ___ No

Civic Participation

7. Did you vote in the 2016 election?

    ___ Yes ___ No

8. Do you agree or disagree with this statement: "Politics is often talked about at work."

___ Strongly Disagree
___ Disagree
___ Neutral
___ Agree
___ Strongly Agree

9. How often do you feel uncomfortable about expressing your political opinions at work?

___ Hardly ever ___ Sometimes ___ Often ___ Almost always

10. How often do you feel uncomfortable about expressing your political opinions on social media sites like Facebook or Twitter?

___ Hardly ever
___ Sometimes
___ Often
___ Almost always
___ I do not use social media

11. If you indicated you use social media in Question 10, to what extent do you agree or disagree with this statement: "My active-duty military friends often talk about politics on social media sites."

___ Strongly Disagree
___ Disagree
___ Neutral
___ Agree
___ Strongly Agree
___ Not applicable

12. If you indicated you use social media in Question 10, have you ever observed your active-duty friends use or share insulting, rude, or disdainful comments directed against the President of the United States or other elected leaders on social media networking sites?

___ Yes ___ No ___ Not applicable

Civil-Military Relations

13. This question asks for your opinion on a number of statements concerning the military's role in society.

a. Members of the active-duty military should not publicly criticize senior members of the civilian branch of the government.

___ Strongly Disagree
___ Disagree
___ Neutral
___ Agree
___ Strongly Agree

b. Members of the active-duty military should be allowed to publicly express their political views just like any other citizen.

___ Strongly Disagree
___ Disagree
___ Neutral
___ Agree
___ Strongly Agree

c. Members of the military should vote.

___ Strongly Disagree
___ Disagree
___ Neutral
___ Agree
___ Strongly Agree

14. This question asks for your opinion on the role of retired officers in civilian society.

a. Retired officers should not publicly criticize senior members of the civilian branch of government.

___ Strongly Disagree
___ Disagree
___ Neutral
___ Agree
___ Strongly Agree

b. Retired officers should be allowed to publicly express their political views just like any other citizen.

___ Strongly Disagree
___ Disagree
___ Neutral
___ Agree
___ Strongly Agree

c. It is appropriate for retired generals/admirals to publicly express their political views.

___ Strongly Disagree
___ Disagree
___ Neutral
___ Agree
___ Strongly Agree

d. More retired four-star generals/admirals should be encouraged to serve as political appointees.

___ Strongly Disagree
___ Disagree
___ Neutral
___ Agree
___ Strongly Agree

15. This question asks you to specify the proper role of senior military leadership in decisions to commit U.S. armed forces abroad. The following are typical elements of the decisions the President must make. Please specify the proper role of the military for each element.

a. Deciding whether to intervene

___ Be neutral ___ Advise ___ Advocate ___ Insist ___ No opinion

b. Setting rules of engagement

___ Be neutral ___ Advise ___ Advocate ___ Insist ___ No opinion

c. Ensuring that clear political and military goals exist

___ Be neutral ___ Advise ___ Advocate ___ Insist ___ No opinion

d. Deciding what the goals or policy should be

___ Be neutral ___ Advise ___ Advocate ___ Insist ___ No opinion

e. Generating public support for the intervention

___ Be neutral ___ Advise ___ Advocate ___ Insist ___ No opinion

f. Developing an exit strategy

___ Be neutral ___ Advise ___ Advocate ___ Insist ___ No opinion

g. Deciding what kinds of military units (air vs. naval, heavy vs. light) will be used to accomplish all tasks

___ Be neutral ___ Advise ___ Advocate ___ Insist ___ No opinion

16. This question asks for your opinion on a number of statements concerning relations between the military and senior civilian leaders.

a. When civilians tell the military what to do, domestic partisan politics rather than national security requirements are often the primary motivation.

___ Strongly Disagree
___ Disagree
___ Neutral

___ Agree
___ Strongly Agree

b. In wartime, civilian government leaders should let the military take over running the war.

___ Strongly Disagree
___ Disagree
___ Neutral
___ Agree
___ Strongly Agree

c. To be respected as Commander in Chief, the President should have served in uniform.

___ Strongly Disagree
___ Disagree
___ Neutral
___ Agree
___ Strongly Agree

17. This question asks for your opinion on a number of statements concerning relations between the military and civil society.

a. The American public understands the sacrifices members of the military make today.

___ Strongly Disagree
___ Disagree
___ Neutral
___ Agree
___ Strongly Agree

b. The American public is grateful for the sacrifices members of the military make today.

___ Strongly Disagree
___ Disagree
___ Neutral

___ Agree
___ Strongly Agree

c. It is good for the U.S. military to look like and reflect society.

    ___ Strongly Disagree
    ___ Disagree
    ___ Neutral
    ___ Agree
    ___ Strongly Agree

d. People who haven't served in the military generally shouldn't question or criticize the military.

    ___ Strongly Disagree
    ___ Disagree
    ___ Neutral
    ___ Agree
    ___ Strongly Agree

e. Military culture is generally superior to the rest of society today.

    ___ Strongly Disagree
    ___ Disagree
    ___ Neutral
    ___ Agree
    ___ Strongly Agree

f. I am proud of my military service.

    ___ Strongly Disagree
    ___ Disagree
    ___ Neutral
    ___ Agree
    ___ Strongly Agree

h. I would encourage a young person close to me to join the military today.

    ___ Strongly Disagree

___ Disagree
___ Neutral
___ Agree
___ Strongly Agree

Personal Beliefs

18. Here is a 7-point scale on which the political views that people might hold are arranged from very liberal to very conservative. Where would you place yourself on this scale?

    ___ Very liberal
    ___ Liberal
    ___ Somewhat liberal
    ___ Moderate
    ___ Somewhat conservative
    ___ Conservative
    ___ Very conservative

19. Where would you place the officer corps on this scale?

    ___ Very liberal
    ___ Liberal
    ___ Somewhat liberal
    ___ Moderate
    ___ Somewhat conservative
    ___ Conservative
    ___ Very conservative

20. Since joining the military, have your political views changed?

    ___ I am more liberal
    ___ I am less conservative
    ___ I am more moderate
    ___ I am less liberal
    ___ I am more conservative
    ___ My political views have not changed much at all

21. Generally speaking, how do you usually think of yourself politically?

___ Strong Democrat
___ Not very strong Democrat
___ Independent who leans Democrat
___ Independent
___ Independent who leans Republican
___ Not very strong Republican
___ Strong Republican
___ Other

22. Generally speaking, how would you describe your parents' political leanings?

___ Democrats
___ Independents
___ Split Affiliations (they vote for different parties)
___ Republicans
___ Other

23. Generally speaking, how would you describe the officer corps as a whole?

___ Most are Democrats
___ Most are Republicans
___ It's a mix of Democrats and Republicans
___ Not sure

24. Since joining the military, has your party affiliation changed?

___ I feel more attached to the Democratic Party
___ I feel less attached to the Democratic Party
___ I feel less attached to either party
___ I feel less attached to the Republican Party
___ I feel more attached to the Republican Party
___ My party affiliation has not changed much at all

Background

25. What is your age group?

___ 18–24 years old
___ 25–29 years old
___ 30–34 years old
___ 35–39 years old
___ 40–44 years old
___ 45–49 years old
___ 50–54 years old
___ 55 or older

26. Are you male or female? ___ Male ___ Female

27. What best describes your racial or ethnic identity?

___ White or Caucasian
___ Hispanic
___ Black or African American
___ American Indian or Eskimo
___ Native Hawaiian or Pacific Islander
___ Asian American
___ Mixed race
___ Other

28. Have you obtained a graduate degree from a civilian institution?

___ Yes ___ No

Thank you for participating in this study.

Bibliography

Abramowitz, Alan I., and Steven W. Webster. "Negative Partisanship: Why Americans Dislike Parties But Behave Like Rabid Partisans." *Political Psychology* 39 (2018): 119–135.

————, and Steven Webster. "The Rise of Negative Partisanship and the Nationalization of U.S. Elections in the 21st Century." *Electoral Studies* 41 (2016): 12–22.

The American Presidency Project. "Voter Turnout in Presidential Elections: 1828–2016." https://www.presidency.ucsb.edu/statistics/data/voter-turnout-in-presidential-elections.

Associated Press. "The 1992 Campaign; A Letter by Clinton on His Draft Deferment: 'A War I Opposed and Despised,'" *New York Times*, February 13, 1992.

Babcock-Lumish, Brian. "Uninformed, not Uniformed? The Apolitical Myth." *Military Review*, September-October 2013. https://www.armyupress.army.mil/Portals/7/military-review/Archives/English/MilitaryReview_20131031_art009.pdf.

Bacevich, Andrew J. "Tradition Abandoned: America's Military in a New Era." *The National Interest* 48 (Summer 1997): 16–25.

————, and Richard H. Kohn, "Grand Army of the Republicans? Has the U.S. Military Become a Partisan Force?" *New Republic*, December 8, 1997.

Beehner, Lionel, Risa Brooks, and Daniel Maurer. *Reconsidering American Civil-Military Relations: The Military, Society, Politics, and Modern War.* New York, NY: Oxford University Press, 2020.

Barno, David, and Nora Bensahel. "How to Get Generals Out of Politics." *War on the Rocks*, September 27, 2016. https://warontherocks.com/2016/09/how-to-get-generals-out-of-politics/.

———. "The Increasingly Dangerous Politicization of the U.S. Military." *War on the Rocks*, June 28, 2019. https://warontherocks.com/2019/06/the-increasingly-dangerous-politicization-of-the-u-s-military/.

———. "Why No General Should Serve as White House Chief of Staff." *War on the Rocks*, September 12, 2017. https://warontherocks.com/2017/09/why-no-general-should-serve-as-white-house-chief-of-staff/.

Bartels, Larry. "Beyond the Running Tally: Partisan Bias in Political Perceptions." *Political Behavior* 24, no. 2 (2002): 117–150.

Bender, Bryan. "'Disturbing and Reckless': Retired Brass Spread Election Lie in Attack on Biden, Democrats." *Politico*, May 11, 2021. https://www.politico.com/news/2021/05/11/retired-brass-biden-election-487374.

Berube, Claude. "Presidential Military Service: The Service Gap and the Validation Surge." *War on the Rocks*, January 23, 2020. https://warontherocks.com/2020/01/presidential-military-service-the-service-gap-and-the-validation-surge/.

Betros, Lance. "Political Partisanship and the Military Ethic in America." *Armed Forces & Society* 27, no. 4 (2001): 501–523.

Binkley, John C. "Revisiting the 2006 Revolt of the Generals." *Parameters* 50, no.1 (Spring 2020): 23–37.

Brady, Henry, Lee Rainie, Kay Lehman Schlozman, Aaron Smith, and Sidney Verba. "Social Media and Political Engagement." *Pew Research Center*, October 19, 2012. https://www.pewresearch.org/internet/2012/10/19/social-media-and-political-engagement/.

Brenan, Megan. "Amid Pandemic, Confidence in Key U.S. Institutions Surges." *Pew Research Center*, August 12, 2020. https://news.gallup.com/poll/317135/amid-pandemic-confidence-key-institutions-surges.aspx.

Brooks, Risa A. "Paradoxes of Professionalism: Rethinking Civil-Military Relations in the United States," *International Security* 44, no. 4 (Spring 2020): 7–44.

———. "The Real Threat to Civilian Control of the Military: The Officer Corps Can No Longer Simply Ignore Politics." *Foreign Affairs*, January

18, 2021, https://www.foreignaffairs.com/articles/united-states/2021
-01-18/real-threat-civilian-control-military.

———. "What Can Military and Civilian Leaders Do to Prevent the
Military's Politicization." *War on the Rocks*, April 27, 2020, https://
warontherocks.com/2020/04/what-can-military-and-civilian-leaders-
do-to-prevent-the-militarys-politicization/.

———, Michael Robinson, and Heidi Urben, "What Makes a Military
Professional? Evaluating Norm Socialization in West Point Cadets,"
Armed Forces and Society, June 20, 2021.

Brooks, Rosa. *How Everything Became War and the Military Became
Everything: Tales from the Pentagon*. New York: Simon & Schuster,
2017.

Bucella, Matthew. "No, Retired Military Officers Don't Check Their
Free Speech at the Door." *The Federalist*, October 29, 2019.
https://thefederalist.com/2019/10/29/no-retired-military-officers-
dont-check-their-free-speech-at-the-door/

Burden, Barry C. "Voter Turnout and the National Election Studies." *Political Analysis* 8, no. 4: (July 2000): 389–398.

Bryant, Susan, and Heidi A. Urben. "Reconnecting Athens and Sparta:
A Review of OPMS XXI at 20 Years." *Association of the U.S. Army
Institute of Land Warfare* no. 114 (October 2017). https://www.ausa.
org/sites/default/files/publications/LWP-114-Reconnecting-Athens-
and-Sparta-A-Review-of-OPMS-XXI-at-20-Years.pdf.

Campbell, Angus, Philip E. Converse, Warren E. Miller, and Donald E.
Stokes. *The American Voter*. Chicago, IL: University of Chicago Press,
1980.

Canter, Sam. "Generals Are People Too: And Their Involvement in
Politics Is Part of the American Tradition." *Real Clear Defense*,
July 1, 2020. https://www.realcleardefense.com/articles/2020/07/01
/generals_are_people_too__and_their_involvement_in_politics_is_
part_of_the_american_tradition_115429.html.

Carter, Philip, and Loren DeJonge Schulman. "Trump is Surrounding
Himself with Generals. That's Dangerous." *Washington Post*,
November 30, 2016. https://www.washingtonpost.com/opinions/

trump-is-surrounding-himself-with-generals-thats-dangerous/2016/11/30/e6a0a972-b190-11e6-840f-e3ebab6bcdd3_story.html.

Cavanaugh, M.L. "I Fight for Your Right to Vote. But I Won't Do It Myself." *New York Times*, October 19, 2016. https://www.nytimes.com/2016/10/19/opinion/i-fight-for-your-right-to-vote-but-i-wont-do-it-myself.html.

Chadwick, Alex. "Gen. Petraeus Addresses his 'Legacy.'" *NPR*, March 19, 2008. https://www.npr.org/templates/story/story.php?storyId=88584830.

Chesney, Robert. "Trump Will Need a New Law to Put Mattis Back in the Pentagon." *War on the Rocks*, November 22, 2016. https://warontherocks.com/2016/11/trump-will-need-a-new-law-to-put-mattis-back-in-the-pentagon/.

Cloud, David S., Eric Schmitt, and Thom Shanker. "Rumsfeld Faces Growing Revolt by Retired Generals." *New York Times*, April 13, 2006. https://www.nytimes.com/2006/04/13/washington/rumsfeld-faces-growing-revolt-by-retired-generals.html.

Cohen, Eliot A. *Supreme Command: Soldiers, Statesmen, and Leadership in Wartime.* New York: Simon and Schuster, 2002.

Collins, Joseph J. "Combining the Roles of Actor and Observer: Comments on Russell Burgos's 'An N of 1.'" *Perspectives on Politics* 2, no. 3 (2004): 561–562.

Contempt Toward Officials, U.S. Code 10 (2006), § 888, Article 88.

Converse, Philip E. "The Nature of Belief Systems in Mass Publics." In *Ideology and Discontent*, edited by David E. Apter. New York: Free Press, 1964.

Conway, Madeline. "9 Unforgettable Quotes by James Mattis." *Politico*, December 1, 2016. https://www.politico.com/blogs/donald-trump-administration/2016/12/james-mattis-quotes-232097.

Cook, Martin L. "Revolt of the Generals: A Case Study in Professional Ethics." *Parameters* (Spring 2008): 4–15.

Corasaniti, Nick Annie Karni, and Isabella Grullón Paz. "'There's Nothing Left': Why Thousands of Republicans Are Leaving the Party." *New*

York Times, February 10, 2021. https://www.nytimes.com/2021/02/10
/us/politics/republicans-leaving-party.html.

Corbett, Steve, and Michael J. Davidson. "The Role of the Military in
Presidential Politics." *Parameters* 39, no. 4 (Winter 2009/2010): 69–70.

Cronk, Terri Moon. "Service Members, Civilians Bound By DOD Rules
During Election Campaigns." *DOD News*, June 4, 2020. https://www.
defense.gov/Explore/News/Article/Article/2208332/service-members-
civilians-bound-by-dod-rules-during-election-campaigns/.

Davidson, Michael J. "Contemptuous Speech Against the President." *The
Army Lawyer* (July 1999): 1–2.

Dempsey, Jason K. "John Kelly Lent His Military Credibility to Trump.
It's Too Late Now to Stay Neutral." *Washington Post*, September
8, 2020. https://www.washingtonpost.com/outlook/2020/09/08/john-
kelly-trump-military/.

———. *Our Army: Soldiers, Politics, and American Civil-Military Relations.*
Princeton, NJ: Princeton University Press, 2010.

Dempsey, Martin E. "Civil-Military Relations and the Profession of Arms."
Chairman's Corner Blog, June 25, 2012. http://www.dodlive.mil/index.
php/2012/06/civil-military-relations-and-the-profession-of-arms/.

———. "From the Chairman: Putting Our Nation First." *Joint Force Quarterly* 65 (April 2012): 4.

———. "Keep Your Politics Private, My Fellow Generals and Admirals."
Defense One, August 1, 2016. https://www.defenseone.com/ideas/20
16/08/keep-your-politics-private-my-fellow-generals-and-admirals/
130404/.

———. "Military Leaders Do Not Belong at Political Conventions."
Washington Post, July 30, 2016. https://www.washingtonpost.com/
opinions/military-leaders-do-not-belong-at-political-conventions/20
16/07/30/0e06fc16-568b-11e6-b652-315ae5d4d4dd_story.html.

Department of the Air Force. "Air Force Social Media Guidelines." *https://
www.publicaffairs.af.mil/Programs/Air-Force-Social-Media/.*

———. *Public Web and Social Information.* Air Force Instruction 35-107.
Washington, DC: Department of the Air Force, 2017. https://static.

e-publishing.af.mil/production/1/saf_pa/publication/afi35-107/afi35 -107.pdf.

Department of the Army. *Army Command Policy.* Army Regulation 600-20. Washington, DC: 2020. https://armypubs.army.mil/epubs/ DR_pubs/DR_a/ARN30511-AR_600-20-002-WEB-3.pdf.

———. *Army Leadership and the Profession.* Army Doctrine Publication 6-22. Washington, DC: 2019. https://armypubs.army.mil/epubs/DR_ pubs/DR_a/ARN20039-ADP_6-22-001-WEB-0.pdf.

———. "Army Social Media: Policies and Resources." https://www.army. mil/socialmedia/.

———. *Information Management Control Requirements Program.* Army Regulation 25-98. Washington, DC: Department of the Army, 2019. https://armypubs.army.mil/epubs/DR_pubs/DR_a/pdf/web/ARN209 10_R25_98_ADMIN_FINAL.pdf.

Department of Defense. *Department of Defense (DoD Surveys).* DoD Directive 1100.13. Washington, DC: Department of Defense, 2017. https://www.esd.whs.mil/Portals/54/Documents/DD/issuances/dodi/ 110013p.pdf?ver=2019-04-08-125316-290.

———. *Federal Voting Assistance Program 2016 Post-Election Report to Congress.* Washington, DC: U.S. Department of Defense, 2017. https:// www.fvap.gov/uploads/FVAP/Reports/TabB_2017Report_20180301_ v10_Final.pdf

———. *Federal Voting Assistance Program 2012 Post-Election Report to Congress.* Washington, DC: U.S. Department of Defense, 2013. https:// www.fvap.gov/uploads/FVAP/Reports/FVAP2014ReporttoCongress_ 20150724_final.pdf

———. *Federal Voting Assistance Program 2008 Post-Election Report to Congress.* Washington, DC: U.S. Department of Defense, 2011. https:// www.fvap.gov/uploads/FVAP/Reports/18threport.pdf

———. *Federal Voting Assistance Program 2004 Post-Election Report to Congress.* Washington, DC: U.S. Department of Defense, 2005. https:// www.fvap.gov/uploads/FVAP/Reports/17threport.pdf

———. *Federal Voting Assistance Program 2000 Post-Election Report to Congress.* Washington, DC: U.S. Department of Defense, 2001. https://www.fvap.gov/uploads/FVAP/Reports/16threport.pdf

———. *Political Activities by Members of the Armed Forces.* DoD Directive 1344.10. Washington, DC: Department of Defense, 2008. https://www.esd.whs.mil/Portals/54/Documents/DD/issuances/dodd/134410p.pdf.

———. *Prohibition of Lobbying Activity by Former DoD Senior Officials.* Department of Defense Instruction 1000.32. Washington, DC: 2020.

———. *Statistical Report on the Military Retirement System.* Washington, DC: Department of Defense, Office of the Actuary, 2020. https://media.defense.gov/2020/Aug/12/2002475697/-1/-1/0/MRS_STATRPT_2019_FINAL.PDF.

Department of Justice. "*Fact Sheet: Move Act,*", 2010. https://www.justice.gov/opa/pr/fact-sheet-move-act.

Department of the Navy. *Navy Social Media Handbook.* Washington, DC: Navy Office of Information, 2019. https://www.csp.navy.mil/Portals/2/documents/downloads/navy-social-media-handbook-2019.pdf.

Desch, Michael C. "Bush and the Generals." *Foreign Affairs* 86, no. 3 (May/June 2007): 97–108.

DeYoung, Karen. "Nearly 500 Former Senior Military, Civilian Leaders Signal Support for Biden." *Washington Post,* September 24, 2020. https://www.washingtonpost.com/national-security/nearly-500-former-senior-military-civilian-leaders-signal-support-for-biden/2020/09/23/81196288-fdf9-11ea-9ceb-061d646d9c67_story.html.

Dillman, Don. *Mail and Internet Surveys: The Tailored Design Method.* 2nd ed. New York: Wiley & Sons, 2007.

Dimock, Michael, Carroll Doherty, Jocelyn Kiley, and Russ Oates. "Political Polarization in the American Public." *Pew Research Center,* June 12, 2014. https://www.pewresearch.org/politics/2014/06/12/political-polarization-in-the-american-public/.

Dinan, Stephen. "Retired Top Military Brass Push for Romney." *Washington Times,* November 4, 2012. https://www.washingtontimes.

com/blog/inside-politics/2012/nov/4/retired-top-military-brass-push-romney/.

Duggan, Maeve. "The Demographics of Social Media Users." *Pew Research Center,* August 19, 2015. http://www.pewinternet.org/2015/08/19/mobile-messaging-and-social-media-2015/2015-08-19_social-media-update_10/.

Dunford, Joseph F., Jr. "Upholding Our Oath." *Joint Force Quarterly* 82 (July 2016): 2–3.

Dunlap, Charles J., Jr. "It's Wrong to Suppress the Military Vote." *The Hill,* October 20, 2016. https://thehill.com/blogs/pundits-blog/defense/302082-its-wrong-to-suppress-the-military-vote.

———. "Should Retired Servicemembers Be Subject to Military Jurisdiction? A Retiree's Perspective." *Lawfire,* February 16, 2019. https://sites.duke.edu/lawfire/2019/02/16/should-retired-servicemembers-be-subject-to-military-jurisdiction-a-retirees-perspective/.

Exum, Andrew. "The Dangerous Politicization of the U.S. Military." *The Atlantic,* July 24, 2017. https://www.theatlantic.com/politics/archive/2017/07/the-danger-of-turning-the-us-military-into-a-political-actor/534624/.

———. *This Man's Army: A Soldier's Story from the Front Lines of the War on Terrorism.* New York: Gotham Books, 2004.

Fahrenthold, David A., Rosalind S. Helderman, and Tom Hamburger. "In Poll Watcher Affidavits, Trump Campaign Offers No Evidence of Fraud in Detroit Ballot-Counting." *Washington Post,* November 11, 2020. https://www.washingtonpost.com/politics/michigan--poll-watcher-affidavits/2020/11/11/4d073d7a-2447-11eb-a688-5298ad5d580a_story.html.

Feaver, Peter D. *Armed Servants: Agency, Oversight, and Civil-Military Relations.* Cambridge, MA: Harvard University Press, 2003.

———. "The Right to Be Right: Civil-Military Relations and the Iraq Surge Decision." *International Security* 35, no.4 (Spring 2011): 87–125.

———. "We Don't Need Generals to Become Cheerleaders at Political Conventions," *Foreign Policy,* July 29, 2016. https://foreignpolicy.

com/2016/07/29/we-dont-need-generals-to-become-cheerleaders-at-political-conventions/.

———, and Richard H. Kohn. *Soldiers and Civilians: The Civil-Military Gap and American National Security.* Cambridge, MA: MIT Press, 2001.

Fidell, E.R. "Free Speech v. Article 88" *Proceedings* 124, no. 12 (December 1998): 2.

Fink, Jenni. "West Point's Newest Class Has More Minority New Cadets Than Last Year." *Newsweek*, July 1, 2019. https://www.newsweek.com/west-point-class-2023-minority-cadets-1446958.

Finney, Nathan K. "Views on the #Profession from the Professional." *The Strategy Bridge*, January 28, 2015. https://thestrategybridge.org/the-bridge/2016/1/28/views-on-the-profession-from-the-professional.

Fiorina, Morris P. "Has the American Public Polarized?" *Hoover Institution*, September 14, 2016. https://www.hoover.org/sites/default/files/research/docs/fiorina_finalfile_0.pdf.

———. *Retrospective Voting in American National Elections.* New Haven, CT: Yale University Press, 1981.

Fort Hood Independent Review Committee. *Report of the Fort Hood Independent Review Committee.* November 6, 2020, https://www.army.mil/e2/downloads/rv7/forthoodreview/2020-12-03_FHIRC_report_redacted.pdf.

Foster, Gregory. "The Real Problem With 'Politicizing the Military.'" *Defense One*, July 30, 2020. https://www.defenseone.com/ideas/2020/07/politicizing-military/167361/.

Friend, Alice Hunt. "Mattis is Outstanding, So What's the Problem?" *War on the Rocks*, December 7, 2016. https://warontherocks.com/2016/12/mattis-is-outstanding-so-whats-the-problem/.

———. "A Military Litmus Test? Evaluating the Argument that Civilian Defense Leaders Need Military Experience." *Just Security*, August 19, 2020. https://www.justsecurity.org/72084/a-military-litmus-test-evaluating-the-argument-that-civilian-defense-leaders-need-military-experience/.

———. "Military Politicization." *Center for Strategic and International Studies*, May 5, 2017. https://www.csis.org/analysis/military-politicization.

———. "Navigating Politics in 2020 and Beyond" (unpublished manuscript, July 2020).

———, and Jim Golby. "The Military and the Election." In *Thank You for Your Service*, October 30, 2020. Podcast, MP3 audio, 34:35. https://www.csis.org/node/58716.

Garamone, Jim. "Active Duty Personnel Must Remain Apolitical, Nonpartisan, Dunford Says." *DOD News*, August 1, 2016. https://www.defense.gov/Explore/News/Article/Article/881624/active-duty-personnel-must-remain-apolitical-nonpartisan-dunford-says/.

———. "Joint Chiefs Vision Changes Military Education Philosophy." *DOD News*, June 1, 2020. https://www.defense.gov/Explore/News/Article/Article/2204041/joint-chiefs-vision-changes-military-education-philosophy/.

Garrett, R. Sam. *Absentee Voting for Uniformed Services and Overseas Citizens: Roles and Process, In Brief.* CRS Report No. IF11642. Washington, DC: Congressional Research Service, 2020.

Gelpi, Chris. "Retired Generals are People Too!" *Duck of Minerva* (blog). August 9, 2016. https://duckofminerva.com/2016/08/retired-generals-are-people-too.html.

———. "In the Wake of Chaos: Civil-Military Relations Under Secretary Jim Mattis." *War on the Rocks*, February 4, 2019. https://warontherocks.com/2019/02/in-the-wake-of-chaos-civil-military-relations-under-secretary-jim-mattis/.

Golby, Jim, and Peter Feaver. "Former Military Leaders Criticized the Election and the Administration. That Hurts the Military's Reputation." *Washington Post*, May 15, 2021.

———, Heidi Urben, Kyle Dropp, and Peter D. Feaver. "Brass Politics: How Retired Military Officers Are Shaping Elections." *Foreign Affairs*, November 5, 2012. https://www.foreignaffairs.com/articles/2012-11-05/brass-politics.

———, Peter D. Feaver, and Kyle Dropp. "Elite Military Cues and Public Opinion About the Use of Military Force." *Armed Forces & Society* 44, no. 1 (2017): 44-71.

———, Kyle Dropp, and Peter D. Feaver. *Military Campaigns: Veterans' Endorsements and Presidential Elections.* Washington, DC: Center for a New American Security, 2012. https://s3.amazonaws.com/files.cnas. org/documents/CNAS_MilitaryCampaigns_GolbyDroppFeaver.pdf? mtime=20160906081631.

———, Lindsay P. Cohn, and Peter D. Feaver, "Thanks For Your Service: Civilian and Veteran Attitudes After Fifteen Years of War." In *Warriors and Citizens*, edited by Kori Schake and Jim Mattis, [97–141] (Stanford: Hoover Institute Press, 2016).

Gourley, Jim. "What Is the Tipping Point for America's Trust in the Military? And Are We Near It?" *Foreign Policy*, February 14, 2014. https://foreignpolicy.com/2014/02/14/where-is-the-tipping-point-for-americas-trust-in-the-military-and-are-we-near-it/.

Green, Donald P., Bradley Palmquist, and Eric Schickler. *Partisan Hearts and Minds: Political Parties and the Social Identities of Voters.* New Haven, CT: Yale University Press, 2002.

Griffiths, Zachary. "Let's Use Peer Pressure to End Political Endorsements by Retired Generals." *Defense One*, February 18, 2020. https:// www.defenseone.com/ideas/2020/02/use-peer-pressure-stop-retired-generals-making-political-endorsements/163034/.

———, and Olivia Simon. "Not Putting Their Money Where Their Mouth Is: Retired Flag Officers and Presidential Endorsements." *Armed Forces & Society*, December 9, 2019.

Hageman, Theresa Schroeder, Jeremy Teigen, and Rebecca Best. "The Democrats Are Running More Female Veterans for Office Than Ever Before—But Can They Win?" *The Conversation*, November 15, 2019. https://theconversation.com/the-democrats-are-running-more-female-veterans-for-office-than-ever-before-but-can-they-win-125417.

Ham, Carter F. "Get Out and Vote but Obey Your Oath, General Tells Officers." *Military Times*, October 19, 2016. https://www.

armytimes.com/opinion/2016/10/19/get-out-and-vote-but-obey-your-oath-general-tells-officers/.

Hattem, Michael. "Newburgh Conspiracy." *The Digital Encyclopedia of George Washington at the Fred W. Smith National Library for the Study of George Washington at Mount Vernon,* https://www.mountvernon.org/library/digitalhistory/digital-encyclopedia/article/newburgh-conspiracy/.

Headquarters, U.S. Marine Corps. *The Social Corps: U.S.M.C. Social Media Principles.* Washington, DC: Marine Corps Production Directorate, 2017. https://www.marines.mil/Portals/1/Docs/Social-Media-Handbook20170308.pdf.

Hicks, Kathleen, Alice Hunt Friend, Phillip Carter, and Charles J. Dunlap, Jr. "Civil-Military Relations, Part 1: The 2020 Legacy." Produced by Center for Strategic and International Studies. In *Defense 2020,* July 7, 2020. Podcast, MP3 audio, 35:07, https://www.csis.org/podcasts/defense-2020.

Hill, Samantha. "Hatch Act, DOD Regulations Govern Political Activities on Social Media." June 8, 2020. https://www.army.mil/article/236270/hatch_act_dod_regulations_govern_political_activities_on_social_media.

Hohmann, James. "The Kabul Evacuation Illuminated a Dangerous Strain of Thought in the Military About Civilian Control." *Washington Post,* September 1, 2021. https://www.washingtonpost.com/opinions/2021/09/01/stuart-scheller-civilian-control-military-kabul/.

Hoffman, Frank G. "Dereliction of Duty *Redux?* Post-Iraq American Civil-Military Relations." *Orbis* 52, no. 2 (Spring 2008): 217–235.

Holsti, Ole R. "Of Chasms and Convergences: Attitudes and Beliefs of Civilians and Military Elites at the Start of a New Millennium." In *Soldiers and Civilians: The Civil-Military Gap and American National Security,* edited by Peter D. Feaver and Richard H. Kohn. Cambridge, MA: MIT Press, 2001.

———. "Politicization of the United States Military: Crisis or Tempest in a Teapot?" *International Journal* 57, no. 1 (Winter 2001-02): 1–18.

———. "A Widening Gap Between the U.S. Military and Civilian Society: Some Evidence, 1976–1996." *International Security* 23, no. 3 (Winter 1998–1999): 5–42.

Hooker, Richard. "Soldiers of the State: Reconsidering American Civil-Military Relations." *Parameters* (Winter 2003-04): 4–18.

Houghton, Rick. "The Law of Retired Military Officers and Political Endorsements: A Primer." *Lawfare*, October 3, 2016. https://www.lawfareblog.com/law-retired-military-officers-and-political-endorsements-primer.

Huntington, Samuel P. *The Soldier and the State: The Theory and Politics of Civil-Military Relations.* Cambridge, MA: Belknap Press, 1957.

Hutzler, Alexandra. "Over 200 Retired Senior Military Leaders Endorse Donald Trump, Criticize Biden's Record." *Newsweek*, September 14, 2020. https://www.newsweek.com/over-200-retired-senior-military-leaders-endorse-donald-trump-criticize-bidens-record-1531765.

Inbody, Donald S. *The Soldier Vote: War, Politics, and the Ballot in America.* New York: Palgrave Macmillan, 2016.

Iyengar, Shanto, Gaurav Sood, and Yphtach Lelkes. "Affect, Not Ideology: A Social Identity Perspective on Polarization." *Public Opinion Quarterly* 76, no. 3 (Fall 2012): 405–431.

Jackman, Sidney, and Bradley Spahn. "Why Does the American National Election Study Overestimate Voter Turnout?" *Political Analysis* 27, no. 2 (Spring 2019): 193–207.

James, Michael S., and Marisa Taylor. "Marine Sgt. Gary Stein Gets 'Other Than Honorable' Discharge Over Anti-Obama Facebook Comment." *ABC News*, April 14, 2012. https://abcnews.go.com/US/marine-sgt-gary-stein-honorable-discharge-anti-obama/story?id=16216279.

Joe Biden for President 2020. "No Wonder." October 30, 2020. Campaign advertisement video, 1:00.https://www.youtube.com/watch?v=d1Kwr1eJQMw.

Kablack, Brianna, Tammy Kupperman Thorp, Peter Bergen, Melissa Salyk-Virk, and David Sterman. "The Military Speaks Out: Serving and Retired U.S. Military Leaders' Views About the Trump

Administration." *New America* (blog). January 19, 2021. https://www.newamerica.org/international-security/blog/military-speaks-out/.

Kaplan, Lawrence F. "Officer Politics." *New Republic*, September 13, 2004. https://newrepublic.com/article/75794/officer-politics.

Keith, Bruce E., David B. Magleby, Candice J. Nelson, Elizabeth A. Orr, Mark C. Westlye, and Raymond E. Wolfinger. *The Myth of the Independent Voter*. Berkeley, CA: California University Press, 1992.

Kilmeade, Brian. "General Michael Flynn Sounds Off on Generals Allen and Dempsey, Khizr Khan." *Fox News*, August 1, 2016. https://radio.foxnews.com/2016/08/01/general-michael-flynn-sounds-off-on-generals-allen-and-dempsey-khizr-khan/.

Kime, Patricia and Oriana Pawlyk. "'Beijing Biden Is Not My President:' Troops' Social Media Posts in Spotlight After Capitol Riots." *Military.com*, February 4, 2021. https://www.military.com/daily-news/2021/02/04/beijing-biden-not-my-president-troops-social-media-posts-spotlight-after-capitol-riots.html.

King, Gary, Michael Tomz, and Jason Wittenberg. "Making the Most of Statistical Analyses: Improving Interpretation and Presentation." *American Journal of Political Science* 44, no. 2 (April 2000), 347–361.

Kitfield, James. "Trump's Generals Are Trying to Save the World. Starting with the White House." *Politico*, August 4, 2017. https://www.politico.com/magazine/story/2017/08/04/donald-trump-generals-mattis-mcmaster-kelly-flynn-215455.

Kohn, Richard H. "The Erosion of Civilian Control of the Military in the United States Today." *Naval War College Review* 40, no. 3 (2002): 8–49.

———. "General Elections: The Brass Shouldn't Do Endorsements." *Washington Post*, September 19, 2000.

———. "Military Endorsements Harm National Interest." *The Washington Times*, October 15, 2000. https://www.washingtontimes.com/news/2000/oct/15/20001015-012137-3090r/.

———. "Out of Control: The Crisis in Civil-Military Relations." *The National Interest* 35 (Spring 1994): 3–17.

Kollman, Ken, and John Jackson. "Trump Radicalized the Republican Party. If it Doesn't Change Course, Many Supporters Will Flee." *Washington Post*, October 29, 2020. https://www.washingtonpost.com/politics/2020/10/29/trump-radicalized-republican-party-if-it-doesnt-change-course-many-supporters-will-flee/.

Krebs, Ronald R., and Robert Ralston. "Civilian Control of the Military is a Partisan Issue: Too Many Americans Don't Subscribe to a Basic Tenet of Democracy." *Foreign Affairs*, July 14, 2020. https://www.foreignaffairs.com/articles/united-states/2020-07-14/civilian-control-military-partisan-issue.

———, Robert Ralston, and Aaron Rapport. "No Right to Be Wrong: What Americans Think About Civil-Military Relations," *Perspectives on Politics*, March 11, 2021.

Krogstad, Jens Manuel, Antonio Flores, and Mark Hugo Lopez. "Key Takeaways About Latino Voters in the 2018 Midterm Elections." *Pew Research Center*, November 9, 2018. https://www.pewresearch.org/fact-tank/2018/11/09/how-latinos-voted-in-2018-midterms/.

Lacey, James. "Finally Getting Serious About Professional Military Education." *War on the Rocks*, May 18, 2020. https://warontherocks.com/2020/05/finally-getting-serious-about-professional-military-education/.

Lauderdale, Benjamin E. "Partisan Disagreements Arising from Rationalization of Common Information." *Political Science Research and Methods* 4, no. 3 (September 2016): 477–492.

Lewis-Beck, Michael S., William Jacoby, and Helmut Norpoth. *The American Voter Revisited*. Ann Arbor, MI: University of Michigan Press, 2008.

Liebert, Hugh, and Jim Golby. "Midlife Crisis? The All-Volunteer Force at 40." *Armed Forces and Society* 43, no. 1 (January 2017): 115–138.

Lodge, Milton, and Charles S. Taber. *The Rationalizing Voter*. New York: Cambridge University Press, 2013.

Lopez, Mark Hugo. "The Hispanic Vote in 2008." *Pew Research Center*, November 5, 2008. https://www.pewresearch.org/hispanic/2008/11/05/the-hispanic-vote-in-the-2008-election/.

Lowther, Adam, and Brooke Mitchell. "Professional Military Education Needs More Creativity, Not More History." *War on the Rocks*, May 28, 2020. https://warontherocks.com/2020/05/professional-military-education-needs-more-creativity-not-more-history/.

Macias, Amanda, and Dan Mangan, "Joint Chiefs of Staff Chairman Milley Apologizes for Appearing with Trump at Church Photo-Op," *CNBC*, June 11, 2020, https://www.cnbc.com/2020/06/11/george-floyd-joint-chiefs-chairman-milley-apologizes-for-appearing-with-trump.html.

MacKuen, Michael B., Robert S. Erikson, and James A. Stimson, "Macropartisanship," *American Political Science Review* 83, no. 4 (December 1989): 1125–1142.

MacQuarrie, Brian. "Last Year, He Was the Country's Top Military Officer. Now He is Retired on the South Shore." *Boston Globe*, September 6, 2020. https://www.bostonglobe.com/2020/09/06/metro/last-year-he-was-countrys-top-military-officer-now-he-is-retired-south-shore/.

Mann, James. "The Adults in the Room." *New York Review of Books*, October 26, 2017. https://www.nybooks.com/articles/2017/10/26/trump-adult-supervision/.

Margolik, David. "The Night of the Generals." *Vanity Fair*, April 2007. https://www.vanityfair.com/news/2007/04/iraqgenerals200704.

Martinez, Jessica, and Gregory A. Smith. "How the Faithful Voted: A Preliminary 2016 Analysis." *Pew Research Center*, November 9, 2016. https://www.pewresearch.org/fact-tank/2016/11/09/how-the-faithful-voted-a-preliminary-2016-analysis/.

Maury, Rosalinda, Brice Stone, Nathaniel George Birnbaum, Deborah Bradbard, Ryan David Van Slyke, and Nicholas Armstrong. *Military Families: Perceptions, Challenges, and Barriers to Voting Participation and Absentee Voting*. Syracuse, NY: Institute for Veterans and Military Families, 2018. https://ivmf.syracuse.edu/wp-content/uploads/2019/10/MOAA_Voting-Participation-and-Absentee-Voting-Report-Sept-2018-Full-Report.pdf.

McDonald, Michael P. "On the Over-Report Bias of the National Election Study." *Political Analysis* 11, no. 2 (Spring 2003): 180–186.

McLaughlin, Elizabeth. "'Sickening': Here's Why One Retired Military Officer Spoke Out Against Trump." *ABC News*, June 4, 2020. https://abcnews.go.com/Politics/sickening-retired-military-officer-spoke-trump/story?id=71074748.

McMaster, H.R. *Dereliction of Duty: Lyndon Johnson, Robert McNamara, the Joint Chiefs of Staff and the Lies That Led to Vietnam.* New York: Harper Collins, 1997.

McRaven, William H. "Our Republic Is Under Attack from the President." *New York Times*, October 17, 2019. https://www.nytimes.com/2019/10/17/opinion/trump-mcraven-syria-military.html.

Miller, Hannah M. "Generals & General Elections: Legal Responses to Partisan Endorsements by Retired Military Officers," *Vanderbilt Law Review* 73, no. 4 (May 2020): 1209–1258.

Milley, Mark A. "A Conversation with Chairman of the Joint Chiefs of Staff General Mark A. Milley." Interview with Michael O'Hanlon, *Brookings Institution*, December 2, 2020. https://www.brookings.edu/events/a-conversation-with-chairman-of-the-joint-chiefs-of-staff-general-mark-a-milley/.

Mitchell, Amy, Jeffrey Gottfried, Jocelyn Kiley, and Katerina Eva Matsa. "Political Polarization and Media Habits." *Pew Research Center*, October 21, 2014. http://www.journalism.org/files/2014/10/Political-Polarization-and-Media-Habits-FINAL-REPORT-7-27-15.pdf.

———, Jeffrey Gottfried, and Katerina Eva Matsa. "Millennials and Political News: Social Media—the Local TV for the Next Generation?" *Pew Research Center*, June 1, 2015. http://www.journalism.org/2015/06/01/millennials-political-news/.

Moran, Michael. "In New England, a Sense of Abandonment." *NBC News*, June 15, 2005. http://www.nbcnews.com/id/8228127/ns/us_news-security/t/new-england-sense-abandonment/.

Moreland, Laurence W., Tod A. Baker, and Robert P. Steed. *The 1988 Presidential Election in the South: Continuity amidst Change in Southern Party Politics.* New York, NY: Praeger, 1991.

Mullen, Michael G. "From the Chairman: Military Must Stay Apolitical." *Joint Force Quarterly* 50 (July 2008): 2–3.

———. "Speech Delivered at National Defense University Commencement." Washington, DC: June 11, 2009.

Myers, Richard B., Richard H. Kohn, Mackubin T. Owens, Lawrence J. Korb, Michael C. Desch. "Salute and Disobey? The Civil-Military Balance, Before Iraq and After," *Foreign Affairs* 86, no. 5 (September/October 2007): 147–156.

Nielsen, Suzanne C., and Don M. Snider. *American Civil-Military Relations: The Soldier and the State in a New Era.* Baltimore, MD: Johns Hopkins University Press, 2009.

Nix, Dayne E. "American Civil-Military Relations: Samuel P. Huntington and the Political Dimensions of Military Professionalism." *Naval War College Review* 65, no. 2 (Spring 2012): 88–104.

O'Hanlon, Michael. "Civil-Military Relations and the 2016 Presidential Race." *Las Vegas Sun*, August 15, 2016, https://lasvegassun.com/news/2016/aug/15/civil-military-relations-and-the-2016-presidential/.

Owens, Mackubin T. "Rumsfeld, the Generals, and the State of U.S. Civil-Military Relations." *Naval War College Review* 59, no. 4 (Autumn 2006): 68–80.

Pew Research Center. "A Deep Dive into Party Affiliation: Sharp Differences by Race, Gender, Generation, Education." April 7, 2015. https://www.pewresearch.org/politics/2015/04/07/a-deep-dive-into-party-affiliation/#survey-report.

Prensky, Marc. "Digital Natives, Digital Immigrants." *On the Horizon* 9, no. 5 (October 2001): 1–6.

Priest, Dana, and Greg Miller. "He Was One of the Most Respected Intel Officers of His Generation. Now He's Leading 'Lock Her Up' Chants." *Washington Post*, August 15, 2016. https://www.washingtonpost.com/world/national-security/nearly-the-entire-national-security-establishment-has-rejected-trumpexcept-for-this-man/2016/08/15/d5072d96-5e4b-11e6-8e45-477372e89d78_story.html?utm_term=.63bcadd88b7a.

Rapp, William E. "Civil-Military Relations: The Role of Military Leaders in Strategy Making," *Parameters*, 45, no. 3 (Autumn 2015): 13–26.

Ricks, Thomas E. "Can the Military Learn From Its Mistakes?" *Washington Post*, October 25, 2013. https://www.washingtonpost.com/opinions/can-the-military-learn-from-its-mistakes/2013/10/25/ce8df7e6-3b31-11e3-b6a9-da62c264f40e_story.html.

———. *Making the Corps*. New York: Scribner, 1997.

———. "The Widening Gap Between the Military and Society." *Atlantic Monthly* 280 (July 1997): 67–78.

Robinson, Michael. "Danger Close: Military Politicization and Elite Credibility." PhD diss., Stanford University, 2018.

———. "Danger Close: Military Politicization and Elite Credibility." *War on the Rocks*, August 21, 2018. https://warontherocks.com/2018/08/danger-close-military-politicization-and-elite-credibility/.

———, Risa Brooks, and Heidi Urben. "How Biden's Pick for Defense Secretary Might Shake Up Civil-Military Relations." *Political Violence at a Glance*, December 8, 2020. https://politicalviolenceataglance.org/2020/12/08/how-bidens-pick-for-defense-secretary-might-shake-up-civil-military-relations/.

Ryan, Missy, and Dan Lamothe. "Trump Administration to Significantly Expand Military Response in Washington Amid Unrest," *Washington Post*, June 1, 2020. https://www.washingtonpost.com/national-security/defense-secretary-pledges-pentagon-support-to-help-dominate-the-battlespace-amid-unrest/2020/06/01/7c5b4630-a449-11ea-8681-7d471bf20207_story.html.

Saad, Lydia. "Trump and Clinton Finish with Historically Poor Images." *Gallup*, November 8, 2016. https://news.gallup.com/poll/197231/trump-clinton-finish-historically-poor-images.aspx.

Schaul, Kevin, Kate Rabinowitz, and Ted Mellnik. "2020 Turnout is on Pace to Break Century-Old Records." *Washington Post*, November 4, 2020. https://www.washingtonpost.com/graphics/2020/elections/voter-turnout/.

Schmitt, Eric. "General to Be Disciplined for Disparaging President." *New York Times*, June 16, 1993. https://www.nytimes.com/1993/06/16/us/general-to-be-disciplined-for-disparaging-president.html.

Schake, Kori. "Why Donald Trump's Endorsement by 88 Generals Is So Dangerous." *Foreign Policy*, September 6, 2016. https://foreignpolicy. com/2016/09/06/why-donald-trumps-endorsement-by-88-generals-is-so-dangerous-civilian-military-relations/;

———, and Jim Mattis. *Warriors and Citizens: American Views of Our Military*. Stanford, CA: Hoover Institution Press, 2016.

Shane, Leo, III. "Here are the 181 Veterans Running for Congress This Year." *Military Times*, October 21, 2020. https://www.militarytimes. com/news/pentagon-congress/2020/10/21/here-are-the-181-veterans-running-for-congress-this-year/.

———. "Military Times Poll: What You Really Think About Trump." *Military Times*, October 23, 2017. https://www.militarytimes.com/ news/pentagon-congress/2017/10/23/military-times-poll-what-you-really-think-about-trump/.

———. "Trump's Popularity Slips in Latest Military Times Poll—and More Troops Say They'll Vote for Biden." *Military Times*, August 31, 2020. https://www.militarytimes.com/news/pentagon-congress/ 2020/08/31/as-trumps-popularity-slips-in-latest-military-times-poll-more-troops-say-theyll-vote-for-biden/.

Shelbourne, Mallory. "'Apolitical' Petraeus Says He Did Not Vote in Election." *The Hill*, December 4, 2016. https://thehill.com/homenews/ campaign/308673-petraeus-says-he-did-not-cast-a-ballot-in-election.

Sherill, Robert. *Military Justice Is to Justice as Military Music Is to Music*. New York: Harper Collins, 1970.

Schogol, Jeff. "MARSOC Facebook Page Takes Down Meme of 'Saint Mattis.'" *Marine Corps Times*, December 2, 2016. https://www. marinecorpstimes.com/news/your-marine-corps/2016/12/02/marsoc-facebook-page-takes-down-meme-of-saint-mattis/.

Schulman, Loren DeJonge, and Amy Schafer. "Too Many Generals in the Situation Room?" *Lawfare*, June 25, 2017. https://www.lawfareblog. com/too-many-generals-situation-room.

Shanker, Thom. "The Wars on Three Fronts: Iraq, the Pentagon, and Main Street." Lecture at Stanford University, Center for International Security and Cooperation, Freeman Spogli Institute, Stanford, CA,

March 8, 2007. https://cisac.fsi.stanford.edu/events/the_wars_on_three_fronts_iraq_the_pentagon_and_main_street.

Simpson, Erin. "I Love Mattis, But I Don't Love Him as SECDEF." *War on the Rocks*, November 25, 2016. https://warontherocks.com/2016/11/i-love-mattis-but-i-dont-love-him-as-secdef/.

Swain, Richard. "Reflection on an Ethic of Officership." *Parameters* (Spring 2007): 4–22.

Taber, Charles S., and Milton Lodge. "Motivated Skepticism in the Evaluation of Political Beliefs." *American Journal of Political Science* 50, no. 3 (July 2006): 755–769.

Teigen, Jeremy. "Enduring Effects of the Uniform: Previous Military Experience and Voting Turnout." *Political Research Quarterly* 59, no.4 (December 2006): 601–607.

Thompson, Alex. "Why the Right Wing Has a Massive Advantage on Facebook." *Politico*, September 26, 2020, https://www.politico.com/news/2020/09/26/facebook-conservatives-2020-421146.

Thornhill, Paula. "How to Teach Troops About the Constitution." *Defense One*, February 18, 2021, https://www.defenseone.com/ideas/2021/02/how-teach-troops-about-constitution/172117/.

Timberg, Craig. "How Conservatives Learned to Wield Power Inside Facebook." *Washington Post*, February 20, 2020, https://www.washingtonpost.com/technology/2020/02/20/facebook-republican-shift/.

Toner, Kevin. "Officers Should Not Vote." *The Professional Ethic and the State Symposium Report*, ed. Kristy G. Russell and Ted G. Ihrke. Fort Leavenworth, KS: Command and General Staff College Press, 2015.

Uniformed and Overseas Citizens Absentee Voting Act, 52 U.S. Code (1986), § 20301-2-311.

Urben, Heidi A. "Generals Shouldn't Be Welcome at These Parties: Stopping Retired Flag Officer Endorsements." *War on the Rocks*, July 27, 2020, https://warontherocks.com/2020/07/generals-shouldnt-be-welcome-at-these-parties-stopping-retired-flag-officer-endorsements/.

———. *Like, Comment, Retweet: The State of the Military's Nonpartisan Ethic in the World of Social Media.* Washington, DC: National Defense University Press, 2017. https://ndupress.ndu.edu/Portals/6 8/Documents/casestudies/cco_casestudy-1.pdf?ver=2017-05-22-0901 56-523.

———. "Partisan Activity on Social Media Hurts the Military Profession." *Proceedings* 147, no. 9 (September 2021): 64–67.

———. "Party, Politics, and Deciding What Is Proper: Army Officers' Attitudes after Two Long Wars." *Orbis* 57, no. 3 (Summer 2013): 351–368.

———. "Wearing Politics on Their Sleeves? Levels of Political Activism of Active Duty Army Officers." *Armed Forces & Society* 40, no. 3 (2014): 568–591.

Verba, Sidney, and Norman H. Nie. *Participation in America: Political Democracy and Social Equality.* Chicago, IL: The University of Chicago Press, 1991.

Vespa, Jonathan E. *Those Who Served: America's Veterans From World War II to the War on Terror.* ACS-43. Washington, DC: U.S. Census Bureau, 2020. https://www.census.gov/content/dam/Census/library/publications/2020/demo/acs-43.pdf.

Votel, Joseph. "An Apolitical Military Is Essential to Maintaining Balance Among American Institutions." *Military Times*, June 8, 2020. https://www.militarytimes.com/opinion/commentary/2020/06/08/an-apolitical-military-is-essential-to-maintaining-balance-among-american-institutions/.

Wagner, John. "White House Press Secretary: It's 'Highly Inappropriate' to Question a 4-star Marine General." *Washington Post*, October 20, 2017. https://www.washingtonpost.com/news/post-politics/wp/2 017/10/20/white-house-press-secretary-its-highly-inappropriate-to-question-a-4-star-marine-general/

Washington, George. *Newburgh Address: George Washington to Officers of the Army, March 15, 1783.* https://www.mountvernon.org/education/primary-sources-2/article/newburgh-address-george-washington-to-officers-of-the-army-march-15-1783/#.

Werner, Erica. "Dunford Signals He Won't Chair Coronavirus Panel in Latest Blow to New Oversight Body," *Washington Post*, July 14, 2020. https://www.washingtonpost.com/us-policy/2020/07/14/dunford-signals-he-wont-chair-coronavirus-panel-latest-blow-new-oversight-body/.

Westlye, Mark C. "The Myth of the Independent Voter Revisited." In *Facing the Challenge of Democracy: Explorations in the Analysis of Public Opinion and Political Participation*, edited by Paul M. Sniderman and Benjamin Highton. Princeton, NJ: Princeton University Press, 2011.

Winkie, Davis. "'Accountability' Marine gets light sentence; judge blasts command." *Marine Corps Times*, October 15, 2021. https://www.marinecorpstimes.com/news/your-marine-corps/2021/10/15/judge-blasts-command-gives-light-sentence-to-marine-who-demanded-accountability-on-social-media/.

Wolfinger, Raymond E. and Steven J. Rosenstone. *Who Votes?* New Haven, CT: Yale University Press, 1980.

Zaller, John. *The Nature and Origins of Mass Opinion.* New York: Cambridge University Press, 1992.

INDEX

About the Author

Heidi A. Urben is a Chamberlain Teaching Fellow at Howard University, an adjunct associate professor in Georgetown University's Security Studies Program, and a retired U.S. Army colonel. She writes on US civil-military relations and also serves as a senior associate (non-resident) at the Center for Strategic and International Studies, an adjunct scholar at West Point's Modern War Institute, and a visiting Research Fellow at the Institute for National Strategic Studies at the National Defense University. She holds a PhD, MA, and MPM from Georgetown University, an MS from the National War College, and a BA from the University of Notre Dame.

PRAISE FOR THE BOOK

"The relationships among our military, fellow citizens, and those elected to serve in public office are changing. However, few seem to appreciate the implications of such changes, even though civil-military relations are at the very heart of our democracy. This book addresses these issues with timely, important insights and refreshingly pragmatic advice. In my time as Chairman of the Joint Chiefs of Staff, I valued Dr. Heidi Urben's wisdom, balance, and discipline in dealing with the most complex national security issues—and readers will appreciate those same traits being applied in this book, which I highly recommend."

—General Martin Dempsey, US Army (ret.),
18th Chairman of the Joint Chiefs of Staff,
and 37th Chief of Staff of the Army

"While lots of us talk about what the military thinks, Professor Urben brings the data on Army officers. If this book just presented that it'd be an important addition to civil-military scholarship. But her analysis and practical appendix for use by Army leaders to instill the nonpartisan ethic in their units will help civilians better understand our military, and help our military better serve our country."

—Dr. Kori Schake,
Director of Foreign and Defense Policy,
American Enterprise Institute

"This book provides a particularly valuable window into the political beliefs and behavior of active duty (primarily US Army) officers. The idea that leaders of tactical units (battalions, brigades, and other service equivalents) should bear responsibility for the inculcation of nonpartisanship and healthy civil-military norms is novel and even somewhat provocative, but it flows logically from the author's arguments. This focus and the book's accessible length make it likely to become a required touchstone. This book is highly relevant to policy makers, with particular strengths that include its clear presentation of contemporary data on the political beliefs and behaviors of active duty cadets and officers, its discussion of new dynamics created by social media, its large number of questions for future research, its pragmatic policy recommendations, and its guide for O5 and O6 commanders to use in teaching their units about the nonpartisan ethic."

—Dr. Suzanne C. Nielsen,
coeditor of *American Civil-Military Relations:
The Soldier and the State in a New Era*

"This book is a highly useful reference that could be used readily by professors of civil-military relations. It uses a range of survey tools to glean insights into changing norms within the US military. The breadth and depth of data is highly compelling and rigorous. Dr. Heidi Urben does a superb job laying out her argument clearly and logically. Each chapter is written in a manner that is easy to follow and, importantly, successfully ties in the implications that can be drawn from the statistics. Readers will find themselves carefully reading the conclusions at the end of each chapter and gaining new, important insights. This book offers significant findings to be pulled that will improve the dialogue within professional military education as well as senior military leaders' writings to their colleagues and guidance to the forces."

—Major General William E. Rapp, US Army (ret.),
Lecturer in Military Affairs, Belfer Center,
Harvard Kennedy School

CAMBRIA RAPID COMMUNICATIONS IN CONFLICT AND SECURITY (RCCS) SERIES

General Editor: Geoffrey R. H. Burn

The aim of the RCCS series is to provide policy makers, practitioners, analysts, and academics with in-depth analysis of fast-moving topics that require urgent yet informed debate. Since its launch in October 2015, the RCCS series has the following book publications:

- *A New Strategy for Complex Warfare: Combined Effects in East Asia* by Thomas A. Drohan
- *US National Security: New Threats, Old Realities* by Paul R. Viotti
- *Security Forces in African States: Cases and Assessment* edited by Paul Shemella and Nicholas Tomb
- *Trust and Distrust in Sino-American Relations: Challenge and Opportunity* by Steve Chan
- *The Gathering Pacific Storm: Emerging US-China Strategic Competition in Defense Technological and Industrial Development* edited by Tai Ming Cheung and Thomas G. Mahnken
- *Military Strategy for the 21st Century: People, Connectivity, and Competition* by Charles Cleveland, Benjamin Jensen, Susan Bryant, and Arnel David
- *Ensuring National Government Stability After US Counterinsurgency Operations: The Critical Measure of Success* by Dallas E. Shaw Jr.
- *Reassessing U.S. Nuclear Strategy* by David W. Kearn, Jr.
- *Deglobalization and International Security* by T. X. Hammes
- *American Foreign Policy and National Security* by Paul R. Viotti

- *Make America First Again: Grand Strategy Analysis and the Trump Administration* by Jacob Shively
- *Learning from Russia's Recent Wars: Why, Where, and When Russia Might Strike Next* by Neal G. Jesse
- *Restoring Thucydides: Testing Familiar Lessons and Deriving New Ones* by Andrew R. Novo and Jay M. Parker
- *Net Assessment and Military Strategy: Retrospective and Prospective Essays* edited by Thomas G. Mahnken, with an introduction by Andrew W. Marshall
- *Deterrence by Denial: Theory and Practice* edited by Alex S. Wilner and Andreas Wenger
- *Negotiating the New START Treaty* by Rose Gottemoeller
- *Party, Politics, and the Post-9/11 Army* by Heidi A. Urben

For more information, visit www.cambriapress.com.

www.ingramcontent.com/pod-product-compliance
Lightning Source LLC
Chambersburg PA
CBHW022301280326
41932CB00010B/943